WORLD MODERNIZATION

WORLD MODERNIZATION
The Limits of Convergence

Wilbert E. Moore
Professor of Sociology and Law
University of Denver

Elsevier · New York

NEW YORK · OXFORD

Elsevier North Holland, Inc.
52 Vanderbilt Avenue, New York 10017

Distributors outside the United States and Canada:

Thomond Books
(A Division of Elsevier/North-Holland Scientific Publishers, Ltd.)
P.O. Box 85
Limerick, Ireland

Library of Congress Cataloging in Publication Data

Moore, Wilbert Ellis.
    World modernization: the limits of convergence.

    Bibliography: p.
    Includes index.
    1. Economic history—20th century. 2. Economic
    development. 3. Underdeveloped areas. I. Title.
HC59.M64   301.5'1   79-14769
ISBN 0-444-99062-3

Design: Edmée Froment
Mechanicals/Opening pages and Art: José Garcia

Manufactured in the United States of America

This book is dedicated to
Alfred J. Lockett
English friend and admirer of the language
we sometimes share

CONTENTS

Preface   ix

1 THE QUEST FOR A RATIONAL SOCIETY   1
Beliefs and Practical Matters   2
Rational Men and Rational Society   7
Sources of Unease   14
Notes   17

2 MODERNIZATION: From Industrialization to Rationalization   19
Joining the Modern World   21
Economic Development and Its Social Setting   23
Convergence Theory and the Model Modernized Society   26
Modernization as Rationalization   29
Notes   31

3 COMMERCIALIZATION   33
Monetization of Exchange   34
Accounting: Credits and Debts   41
Normative and Particularistic Elements   44
Notes   45

4 DIFFERENTIATION   46
Occupational Specialization   48
New and Multiplied Forms of Inequality   52
Functional Specialization of Organizations   56
Overspecialization and Alienation   58
Notes   60

5   TECHNIFICATION   63
     Rationalization of Production and Distribution   64
     Alternative Technologies   71
     The Price of Progress   73
     Notes   75

6   EDUCATION   77
     Functional Literacy and Technical Skills   79
     Knowledge and Character   82
     Hazards and Virtues of Irrelevance   85
     Notes   88

7   BUREAUCRATIZATION   90
     The Social Machine   93
     Organization of Change   98
     Pathologies, Amendments, and Purposes   102
     Notes   104

8   RATIONALIZING BIRTH, LIFE, AND DEATH   106
     Health and Longevity as Universal Values   107
     Fertility Control   110
     Demographic Transition   113
     Limits and Resistances to Rationalization   116
     Notes   119

9   SECULARIZATION   121
     Questioning Beliefs and Assumptions   122
     The Problem of Legitimacy   124
     The Quest for Meaning   131
     Notes   134

10   THE LIMITS OF RATIONALITY   136
     Expression and Affectivity   138
     Tradition and Modernity   143
     Collective Goals and Values   146
     Notes   148

11   PERSISTENT PLURALISM   150
     Failed Initiatives   152
     Dependency Theory   154
     Increasing Convergence and Accentuated Diversity   156
     Notes   158

     METHODOLOGICAL NOTE   160

     Index   163

PREFACE

Nearly four decades ago when I had completed my doctoral studies at Harvard, I started work on what I envisaged as a multi-volumed scholarly study of comparative (historical and contemporary) property and labor systems. At that time, much of Max Weber's *Wirtschaft und Gesellschaft* was relatively unknown to me, because I did not then and do not now comfortably read German—especially Weber's German. By the time that the partial* or full† translations became available, I had grown impatient with my grandiose scheme (I was a young man in a hurry) and began publishing work in industrial sociology, economic demography, social inequality, African labor migration, and other aspects of what might be called economic sociology. I saw this work as consistent with my original ambition, but certainly in no orderly and systematic way. My investment in historical research had not been nearly as great as that reflected in Reinhard Bendix's *Kings or People,*‡ and my interest was in the normative structure of economic activity rather than the bases of political legitimacy. When I discovered that Weber had not really done what I had in mind, Weber's scholarship being founded in economic history but not comparative anthropology, nor had Émile Durkheim and his associates and students, who did have an anthropological perspective, I had begun what proved to be an enduring commitment to the analysis of modernization.

---

*Max Weber, *The Theory of Social and Economic Organization*, trans. by A. M. Henderson and Talcott Parsons (New York: Oxford University Press, 1947).

†Max Weber, *Economy and Society*, trans. by Guenther Roth and Claus Wittich (New York: Bedminster Press, 1968).

‡Reinhard Bendix, *Kings or People: Power and the Mandate to Rule* (Berkeley: University of California Press, 1978).

I came upon that interest through no orderly intellectual progression. In 1948, Adolf Lowe, a German-trained "institutional" economist then at the Institute of World Affairs, The New School for Social Research, asked me concerning my possible interest in the impact of industrialization on "native" labor, as economic development had begun its ever-expanding influence as a prime goal of those places that were still candidly called the "backward" areas of the world. (The semantic transformation from backward to undeveloped to underdeveloped—or the United Nations' "less developed countries"—to the more currently acceptable "newly developing" is itself an interesting case study in euphemisms.) That initiative by Lowe led to my undertaking a survey of the research literature and a "field study" in south-central Mexico, reported in my *Industrialization and Labor*.*

With the establishment in 1950 of the Committee on Economic Growth of the Social Science Research Council, at the initiative and under the chairmanship of Simon Kuznets, I had the opportunity of participation in a series of interdisciplinary conferences—extending over some 15 years—on comparative economic development. As I have noted in Chapter 2 of this book, the term "modernization" gradually gained currency, as social scientists, other than economists, became increasingly involved in studying the world's first truly global social movement. Although I was continuing to write conference papers, subsequently published in symposia, both under the auspices of the SSRC Committee and of the (then still professional) Social Science Division of UNESCO, as well as other symposium chapters and a short book (*The Impact of Industry*, 1965), I was increasingly uneasy about the underlying theoretical structure and related methodological procedures that most social scientists analyzing modernization were using. The theoretical structure seemed to be based, at least implicitly, on "convergence theory," leading to the expectation of far greater uniformity in process and result than was observationally justified, and therefore on an application of "functionalism," with its emphasis (and exaggeration) of systemic interdependence. Put crudely, the argument was essentially that economic modernization, using borrowed technology and principles of organization, would inevitably produce a highly homogeneous category of "post-industrial societies." I began to express my doubts in some short papers (two with Arnold Feldman), in *The Impact of Industry*, and in some subsequent papers—mainly in symposia. The theoretical issues are explored, and I believe mainly resolved, in this book. Some of the methodological issues are discussed in a "Methodological Note" at the end of the volume.

The stimulus to re-think the theory and conceptualization of moderniza-

---

*Wilbert E. Moore, *Industrialization and Labor: Social Aspects of Economic Development* (Ithaca, NY: Cornell University Press, 1951; reprinted, New York: Russell and Russell, 1965).

tion came, almost by chance, from Neil H. Cheek, Jr., when he was Visiting Professor of Sociology at the University of Denver for the academic year 1972–1973. Cheek was organizing a session on the sociology of leisure for the 1973 annual meeting of the American Sociological Association and he asked me to prepare a paper on "Modernization and Recreation." Now I flattered myself that I knew a good bit about modernization and something about leisure, reflected in my short book, *Man, Time, and Society* (1963), but I had given little thought to their relationship. In attempting to formulate something worth saying on the subject, it struck me (I now believe tardily) that every aspect of what social scientists appeared to mean by modernization (or development) represented a form of structural rationalization. That seemed, and still seems, to me to clarify the sources of my theoretical and methodological unease and, after some further explorations in one published paper* and several deservedly unpublished papers presented at conventions, the present book is the result.

Prompt completion of the book was greatly aided by a one-term sabbatical leave from the University of Denver, and for that I wish to express my gratitude. Susan Bockhoff, a graduate assistant in the Department of Sociology at the University of Denver, helped me partially repair my deficient knowledge of philosophical rationalism. Cathy Atkinson, secretary extraordinary and general custodian of my professional activities, typed the entire manuscript with indefatigable good humor. William L. Gum of Elsevier, personal friend of long standing and favorite editor, did me the honor of personally editing the manuscript. He caught me in a few grammatical errors and many infelicities of expression. Our friendship has safely survived various small differences of view on style and content, with a score perhaps about even on arguments won and lost. I am pleased to record here my thanks to those I have just mentioned, and to other colleagues and friends whom I may too often take for granted.

Wilbert E. Moore

Denver, Littleton, and
South Turkey Creek,
Colorado
January 1979

---

*Wilbert E. Moore, "Modernization as Rationalization: Processes and Restraints," in Manning Nash, ed., *Essays on Economic Development and Cultural Change in Honor of Bert F. Hoselitz,* Supplement to Vol. 25 of *Economic Development and Cultural Change* (Chicago: University of Chicago Press, 1977).

WORLD MODERNIZATION

1

THE QUEST FOR A RATIONAL SOCIETY

All people everywhere are subject to, and many are actively participating in, a process of social change that is called modernization. In exploring this process and its possible outcomes, this book has a thesis, which can be stated rather briefly. Modernization may be more closely identified as rationalization of the ways social life is organized and social activities performed. By this I mean the use of fact and logic in the choice of instrumental behavior for the achievement of various identified goals: increased economic output, improvement of health and life expectancy, a reliable civil service, an appropriately educated population, the achievement of governable urban areas.

This process of "universal rationalization" has limits of several sorts; logical, bio-psychological, and sociological. The logical limit derives from the proper meaning of rationality, which refers to the criteria in the choice of means (notably causal efficacy and relative efficiency) for *given* ends or goals, but cannot determine those ends. (I am oversimplifying here; for example, if the immediate goal is instrumental to some more general goal or a later stage in a complex process, of course the criteria of rationality do fit.) The bio-psychological limit derives from the reality of emotion, esthetic and expressive propensities, ethical convictions, and attachment to beliefs and values, which are as fundamental to genetic "human nature" as is our capacity to know things cognitively and to manipulate things, people, and ideas instrumentally. The sociological limit, expectably, is a bit more complicated. It derives fundamentally from the fact that we live in organized social units marked by internal differentiation. To maintain the integrity of the "system" (units and their relationships), some mode of coordination is essential, and that mode must be able to claim some form of *legitimacy*. That legitimacy represents, or rests on, goals, beliefs, and values. Thus on both logical and bio-psychological grounds we must exempt legitimacy from a purely rational derivation.

These limits to rationalization apply within societies (which for the moment we can equate with "sovereign" national states)—thus constituting limits to a (or any) rational society. The limits also apply to the global process of rationalization. So, what may increasingly appear to be a homogeneous, "look-alike" world is not in fact headed toward uniformity in belief, in organization, and in many significant aspects of daily life and culture. Despite increasing world interdependence and despite the effect of rationalization—where it is applicable—in reducing the range of variation in the forms of social behavior, significant and indeed fundamental differences will remain.

The thesis just stated in unvarnished assertions in a few brief paragraphs will of course require elaboration, illustration, application. Moreover, that thesis, based on those assertions, is not commonly accepted as self-evident truth. It is contrary to the explicit opinion of many of the social scientists that take comparative modernization as their focus of interest. (Comparativists, of course, represent a small but significant sub-set of social scientists, most of whom have smaller and somewhat more refined issues under inspection.) The thesis is also contrary to the implicit assumptions made by others. Thus, the endeavor at hand is not ended by a simple reminder of homely truths, deserving at most an admonitory note in technical journals of the appropriate disciplines.

The first order of business, as advertised in the chapter title, is to explore the quest for a rational society. This will require some comparative and historical perspective, though of course tracing the detailed nuances of rationalism as a form of social philosophy is not central to our concern with modernization. (However, one of the advantages of viewing modernization as constituting behavioral and structural rationalization is the avoidance of arbitrary decisions on the date or dated event when the modern era began.) The hopes and disappointments associated with rationalism will form the theme of this introductory discourse; the possibilities and limits of rationalization will then be more extensively and intensively explored in subsequent chapters—to the end of the enterprise.

BELIEFS AND PRACTICAL MATTERS

Most people believe that the communities, tribes, societies, or national states to which they owe allegiance, and from which they derive their sense of collective identity, have some form of original—and often current—superhuman support and sanction. No major culture is without its creation myths "at the beginning," supplemented by larger-than-life heroes who have founded, preserved, or reformed the ideologies of political regimes and religious communities.

The pairing of political and religious myths and ideologies is neither accidental nor whimsical. The maintenance of order and the orientation of behavior to supernatural entities are often combined in a single, cohesive organization. Where they seemingly are separated, and where both the "state" and the "church" claim ultimate authority over human conduct, symbolic linkages remain despite tensions arising from disputed jurisdictions. And where it is claimed that a purely secular state has been established, with disavowal and suppression of the "superstitions" of traditional religion—for example, the official atheism of orthodox Marxist regimes—the claim invariably turns out to be spurious. Both the state itself and the charismatic qualities of founders and current leaders become objects for mandatory collective worship. The old gods are dead. Long live the new and true gods.

The secularization of beliefs is one mark of "modernization," as we shall see, though the intellectual roots of such secular ideas may have a considerable antiquity. And the fate of secularization, as we shall also see, has been mixed, ambiguous, often disorderly, and invariably transitory. This set of qualifiers lacks the Anglo-Saxon bite of Thomas Hobbes's famous description of life in his hypothetical state of nature as "solitary, poor, nasty, brutish, and short,"[1] but the ideas have more than a little in common.

The true origins of human social organization remain sufficiently unknown to invite the creation of creation myths that assume some form of supernatural intervention, to the denigration of human ingenuity in inventing social systems (but suitably recognizing a talent for inventing myths). In a nominally less credulous era and intellectual ambience, the same ignorance of origins invites speculation concerning an essentially mindless trial-and-error, survival-of-the-fittest evolutionary model, which is also unflattering to human ingenuity.

For those who prefer naturalistic explanations for observed reality, evolutionary doctrines appear appealing, but only with the dual caution that they remain speculative and inferential, and that they must not be taken as denial of the possibility of purpose and deliberate calculation in human social organization where the evidence warrants that alternative inference.

We know, in those ancient civilizations that had invented writing and have left records for our later inspection, that along with the expected references to traditions of sacred origin, we find rather pragmatic and calculating approaches to such practical matters as military formations and the technology of warfare or the management of estates and the collection of taxes. I have elsewhere argued that the germ of truth in the popular belief that technology is the prime instigator of social change is the universal lack of complete adaptation to and mastery of the environment of human collectivities.[2] This gap between the ideal and the actual provides an opportunity for innovations that narrow the gap. And, following Malinowski,[3] I have rejected the picture of a magic-dominated "primitive mind," noting that non-literate tribesmen just as sophisticated Westerners use known rational techniques directed to achieving their ends, and they supplement those techniques with magic where technology does not guarantee desired results.

Lest this one-sided technological ascendancy go unchallenged, however, it must also be noted that no known society or culture has achieved perfect conformity with rules of conduct or the beliefs that provide their rationale—and that no society fully achieves its professed ideals. This gap, too, is likely to allow innovation, if only in the techniques—always inadequate—of suppression. Now the technology of coping with the environment among extinct cultures and societies may leave sufficient archaeological evidence to permit partial reconstruction, but unfortunately those that left no written records permit scant speculation concerning the social technology of collective cohesion. We are left with inferences from a great diversity of more-or-less-known societies. From that evidence we uniformly find some mixture of punishments (including death or exile but also supernatural retribution after death) for malefactors and rewards (including supernatural ones) for conformity, usually with extra recognition for truly exemplary conduct. In those societies that have organized social problem-solving in executive agencies, legislatures, and courts, we find not only the modification of rules and enunciation of new ones, but also an almost constant preoccupation with the modes for securing compliance. Such problem-solving normally operates within the restraints of established procedures and precedents.

Our concern here is with the quest for a rational society, and I have been attempting to avoid the conventional arrogance that would limit the capacity and practice of rational intervention in the forms and conditions of human existence to "civilized" people and recent history. Yet one bit of conventional wisdom does seem to be approximately right: the sources of order and the rationale for beliefs and practices in most societies for most of human history has been tradition. Rules are followed, beliefs accepted, authority is recognized, obligations fulfilled because they have "always" existed—since sacred creatures established them—or at least have existed since the founder or the "founding fathers" (now sanctified) established them, proving their validity by experience.

Tradition represents one of the three bases of political legitimacy distinguished by Max Weber.[4] The others are charismatic authority, resting upon the special, perhaps super-human, qualities of the leader, and rational-legal or bureaucratic authority. Of the three principles of legitimacy, the traditional is by far the most common over the broad range of human life in organized groups. Charismatic authority is self-limiting because leaders, like ordinary mortals, are mortal. Moderately smooth transition in the succession to the principal position of authority requires what Weber called the "routinization of charisma,"[5] that is, an essentially traditional mode of succession as in hereditary royal dynasties or the "apostolic succession" that supports the divinely sanctioned authority of the Roman Catholic Pope. Weber's rational-legal or bureaucratic mode of claiming political legitimacy does not in fact stand on the same footing as traditional and charismatic authority, as Heinz Hartmann has pointed out,[6] for the ultimate accountability of the bureaucratic state rests with some traditional mode for confirming authority, such as the divine right of hereditary rulers or the sovereign will of the people expressed through their elected representatives.

Weber's three forms of political legitimacy were, as was often the case in his work, "ideal types." That is, they focus on the central or predominant principle in a form of organization (or a belief system) and trace out systematically a coherent set of related characteristics, but they are offered as analytic constructs or models, not as descriptive reality. The circumstance that pure types do not exist is only a factual quibble. The reasons that they do not exist are more interesting. The intrinsic time-limitation on charismatic regimes has already been noted. It must also be observed that the will, or whim, of the leader does not automatically make things happen, without the loyal and more-or-less competent support of trusted agents. Since loyalty will be a prime qualification for appointment, the resulting bureaucracy will be flawed but still recognizable. And, we have also noted, if the regime survives the death of its founder it can do so only by adding some stability in its administrative structure and reliance on a "traditionalized" form of belief in its ideological legitimacy. A rational-legal system is fatally incomplete if it is not accountable to a traditionally ordained source of ultimate legitimacy.

If tradition figures in actuality as one basis for legitimacy in seemingly anti-traditional political orders, what of those that claim no other base? Here the probable impurity of type arises from other sources: the inability of such systems (or any others) to resolve or prevent the uncertainties, ills, and vicissitudes of human life. Traditional systems can scarcely avoid the human propensity to deal with at least some of these imperfections as constituting challenges, problems inviting attempts at partial solutions, not as unquestionable fate or divine will.

Though structural change from internal sources, as distinct from invasions, conquests, or natural disasters, seems relatively infrequent in some long-lived and moderately documented cultures such as those of Egypt, China, or India, they did occur. Medieval Europe is retrospectively conceived as a period of scant change other than endless and somewhat ceremonial disputes among rival lords, yet new forms of government—and indeed of social status—were being tried in the towns and cities, and new forms of agriculture (crop rotation in the three-field system) as well as new productive technology (the horse-drawn plow) and military technology (cavalry units) were developed.[7] The lasting consequences, as well as immediate ones, of these innovations were generally greater than the political clashes that have more commonly attracted the scholarship of historians.

The difficulty with generalizing about predominantly traditional societies arises from ignorance. The non-literate "tribal" groups observed and recorded, with greater or lesser conscientious accuracy, over the last two centuries have, in the nature of the case, only oral histories and only partially mythical pictures of the past. As observed, often for relatively brief periods, authority and conformity appear as purely traditional—that is, up to the time of their contact with inquisitive or avaricious or authoritarian outsiders. And it is just such societies or cultures that have provided the principal examples in the contemporary concern for the impact of modernization on traditional societies, commonly depicted as a confrontation representing fundamental differences in the kind of technology and social organization, and implicitly in the style (and quality?) of thought. The fixity of the social order, even if avowed as the reality by native informants, may represent ignorance or "ideal truth" more than reality. We now know, for example, that highly restrictive and officially mandatory mate-selection patterns must represent "ideal truth," as full implementation over protracted periods would not permit an adequate level of reproduction to sustain the society.[8] And, the anthropologist Marvin Harris has recently observed that the notorious tradition of the sacred cow in Hindu India is of moderately recent origin, has scant foundation in ancient sacred scripture, and has positive and not solely nefarious consequences.[9]

If technology is defined as useful or practical knowledge, as it properly must be,

> it exists in men's minds or in symbols and drawings on paper well before it takes form in processes or products or other palpable results. Technology is no more "material" than beliefs or attitudes or aesthetic responses to perceived beauty or ugliness; it is simply oriented toward "practical" affairs. . . . It is the product of human ingenuity, and without human purpose behind it, it is not the cause of anything.[10]

Technology has a history. And in the full sense of the term, "technology," its history provides some basis for a sweeping evolutionary view of the accumulation, extension, and diversification of useful knowledge. In broad outlines, the progression would run from mechanical manipulation to chemical and metallurgical skills, thence to biological intervention (for example, in animal husbandry and sophisticated agriculture, but proceeding to medical arts) and, finally, to social technology, ranging from applied psychology to national economic planning. But this grand view of the extension of attempts to be informed and to be "practical" is wrong in details, and those details are by no means trivial. For example, the domestication of animals was prehistoric, as were fire, tools, and pots; so, indeed, was symbolic language, which may be the most important social invention of mankind. Yet it does appear that in terms of time and effort, and of results, inanimate nature was more amenable to manipulation—more vulnerable, if you will—than animate nature, and both were more subject to calculating rationality than the forms and processes of social interaction and organization.

The idea of a rational society puts people more-or-less in charge of their own destiny. Or at least it puts those people in charge who have developed both the necessary knowledge and instrumental skills for determining why society exists, what purposes it should serve, and how to achieve those purposes by forms of social organization, rules of conduct, and patterns of action. Warning: the preceding sentence says rather too much, for determining why society exists and the purposes it should serve is not a result of calculation and rational thought. If the rationale for society and its purposes are more-or-less consensually agreed upon, their articulation may aid in their explication and specification in terms of goals; then, and only then, does a rational social technology directed to their attainment make sense. If both social purposes and social arrangements are regarded as essentially sacred, they become immune to profane rationality. As I have noted elsewhere, whether some technology will develop depends

> on what is identified as a *problem*, that is, a situation for which remedies or solutions are at hand or may be seriously attempted—rather than as a *given*, which is a condition defying human intervention. The technical state of mind is secular. It has scant patience with Fate, or with Divine Will, or even with tradition, the wise teachings of the founding fathers, or the shared but un-examined wisdom which "everyone knows."[11]

It is that secular orientation to problem-solving that lies at the base of rationalism—the attempt to construct a rational social order.

RATIONAL MEN AND RATIONAL SOCIETY

On intellectual and philosophical questions in the Western world, it is generally appropriate to start with the classical Greek thinkers. And that is not unsound advice with respect to rationalism or man in charge of his own destiny. Although the Sophists, the Cynics, the Stoics and the Epicureans espoused elements of individualism and hedonism, none of these currents of thought can be said to have attended closely to the problems of social organization or the nature of society.[12] We must turn to Plato and Aristotle for views of the super-individual level of rational conduct. Neither of these philosophers assumed rational conduct as the only attribute of actual human nature, although both exalted rationality as the basis for a "good" or "just" society. Plato identified rational behavior as the distinct mark of human superiority over other creatures. The "appetites," though real, were inferior and regrettable propensities, to be overcome by a select few who thus represented the "good" in their guardianship over those who could not rise above their essentially animal nature.[13] Both Plato and Aristotle were profoundly elitist in their presumptions about the proper character of civic order. Women and children, non-Greeks (barbarians) and the lower orders of Athenian society were essentially regarded as unreasonable, both for deficiencies in intellect and for servitude to appetites and passions. Thus, their "human nature" assumptions stressed genetic differentiation in contrast to the more equalitarian views of human propensities and potentials encountered many centuries later in what came to be called the Age of Reason—or the Enlightenment.

It appears to be nearly as difficult to determine when the Age of Reason began as to decide when it ended. The term has been used by social historians and in other literary sources to refer to rather different periods and indeed to rather different phenomena. Certainly, few would exempt the 18th century in Europe and America as embraced by the era, and few would start it earlier than the 16th century. We have recently (1973) celebrated the 500th anniversary of the birth of Copernicus, but his influence on astrophysics and cosmology was muted until revived by Galileo a century later. Francis Bacon and René Descartes also properly belong to the early 17th century, and Sir Isaac Newton to the 17th and early 18th centuries. These figures in the history of science and what was long called "natural philosophy" are commonly recognized as architects for models of a physical universe that was observable by strict criteria of objectivity and eminently orderly—and indeed in that sense rational. There came to be a kind of comfortable equation between rational models of the universe and the conception of a rational universe. The scientist attended to facts, to uniformities, and to logical inferences to and from principles and laws. That confident conception was shaken only in this century with the enunciation of the principle of relativity and, from this perspective more importantly, the somewhat reluctant admission of chance and uncertainty in quantum mechanics.

Our concern here is properly with social order—not with the arrangement of heavenly bodies or sub-atomic particles. Following an honorable though not unchallenged interpretive canon in intellectual history, I propose that conceptions of a rational cosmos opened the way for ideas and ideals of a rational society. Deistic conceptions of the universe (God as the watchmaker but not its current caretaker) stood at sharp variance with centuries of religious teaching and practice that were mythical, mystical, and magical. And once divine supervisory functions were put in question, notions of society and its polity as the product of a social contract, a rational or perfectible creation of rational men, were promoted as superior to traditional bases for the assertion of authority and propriety. John Locke and Jean-Jacques Rousseau, and their predecessor Thomas Hobbes, the French *Encyclopédistes* and the American "Founding Fathers"—John Adams, Benjamin Franklin, Thomas Jefferson, James Madison—articulated a basis of social order that would unite free men in reasonable agreements to further their common and particular interests.

Here it must be quickly noted that Hobbes, the earliest of those rationalists or contract theorists (*Leviathan,* his master work, was published in 1651[14]), was also a monarchist, and thus reached an essentially "traditional" solution from non-traditional assumptions. Using the assumption of a state of nature lacking any organized society and populated by solely self-seeking individuals, he correctly perceived that the only outcome could be a "war of all against all." Given a plurality of participants, each becomes a potential instrumental means for others' ends. In the absence of rules to the contrary, force and fraud become the most efficient strategies. Perceiving the dismal consequences of such "freedom," the rational actors select a sovereign to make and enforce rules.

Rousseau avoided the problem of order and the problem of goals by making very different human-nature assumptions: an innate benevolence or altruism, leading to an essentially orderly anarchy.[15] But those assumptions virtually removed him from the rationalist position.

Locke[16] and his successors, including the explicit "utilitarians" Jeremy Bentham[17] and John Stuart Mill,[18] avoided the logical problem of the nature of the goals to be pursued by stipulating a finite, uniform, and *given* set of wants. Through exchange there would appear a "natural identity of interests," although a minimal and democratically chosen government would be necessary to ensure that the rules protecting "life, liberty, and property" would be observed.[19] The enthusiasm for individualism and free competition and exchange neglected conspicuous inequality, including the power relationships implicit in control of property, made explicit by Karl Marx, along with the reality of interest conflicts. It also neglected the dismaying capacity for passionately unreasonable conduct. We shall return to both Marx and unreason.

Let us first note how extensively the model, the paradigm, of a rational order was applied. Surely the most famous, influential, and enduring application was to economic affairs, the production and distribution of goods and services. *Homo oeconomicus* was assumed to be hedonic, acquisitive, calculating, and, within his capacity, foresighted. By specializing and trading in an impersonal and atomistic market (greatly facilitated by that most impersonal of social inventions, money), with the terms of trade determined by supply and demand, economic man sought to maximize his own perceived utilities and in so doing sustained a beneficent and self-regulating rational system. Within rules never clearly articulated by the Scotch moral philosophers, including Adam Smith, or by such delineators of pure markets as David Ricardo, competition would both elicit appropriate innovative strategies and keep the market open and its results impersonally just. The "classical" economists did not perceive that unlimited competition would invariably destroy any competitive system, nor did they explicate (though they may have taken for granted) such elementary non-contractual elements as enforcement, or the prohibition on contracts contrary to public order, such as "contracts" for the murder of rival Mafia chieftans.

The enthusiasm for the self-regulating rational economy, characterized with respect to political intervention in the classic French advice, *laissez faire, laissez passer*, may, I have noted, have taken for granted some structure of limiting rules. The rule of reason, in law, was after all an elaborate set of rules, and in the English system they had evolved in both statutes and court decisions around a presumption of at least procedural rationality and with more than a tainted trace of formal logic. Indeed, the Law Merchant, as the rules for trading transactions are known in the history of English law, is probably the most ancient part of the Anglo-American legal system, being fairly well established at least by the 13th century. It affected only a limited trading class until much later, but it required of traders moderate honesty and reliability—as well as assuming their self-interested avarice.

With the extension of commerce, the end of serfdom (and thus the potentiality of genuine labor markets), the transformation of feudal property into private property (and thus the potentiality of enlarged capital markets) and gradual extension of full citizenship at least to persons of property, the legal order was required to cope with all sorts of disputes and divergent claims to rights and privileges, duties and responsibilities. Although the common law is vulgarly characterized as the judicial recognition of established custom, in the course of its evolution it became a set of principles, precedents and procedures. And, although codification is indeed contrary to the spirit of the common law, the quest for moderate consistency, if not certainty, in the law has led to a succession of summarizers and commentators, beginning at least as early as Sir Edward Coke, whose volumes of the *Institutes of the Laws of England* were published from 1628 to 1644.[20] We find Coke writing "How long soever it hath continued, if it be against reason, it is of no force in law."[21] And, in another passage, "Reason is the life of the law, nay the common law itself is nothing else but reason."[22]

The learned and honorable Sir Edward was mistaken, or at least elliptical. The authority of the courts derived from the sovereign power of the crown; the legitimacy of that sovereign power rested on beliefs that were not the product of a rational calculus. In later centuries that legitimate power essentially passed to Parliament, resting there on other non-rational beliefs. Still, once that legitimacy was taken for granted, the operation of reason could provide a criterion for legal decisions. If reason did not ultimately inhere in the law as such, it must be the product of lawyers, possibly lawmakers, and especially of judges. But the notion came to be extended to laymen—to persons involved in activities and transactions reaching the attention of the courts. Thus countless civil and some criminal cases rest upon explicit statements of the expected conduct, in the circumstances, of a *reasonable man*. A special application of such general expectations must guide the behavior of a trustee managing an estate on behalf of particular beneficiaries or managing a charitable endowment. Here the *prudent man* will neither let the corpus of the estate or endowment lie idle or erode nor make investments with unseemly risks. Since reason is related to responsibility, the fulfillment of normal expectations, the problem of normality, that is *sanity*, has long plagued the interpretation of culpability for criminal conduct. And since the reasonable man is alive to his own interests and their improper impairment, and since courts exist as a major mechanism for redress of supposed grievances, the reasonable man may become the *litigious man*—the financial mainstay of much of the practicing bar and the source of much business for the civil courts. The threat, "I'll sue you!", though uttered with intemperate passion, has some advantages over, "I'll kill you!", for both individuals and civil society can survive lost lawsuits.

The rationalists, of course, went beyond the orderly containment of private disputes to the structure of the national state. The emphasis on property did not make them truly equalitarian, and when they wrote "men," they clearly meant males. Yet the notion of a contractual, consensual state owes much to the views of John Locke, particularly among the Americans who rebelled against the British crown. These political philosophers were not so naive as to be unaware of differences in economic interests, but by their assumptions these would be worked out mainly in the market place, or, as a last resort, in the legislatures and the courts.

It remained for Karl Marx to seize upon interest conflicts stemming from the unequal distribution of property, and thus to challenge the consensual or "harmonistic" social order. As Parsons correctly notes,[23] Marx owed some of his notion of capitalist exploitation to David Ricardo's "iron law of wages,"[24] which Ricardo in turn owed in part to Thomas Malthus's observations on the propensity of the poor to have too many children.[25] But Marx went beyond these predecessors to observe that capitalism, and particularly industrial capitalism, expropriated the workers from ownership of tools, the "means and instruments of production."[26] Marx's "historical materialism," that doctrine still espoused by true-believing Marxists, was the essence of a narrowly defined technological rationalism, making the entire shape of society determined by the modes of physical production. I shall soon return to that point. His correct perception of the power implicit in property led him to expect the propertyless workers to recognize their common interests and, overthrowing the capitalist regime, to establish communal ownership and thus a classless society.

Though Marx was self-identified as a historical materialist and is commonly called an economic determinist, this represents faulty thinking to a dismaying degree. Private property, including inheritance of property rights in family lines, is an institutional factor—not an economic or technological one. That is, rules governing rights in scarce values (the proper definition of property) represent part of any society's normative order, highly variable by time and place. Any such institutionalized rules rest on values that support their legitimacy. Those values may not be consensual and the rules are more often imposed by those who most benefit from their operation than truly shared by all. Marx's assertion of that difference in interest set him apart from the exponents of a "natural harmony of interests," but that has nothing to do with historical materialism. The "sanctity of property" in the Western world far predated industrial capitalism. Its ideological foundation was much closer to Greek doctrines of genetic superiority than to the mere rewards for competitive superiority (a kind of Social Darwinist view) that later became the basis of capitalist ideology.

Most "private" business and industrial property in nominally capitalist economies is now corporate in character, which fundamentally alters (by mixing and confusing) the "class" interests of participants in the economy. "Alienation" of the worker from the products of his labor turns out to derive from the division of labor (a point Marx underscored) and the technology of industrialism (a point Marx missed utterly). Private or communal ownership is simply irrelevant to the problem. The "materialist" view that only physical production constitutes labor results in the embarrassing elimination of services from any economic calculus, making it appear that Politbureau members, commissars and their bureaucratic staffs, teachers, ballet performers, physicians, and the police are engaged in useless activities. "Exploitation," that is, withholding part of the product of labor from current consumption, turns out, of course, to be the only way that an economy, from its own resources, can expand its capital capacity to increase production.

By accepting the essentially hedonic view of human motivation put forward by the utilitarians but adding to that one form of interest conflict, the Marxist vision of a rational society, only vaguely articulated in any Marxist literature, appears almost as sterile as that of the classical economists. As some of Marx's early writings indicate, he did regard himself as a humanist and had a (utopian?) vision of man freed from alienating toil for mere survival.[27] In practice, self-styled Marxist regimes have been strongly authoritarian, having, Parsons suggests, more in common with Hobbes than with his "harmonistic" successors among the rationalists. [28]

There is a final irony in the current state of Marxism in its political manifestations, an irony germane to our central concern with modernization. As an ideology (by now, essentially a theology), the image of a socialist future and, more pragmatically, the tactics of a "proletarian dictatorship" have had a wide appeal among the less developed countries. Thus, what should be, from a Marxist perspective, mere "superstructure," derived from technological and economic realities, turns out to be a non-rational source of legitimacy for governmentally sponsored change—the technology and economy being the laggards in the dynamic process.

The hope for reason, and particularly for a rationally constructed civil society, rested on two optimistic errors. The one was a human nature assumption, to the effect that man is by nature rational. That, of course, is at best distortion by omission of the equally valid assertion that man is by nature emotional and not uncommonly stupid and vicious. I shall return to the nature of man later, but it is appropriate to pause here over an anomaly. Though Rousseau has a somewhat sentimental following as a liberal social philosopher, his idealized state of nature before the invention of repressive civil society was not only mythical but analytically false. Hobbes, the conservative royalist, correctly perceived that rational, calculating, hedonic man is not thereby a peaceable or happy one. [29] His description of human life in a state of nature might serve as a caution, if anyone is willing to listen, to those questers after the simple life by a return to nature. [30] This might also stand as ample excuse for the invention of civil society, though for that Rousseau's consensual contract is at least as persuasive a model as Hobbes's presumably wise and benevolent sovereign.

The second optimistic error in the hope for a rational social order is that individual rationality will perforce lead to collective and distributive goals and values and perceptions of justice. This error relates to what I called, in brief comment at the beginning of this discussion, the logical limits of rationalization. Designations such as reasonable and rational refer to procedures, to instrumental acts, but not to the goals or purposes of action. Reasonable men may reasonably differ if their perceptions of relevant facts differ, and, most commonly, if their unspoken goals or values differ. Rationally organized national states may pursue the most nefarious policies, such as international conquest or genocide directed at allegedly inferior ethnic minorities. Bureaucracy, that most rationally constructed complex social system, may be used to put the citizen under total surveillance, to suppress dissent, and (most commonly) to standardize the disposition of quite unstandard problems.

In fact, the advocates of government, law, or even trade based on reason held, and often shared, value assumptions that were not always articulated. In American history, some of these values were most succinctly set forth in the language of the Declaration of Independence and more extensively in the Federalist Papers. The "self-evident truths" were value assumptions, not allegations of established fact. The believers in the rule of reason in law always had an informative value—that of Justice—and Justice is, in terms of the history of legal philosophy, a Natural Law conception, standing prior to and above the outcome of cases.

A purely individualized principle of rationality, without a constraining set of rules, would produce an anarchic state, aptly described by Hobbes. Such individualized conduct also makes no provision for strictly collective goals, such as the integrity of shared culture and its symbols or national survival or preservation of resources for future generations. These omissions were fatal defects of classical economics as a general theory of human conduct, defects still not perceived by contemporary economists who would simply trust our national survival and distributive welfare to the market.

The simple logical point is that *of course* the ends justify the means: what else could? But in a situation with a necessary plurality of ends, those means that would impair other ends must be restricted or prohibited. Thus, winning cases by buying judges or winning athletic events by killing opponents outrages our sense of fair play; it damages a more important end, that is, justice. Or, for that matter, law and order not constrained by conceptions of justice is naked tyranny.

From this simple logical point, applied to the conduct of public affairs, we may note a profound sociological principle. All systems of authority, the claim to legitimacy in the exercise of political power, ultimately rest on non-rational beliefs and values. (I say non-rational, as rationality, to repeat, refers only to procedures.) This value assumption underlying political power is as true of participatory democracy as it is of the collective wisdom of the single minority party, the autocratic sovereign by divine right, the charismatic claims of revolutionary leaders, or the routinized charisma embodied in the doctrine of apostolic succession. I do not mean to be even-handed, however. If the rule of reason has merit as a relatively effective mode for the conduct of public affairs and if we add the value of recognizing the worth and dignity of individuals as citizens or subjects, there is no close rival to some form of democracy as authenticator of political authority.

SOURCES OF UNEASE

The hope for a rational society was not limited to market transactions, the law, or the construction of a contractual state. By the very designation of our particular animal species as *homo sapiens*, we attribute to ourselves special or unique qualities of intelligence. (For apparently intelligent conduct in other species, we use either the explanation of instincts established through long evolutionary selection, or we use the derogatory term, "cunning.") With the interest, dating mainly from the last century, in the biological and cultural evolution of our species, the emergence of distinctively human qualities excited attention and debate. (Of course, evolutionary theory itself represented a startling secularization of religiously based myths of a special, divine creation of mankind.) I believe that it was the tremendous growth in mechanical, chemical, and biological technology that led to one peculiar form of distortion of man's distinctive qualities. We began to see our collective history as a change from adapting to, and in that limited sense coping with, our natural environment to active mastery of our claimed domain. Man came to be identified in the literature of social science as the tool-making animal, *homo faber*. By extension, and by taking some liberties with Latin construction, we may derive *homo technicus*, and even, at a more elevated intellectual plane, *homo scientificus*. Note that these are all variants of rational man, taking charge of his own destiny.

These particular extensions, if meant as a fair characterization of our human qualities, were bad anthropology, bad history, bad psychology. Both in evolutionary terms and in terms of comparison with other species, we are most distinctively described as symbol-creating and symbol-using animals. Our most notable symbolic system is language. Language is so intrinsic to thought that some authorities would say that thought without language is, if you will, unthinkable. (If there is no thought without language, it does not follow that there is no language without thought, for that possibility is daily displayed to our distress.) Symbols indeed extend well beyond language. They include such cultural creations as music and art, marks of identity and exclusion, ceremonies and modes of attire, flags and shrines, gestures of love and hate. We thus come by a rather devious route to the common perception that we are emotional and spiritual as well as rational, prone to attempt destruction of perceived enemies rather than finding a reasoned compromise, consistently credulous concerning cherished myths, given to outbreaks of conduct variously viewed as satanic impulses or animal spirits. In the course of man's biological evolution—and here I follow Loren Eiseley,[31] an outstanding physical anthropologist—the portion of the brain or central nervous system that permits dispassionate analysis and calculated conduct is a late development and always in precarious balance with reactive propensities better suited to our non-symbolic prehistory.

There is little that we can say of human nature in general, of generalized qualities of human personality that would predict behavior in concrete situations. We are safer in speaking of the nature of human potential, for the human infant at birth is totally unequipped to sustain life unaided—

unequipped with instincts that would provide reliable modes of coping with its environment. It does come equipped, however, with an astounding capacity for adaptation, for learning, and eventually for manipulation and innovation.

This leads me to raise a pair of significant questions concerning the conception of the reasonable man: Why was he never a child? Why was he always male? Glib answers to the latter question in terms of male chauvinism are all too accurate and not very helpful. The exclusion of women from the presumption of rationality could be and has been used as a self-confirming theory of sexual differences. If girls are carefully taught that they are mentally and physically and mechanically inferior, decorative but not truly useful outside of sexual and maternal functions, almost exclusively responsible for sentimental, charitable, and many pious concerns, the superior male could safely suppress these important ingredients of social discourse in the knowledge that others would cope. The idea of the intellectual male and the emotional female is biological nonsense, of course.

I think that the question about children is significant, because it says that the learned philosophers forgot their own childhood and its trials, and, needless to say, did not understand what we now know as socialization processes whereby children (and indeed adults) both learn the procedures and values of the social system in which they find themselves, and to a remarkable degree internalize the rules and goals as morally binding standards of personal conduct. But those standards may and certainly do differ among various segments of the social order in any culture or society, and most blatantly differ between cultures.

However, lest we repeat a common error among comparative anthropologists and sociologists in exaggerating cultural differences in values, it is important to note that the hedonic motivations assumed by the classical economists do turn out to be essentially universal. That is, given the possibility of choice, people prefer life to death, health to sickness, and the classic triumvirate of food, clothing, and shelter to their absence of insufficiency. No other-worldly system of value-orientations and cosmology overcomes these homely preferences for most of any society's people. It is also important to note that rational calculation is not limited to "modern man." Primitive societies do not substitute magic for rational technique *if they know one,* but like all people everywhere use magic as a supplement, to bridge the difference between known rational procedures and desired results.[32]

Neither rational, calculating conduct, on the one hand, nor emotional, mystical, or credulous behavior, on the other, distinguishes human beings sharply in human nature terms. Modern Western societies abound not only in violent demonstrations, some of them simply nihilistic in ideology, but also in one form or another of mysticism. Astrology appeals; Oriental or pseudo-

Oriental gurus are clamorously supported in materialistic luxury; witchcraft and demonology are explored; ancient and contemporary invaders from outer space are blamed for current ills or credited with incompletely explained past accomplishments. Since emotion and belief are not to be dismissed as pathological, and forms of rationalization in social organizations such as bureaucracies may become so depersonalized as to treat their inhabitants as somewhat inferior machines, which is pathological, we are dealing once more with the limits of rationality and rationalization. In a discussion of what he calls the sociology of the occult, Edward Tiryakian identifies recent evidence of possibly growing mysticism as a reaction to a "rationalistic-industrial . . . social order."[33]

At the collective level nationalism is taken seriously not only in post-colonial nations but also in old and somewhat stable ones. Charismatic regimes appear in places like post-revolutionary China but also in highly rationalized Germany. Ethnic identification not only survives in multiethnic countries (most are), but actually appears to be getting renewed strength. Ideological conflicts abound, not only between nations or blocks of nations, but within them.

I shall be arguing in this book that although the capacity for rational conduct does not differ widely among human beings, the extent to which rationality is organized and institutionalized (made part of the normative order) does. Increasing rationalization of the social order is the fundamental process underlying what we call modernization. My discussion in this chapter indicates that the process is not exactly new, and that there is ample reason to believe that it must remain incomplete.

After all, were the rule of reason always to prevail, we should be denied a great variety of esthetic and expressive experiences, charming ceremonies, and perhaps even pride in national citizenship, in ethnic identity, in occupational commitment. Love is an unreasonable state, but that does not mean that it is always a pathological state.

NOTES

1. Thomas Hobbes, *Leviathan: Or the Matter, Forme, and Power of a Commonwealth, Ecclesiasticall and Civil*, ed. by Michael Oakesholt (Oxford: Blackwell, 1946); first published in 1651; quotation from Part 1, Chapter 13.
2. Wilbert E. Moore, *Social Change*, 2nd ed. (Englewood Cliffs, NJ: Prentice-Hall, 1974), pp. 19–22, 80–83.
3. Bronislaw Malinowski, "Culture," *Encyclopedia of the Social Sciences* (New York: Macmillan, 1930); also, Malinowski, *Magic, Science, and Religion* (Glencoe, IL: Free Press, 1948).
4. Max Weber, *The Theory of Social and Economic Organization*, trans. by A. M. Henderson and Talcott Parsons (New York: Oxford University Press, 1947), pp. 124–132, 324–363; see also Bert F. Hoselitz, "Tradition and Economic Growth" in Ralph Braibanti and Joseph J.

Spengler, eds., *Tradition, Values, and Socio-Economic Development* (Durham NC: Duke University Press, 1961), pp. 83 – 138.

5. Weber, cited in, note 4, pp. 363 – 373.
6. Heinz Hartmann, *Funktionale Autorität* (Stuttgart: Ferdinand Enke Verlag, 1964), pp. 1 – 61.
7. See Lynn White, Jr., *Medieval Technology and Social Change* (Oxford: Clarendon Press, 1962).
8. See Peter Kunstadter, Roald Buhler, Frederick F. Stephan, and Charles F. Westoff, "Demographic Variables in Preferential Marriage Patterns," *American Journal of Physical Anthropology* N.S. 21: 511 – 519 (December, 1963).
9. Marvin Harris, "India's Sacred Cow," *Human Nature* 1(2):28 – 36 (February 1978).
10. Wilbert E. Moore, "Introduction" to Moore, ed., *Technology and Social Change* (Chicago: Quadrangle Books, 1972), pp. 6 – 8.
11. *Ibid.*, p. 7.
12. See George Boas, *Rationalism in Greek Philosophy* (Baltimore: The Johns Hopkins Press, 1961).
13. *Ibid.* I am relying on this trustworthy secondary source for my brief discussion of the Greeks.
14. Hobbes, *Leviathan*, cited in note 1.
15. Jean-Jacques Rousseau, *The Social Contract* (London: Dent, 1961); first published in French in 1762.
16. John Locke, *Two Treatises of Government*, ed. by Peter Laslett, (Cambridge: Cambridge University Press, 1960); first published in 1690.
17. Jeremy Bentham, *An Introduction to the Principles of Morals and Legislation* (New York: Hafner, 1948); first published in 1780.
18. See especially John Stuart Mill, *Principles of Political Economy, with Some of Their Applications to Social Philosophy*, 7th ed., ed. by W. J. Ashley (New York: Kelley, 1961); first published in 1848.
19. See Talcott Parsons, "Utilitarianism: Sociological Thought," in *International Encyclopedia of the Social Sciences* (New York: Macmillan, 1968); Vol. 16, pp. 229 – 236, see also Parsons, *The Structure of Social Action* (Glencoe, IL: Free Press, 1949); first published in 1937.
20. Sir Edward Coke, *Institutes of the Laws of England*, various editions; originally published in four "Parts." (London: Clarke, 1628 – 1644).
21. Coke, *First Institute*, paragraph 80.
22. *Ibid.*, paragraph 138.
23. Parsons, "Utilitarianism . . . ," cited in note 19.
24. David Ricardo, *Principles of Political Economy and Taxation* (New York: Dutton, 1962); first published in 1817.
25. Thomas R. Malthus, *An Essay on Population* (New York: Dutton, 1958), two volumes; first published in 1798.
26. Karl Marx, *Capital* (Chicago: Kerr, 1925 – 1926), three volumes; Vol. 1 first published in 1867, Vols. 2 and 3 first published posthumously in German in 1885 and 1894.
27. For a discussion of "humanistic" Marxism, see the Editor's Introduction in Robert C. Tucker, *The Marx – Engels Reader* (New York: Norton, 1972).
28. Parsons, "Utilitarianism . . . ," cited in note 19.
29. Hobbes, *Leviathan*, cited in note 1.
30. *Ibid.*, Part 1, Chapter 13.
31. For a brief exposition, see Loren Eiseley, "The Cosmic Orphan," *Saturday Review/World* pp. 16 – 19 (February 23, 1974).
32. See Malinowski, *Magic, Science and Religion* . . . , cited in note 3.
33. Edward A. Tiryakian, "Toward the Sociology of Esoteric Culture," *American Journal of Sociology* 78:491 – 512 (November 1972); quotation from p. 504.

MODERNIZATION:
From Industrialization to Rationalization

We—members of the human species—are in the midst of the first truly global process of social change. And, we are likely to remain in that somewhat precarious predicament for as long into the future as it is at all useful to predict. This global process, which we may call modernization, affects every recognizable political entity—independent nations or their dependancies—and probably every tribe, community, or "culture."

> The "previously unstudied culture," so dear to the dreams of anthropologists, will, if and when discovered by questing ethnographers, not be found in its unsullied and pristine state. The tardy researcher will have been preceded by a military expedition, a tax collector, a missionary, or a Coca-Cola salesman.[1]

Other major discontinuities in cultural change have occurred, which partially fit an evolutionary criterion by exhibiting substantial increases in technical and societal sophistication. (The common association of evolution with gradualism does not fit some previous landmarks.) None has affected all of the extant social units, that is, did not become a cultural universal. The wheel, settled agriculture, and metallurgy were notable "practical" inventions. Written language, money, formal theologies, formal government, and formal legal systems were social inventions for managing human relationships. Each of these provided the basis for further change. But their diffusion was limited and remained so until all have become general only recently, having been caught up in the process of modernization. The one apparent exception is language, about which I previously commented:

> Language as symbolic communication appears to have been coextensive with the species from the beginning or near the beginning of its biological emergence

and differentiation from primate progenitors. It thus constitutes an "evolution-ary universal," but, whether its origins were singular or multiple, it became a principal basis of *differentiation* among human groups. It stands as a major limitation to the structural and cultural de-differentiation or homogenization inherent in the common process of modernization.[2]

Worldwide diffusion of technologies, designed to control "nature," and social technologies, designed to order human relationships, lend substance to the idea of "modernization," as that process is barely five centuries old. The voyages of Columbus to the Americas and of Vasco da Gama and other Portuguese explorers around Africa to India were quickly followed by one form or another of colonialism or imperialism. The European superiority in overseas transportation and in military organization and weaponry brought non-white, non-Christian, often non-literate peoples under European con-trol. But ideologies and beliefs, attitudes and customary practices, were in-creasingly influenced by this essentially European expansion into every sector of the globe—not simply the economic structures or the forms of political organization.

I make no attempt to cast up a balance sheet on colonialism or im-perialism, which have now become unfashionable in international political circles. A warning, however, is appropriate. The places and peoples affected were highly diverse (and, to a remarkable degree remain so), and almost equally diverse were the forms and degrees of external domination, even by the same colonial power. Marxist dogma, with the usual simplification, at-tends only to economic exploitation, which almost invariably occurred. (Many such enterprises, however, turned out to be very poor investments, as the costs of maintaining sufficient political control for exploitative purposes might easily exceed the economic benefits.) It is patently foolish to dismiss as insincere or irrelevant the missionary zeal of religious believers or the almost equal if somewhat more secular zeal of those who wanted to extend such benefits of civilization as medicine and public health, education, and the rule of formal law. And even the purveyors of goods manufactured in the met-ropole or some other industrializing country may have sincerely believed that they were spreading (obviously superior) Western culture while earning hon-orable profits for their pains.

It must also be noted that colonialism has proved to be a generally self-limiting situation, a system containing the seeds of its own destruction. To ease the burden of external rule, colonial authorities "co-opt" native leaders or cultivate new ones, thereby developing an intermediate class of Western-ized natives. Great Britain and France, the largest of the imperial powers until the rapid decline of overt colonialism after World War II, provided education in the home country for selected colonial subjects, and civil service, military, or merely commercial and managerial employment for those (and for others) locally educated. Thus, the rulers also trained the very leaders of independence movements. And, as colonial controls weakened, some native subjects could also travel and study in other countries, including the Soviet Union. Those colonial subjects who had the most direct, and the most favored, relations with the colonial authorities and with the mother country became the "modernizing elites" of the postcolonial national states.

JOINING THE MODERN WORLD

No major part of the world remained immune to what was essentially "Westernization." Africa came totally under European domination, partly with white settlers enjoying local ascendancy over native populations, which was also the pattern in the Americas, Australia, and New Zealand. Eastern Europe, reaching the borders of Russia, was largely under Western European control, once the Ottoman Empire had been restricted to the eastern Mediterranean. Russia's colonialism proceeded by land, extending across northern Asia to the Pacific. British rule in India, Burma, and Malaya was a patchwork of direct and indirect rule, with very unequal forms and degrees of political and legal organization and indeed of economic impact. The French in Indo-China faced comparable complexity, as did the Americans in the Philippines and the Dutch in Indonesia, although all of these colonial areas were in principle subject to more uniform policies than the British followed in India. China, militarily weak and politically disorganized, never became an outright colonial dependency but was forced to cede effective sovereignty in the "treaty ports," such as Shanghai. Japan remained fiercely independent while borrowing Western civilian and military technology and, not least, imperialistic nationalism, which led to a tardy attempt at its own colonial empire.

Western expansionism was probably inevitable, as it stemmed not only from booty-seeking or a later quest for raw materials and expanded markets for industrial capitalist enterprises. It also stemmed from a partly cultural and partly racial belief in Western superiority and in the West's civilizing mission in bringing to the lesser breeds of mankind the law and morals and religion along with more material benefits of prosperous and powerful countries. The outright extinction of some native cultures and the impairment of most others may lead us to sentimental regret, along with the economic exploitation ranging from slavery to more genteel forms of domination such as controlling the terms of trade to the disadvantage of colonial producers of raw-materials. In all fairness, it must be noted that the economic effect of colonialism was not purely negative. Roads, docks and, later, airfields were built, along with irrigation projects, warehouses, and stately governmental buildings. Changes in productive technology, in agriculture as well as industry, were not uniformly nefarious, although the imbalance caused in subsistence economies by the introduction of cash crops had negative as well as positive consequences in terms of traditional institutions and patterns of social organization.

Of the enduring residues of colonialism, or more properly of Westernization as the more general process, the most crucial one is not material but ideological. It is the universal commitment to modernization as a principal goal of national policy, buttressed by a nearly universal commitment to at least some parts of the process by individuals acting on their own behalf and that of their children. As the sociologist Arnold Feldman and I wrote a couple of decades ago:

> There is a kind of unification going on in the world. This unification represents a trend so strong that it is sweeping out of the way many differences in attitudes and beliefs. It proceeds apace despite political difficulties and international tensions, some of which are indeed a direct product of the very force that gives political entities similar goals but without necessarily creating mutual friendship. The unification reflects a commitment to improved material well-being and conditions of life as a goal of public policy and private endeavor. It turns up in the oddest places, and in fact in most places. A worldly doctrine, it is the single most successful conversion movement in the history of ideological diffusion. Its missionaries have been poorly organized, often unwitting, and certainly dissentious. They have succeeded to an often embarrassing extent.[3]

The various aspects of this world unification and its limits comprise the central themes of this book, as noted earlier. The extent to which the formerly exotic places in the world become less so with the establishment of international airports and resort hotels serving American-style or "continental" breakfasts, and the political philosophies expressed in international political debate, say at the United Nations, reflect some form of "Western" political philosophy—liberal, democratic, Marxist-Leninist—including nationalism itself, lends credence to the idea that the world is becoming "just like us." That is, these relatively recent developments support that conclusion if the "us" is made sufficiently comprehensive to include deeply different beliefs and lifestyles, and if we do not get far away from the cosmopolitan components of otherwise persistently different cultures.

Thus, virtually every country or culture has "joined the modern world" in some form and degree, which may be viewed either as confirming the superiority assumed by the missionaries, sacred and profane, who set that as a goal, or with nostalgic regret that traditional cultures of some cohesion and charm have been subverted by external interference over a half millenium of arrogant expansionism.

ECONOMIC DEVELOPMENT AND ITS SOCIAL SETTING

It was "improved material well-being" that Feldman and I believed to provide the common component of public policy in the contemporary world; and that perception is still valid though somewhat too limited. Yet economic development is certainly a major part of any commitment to modernization, for it stands as a goal for the reduction of poverty increasingly perceived and increasingly resented. It also becomes the essential means for increasing administrative efficiency of government; the development of military forces and other seemingly essential trappings of sovereign national states; for support of expanding educational systems, medicine, public health, and perhaps public support for the arts.

Industrialization came to be used as a kind of equivalent for economic growth and development. That equivalence is not technically correct, but it rested on a more fundamental truth. No country has achieved a substantial level of prosperity through increasing agricultural production alone, or even through agriculture and commerce. Indeed, until the formation of the international cartel of oil-producing countries, no country had achieved prosperity solely from raw-materials exploitation. It has been in manufacturing, especially, that productive technology has yielded major increases in the output of goods, with a wondrous diversity of things made as well as in sheer volume of any particular product. In the economic history of the older industrial countries, an agricultural "revolution" preceded the industrial "revolution" (both being revolutionary only figuratively and in retrospect). Continued increases both in agricultural productivity per unit of labor and in total output have depended on a feedback from manufacturing through mechanization, chemical fertilizers, food processing, and transportation. The poor countries of the world were, and remain, primarily agricultural in their economic base; and their problem became that of industrialization.

Since modernization—the term itself is of rather recent vintage—was seen, with some justification, as primarily a problem of economic development, it is scarcely surprising that comparative economists were the first social scientists on the scene. However, as early as 1950, the eminent historical and quantitative economist Simon Kuzenets sponsored formation of the Committee on Economic Growth of the (American) Social Science Research Council. That committee had several other economists in its membership, but also a geographer, an anthropologist, and a sociologist. The principal form of committee activity was the identification of a critical aspect of socioeconomic change about which scholars in various disciplines and universities were thought to have interesting research ideas and theoretical orientations to contribute. Papers were solicited for discussion at a conference, and most conferences resulted in published symposia. One of the first of these was

Economic Growth: Brazil, India, Japan,[4] which, despite its title, had two of its three major topical divisions devoted to "population and labor force" and to "social structure and the state." Other symposia exhibited similar breadth, whatever their somewhat arbitrary titles: *Labor Commitment and Social Change in Developing Areas*,[5] *Economic Transition in Africa*,[6] *Social Structure and Mobility in Economic Development*.[7] It would be unduly cynical to say that the interdisciplinary integration was represented by the binding on each book, for substantial attempts at integration were presented in essays by the editors, at least one of whom for each volume was usually a member of the sponsoring committee. Yet it is fair to say that no integrated theory emerged from 16 years of committee activity.

The interest in economic development was of course not solely an American scholarly concern. UNESCO sponsored several conferences in different world regions on "social aspects of industrialization" in 1959 and 1960, culminating in a roundup conference in 1960, followed by the inevitable symposium, edited by Bert F. Hoselitz and me,[8] both, incidentally, "charter members" of the Committee on Economic Growth.

What was emerging, in effect, was a limited set of scholars, principally economists and sociologists, who were not totally naive about each other's discipline, attempting to become steadily less naive at least with respect to the subject of economic development. For example, when the Committee on Economic Growth was formed in 1950, I was just completing an analysis from published sources (supplemented by field research in Mexico) of the economic and non-economic incentives in industrial labor recruitment and of the structural and attitudinal impediments to this form of rational mobility.[9] Perhaps more significantly, shortly thereafter Hoselitz was responsible for the founding, in 1952, of the journal, *Economic Development and Cultural Change*.[10] The title of that journal represented our conventional wisdom in the social sciences as to both the primarily economic source of change and its consequences for transformed cultures in the broad, anthropological sense of the term.

Yet it must be noted that in the very first article in Volume I, number 1 of the journal, Hoselitz, though using the title "Non-Economic Barriers to Economic Development,"[11] attends to the attitudinal and organizational preconditions for economic development and notes that economic development in fact is not tied to particular forms of government or particular ideologies. This latter empirically accurate observation came to be neglected in much of the writing on modernization over the ensuing quarter-century, not so much by denial, as by implicit assumption that modernization—encompassing economic development, its preconditions, and its structural and "cultural" concomitants and consequences—had led and would lead to increasing uniformity in most significant features of attitudes, values, and actual structured behavior in the world's societies. True, some scholars have issued warnings concerning both initial and persistent sources of differentiation. Hoselitz, for example, noted the historical and situational bases for differentiation in patterns of economic growth.[12] Manning Nash has reviewed the sources of variability in the paths and destinations of modernizing and modernized societies, along with the common features of industrialization (essentially as a proxy for modernization).[13] The political scientist Karl Deutsch, though stressing the rapid spread of some aspects of modernization globally, is cautious both with regard to international peace and with respect to what he terms "residual diversity."[14] And I have noted "persistent pluralism" and, later, attempted a fairly extensive analysis of the reasons for expecting pluralism to continue among industrialized societies and to increase as others move toward the goals of modernization and achieve at least some of them.[15]

It was no doubt the quest for generality, for a unifying theory of modernization, that led many of us to over-generalization. In a recent essay, the anthropologist Manning Nash refers to "the widening gap between the intellectuals and the process" of modernization.[16] Anthropologists, especially, have all along taken a suitably or excessively cautionary position, particularly— and suitably—with respect to the tendency to consider "traditional" societies (that is, non-modernized ones) as a homogeneous category. Those economists actually studying the process in a variety of settings, as distinct from their model-building colleagues, have also learned to take a more cautious view, not only of the uniformity of modernization across time and space but also of the invariance of the results in societies much less closely integrated than the conventional sociological models assume. Thus, Benjamin Higgins asks whether economic development and cultural change are a "seamless web or patchwork quilt," concluding that the latter is the better metaphor.[17] Though he thinks that there is "a dwindling group of sociologists and anthropologists (which) stresses the need for social change as a prerequisite for economic development,"[18] he quickly notes that political organization is crucial. Here, citing Guy Hunter,[19] Higgins properly emphasizes that more than political stability is required. Although political stability is clearly necessary for economic development, in the contemporary world a poor country trying to get a start toward catching up with more prosperous ones will require active political instigation fitted—but not too fitted—to local circumstances.

Higgins's patchwork quilt is at times seamy indeed. The contemporary world continues to offer diversity, not just between the rich and poor countries, but within each category. Some "development" has taken place everywhere, but some of it at high human costs. The invariant circumstance that rapid growth in some aspects of economic activity leads to increases in income inequality has produced some situations in which the poor become absolutely and not simply relatively poorer. Political regimes seeking not only order but development have proceeded to slaughter substantial portions of subject populations and to supress others, sometimes in the name of reactionary nationalism or ethnic ascendancy, sometimes with recourse to the radical rhetoric of some variant of Marxism.

Then the social setting of economic development does make a difference.[20] Transferable property rights in land and other forms of capital, in energy and natural resources, and in consumer goods are essential if a rationalized economy is to operate. (State ownership as in fully socialist systems still requires transferability of rights in use and control from one state unit to another, and eventually to household consumers.) Potential workers must be mobile, probably in physical location, certainly in social (including economic) position. There is no apathy, to say nothing of resistance, to personal or familial economic improvement anywhere. But, any change is likely to affect some interests adversely and some of the unacceptable costs may well be "sentimental," as well as merely economic. No one now seems to argue that members of "primitive" or other traditional societies are "prerational" and thus incapable of perceiving and pursuing their self-interests. There remains, however, some dispute about the relevance of attitudes or personality structures. Alex Inkeles and David Horton Smith, in reporting a highly sophisticated six-country study of the acquisition of "modern" attitudes, demonstrate rather conclusively that factory employment itself is a socializing experience in "becoming modern."[21] Unfortunately, their research still does not answer the question as to why some rural dwellers migrate to seek and secure factory work and others do not. The psychologist David McClelland continues to insist on group differentials in "need achievement," which he views as a more activist orientation than simply making choices among real and present alternatives.[22]

CONVERGENCE THEORY
AND THE MODEL MODERNIZED SOCIETY

Exaggeration of the commonalities among premodernized societies and neglect of the different historical paths to the present among societies that have been subject to varying external influences and local initiatives would be partially forgivable under two assumptions: (1) that all are headed for the same destination despite different starting-points and intermediate routes; and (2) that "success" is assured despite various obstacles such as meager resources, ethnic diversity and conflict, inept political organization, or a condition of "neo-colonial dependency" imposed by powerful and prosperous countries.

Much of the work on the social consequences of modernization has rested on both of these assumptions. The second assumption, the certainty or probability of success, has had less theoretical or empirical foundation than has the assumed common destination. Optimism on this point is scarcely warranted by current observation of recent trends, although some partial successes (on one or another indicator of modernity) do exist. The only theory that would encourage a clearly favorable view of the future is a kind of revived social evolutionism, with its ridiculous assumption that a teleological orientation toward a more advanced "stage" somehow inheres in all social systems but without conscious direction or decision. Otherwise, we are left with the undisputed fact that modernization (particularly economic development) does figure among the articulated purposes of real political officials, though apparently with differing saliency as well as differing competence in actual implementation.

For the assumption of a common destination, both the theoretical base and the actual observation of comparative structural change are somewhat superior to the situation with respect to estimating the probability of universal success. By use of a functional-system model familiar to sociologists (though often properly criticized in the discipline), the stipulation of such a major structural change as, say, advanced industrialization, must have consequences for many other properties of the system. Work organization, the administrative structure of the state, the forms of social control and of social inequality, urbanization, education, norms of mobility and achievement, the structure of the family and kinship—these will not be exactly alike, but approximately so, in part because there are systemic interdependencies that provide limits to structural variability. These commonalities have led modernization theorists to an error less outrageous than the assumption of the homogeneity of all traditional societies, but an error nevertheless.

Convergence theory may be characterized as an unqualified, affirmative answer to the question, "Are industrial societies becoming alike?" By extension, convergence theory predicts the increasing similarity of all societies *if they achieve modernization at some stipulated level*. We have just been noting that neither convergence theory nor its derivative, modernization theory, assesses the probability of "success," but only stipulates the costs and benefits of success, if achieved. The circumstance that the quest for modernization is now an ideological universal (with variant and often internally inconsistent doctrines regarding efficacious means) sets at rest some spurious issues concerning the exportability of values, but leaves some major value differences, along with differences in resources, organizations, and normative structures significant for both the course and the destination of change.

It is well to make explicit the derivation of modernization theory from convergence theory. To the extent that modernization theory, applied to "developing areas," predicts the outcome of economic development, efficacious political mobilization, or educational extension and upgrading, it does so on the basis of the more or less coherent and thus systemic commonalities among highly modernized (or "post-industrial") societies. As Clark Kerr, at the time (1960) at least a true believer in convergence, put it: "This particular history gets written from the future into the present—what is currently happening comes from what is to be. The future is the cause and the present is the effect."[23]

Thus, in effect, the argument presupposes a "model modernized society" as a standard for approximation or achievement. As such, the theory lacks "rates, routes, and timetables"; it neglects the differing historical paths to the present among societies now identified as full members of the modernized club, and the certainty of still different paths for those now seeking admission. The theory is silent on the probabilities of success; and it significantly exaggerates the homogeneity of the present, and a fortiori the possible future, members of the privileged circle.

The identification of the common structural features (and even typical tensions and conflicts) of highly modernized societies, and demonstration of the interrelations and thus systemic properties of those features have been no mean accomplishments. The identification of preconditions, concomitants, and consequences with different temporal orders and degrees of determinateness[24] moves a significant step away from mere comparative statics with its explicit or implicit reliance on correlational analysis toward a dynamic, sequential, and even partially causal analysis. Yet that step has not met most of the objections or deficiencies just noted with respect to convergence-derived modernization theory, for the analysis still lacks measurement and the demonstration of particular causal links, and attention to the real heterogeneity of both structure and change in developing as well as developed societies. It follows that, apart from some economic growth models that precisely fail of practicality because of their neglect of social structure and "culture," modernization theory offers little of practical utility to modernizers other than insistent emphasis on systemic interdependence. That emphasis, without demonstrated and efficacious causal linkages, is likely to be overly cautionary ("change everything at once") or overly optimistic ("every little bit helps").[25]

Modernization has come into increasing use to identify a general process, comprising both "economic development" and "cultural change," the latter in the wide anthropological sense of the term comprising social structure as well as beliefs, values, and norms. The operational definitions of modernization range from Levy's essentially technological indicator (preponderant use of inanimate sources of power)[26] to measures of gross national product, proportions of economic activity outside the primary economic sector (agriculture and extractive activities), extension of relatively uniform law and effective administration throughout the claimed territory of nominally sovereign states, or the institutionalization of change. The systemic character of societies (or national polities) is reconfirmed by the moderately high correlations among these indicators, and indeed others: literacy, low mortality and fertility rates, telephones per capita.[27] Even these relationships are not uniformly confirmed. Higgins, referring to quantitative studies by the United Nations Research Institute for Social Development but not giving a precise reference, indicates a finding of generally low correlations among various economic, demographic, and educational indicators (though other social or political measures were not involved).[28] The closest relationships, Higgins reports, were among strictly economic indicators, and one could scarcely dispute the centrality of economic performance in definitions and indicators of modernization, for it stands both as an autonomous goal distributively and collectively and as an essential means for implementing educational, political, and even some recreational and expressive goals. Ranking countries by various measures and computing rank-order correlations may also help identify anomalies, but, of course, tells nothing of trends, leads and lags, or the consequences of alternative paths and strategies.

MODERNIZATION AS RATIONALIZATION

In recent years I have become convinced that a seemingly simple conceptual or semantic transformation has substantial analytic utility. If modernization is defined as the process of rationalization of social behavior and social organization, one avoids the vagueness of "joining the modern world" and the ethnocentric connotations of "becoming just like us." More positively, rationalization suggests particular aspects or processes that partially cut across the more conventional attention to major functional aspects of society that are analytically and perhaps structurally differentiated (economy, polity, religion, community, education, stratification, family). It also calls attention to the instrumental character of the processes of change, clarifying the significance of differences in beliefs and values, in attitudes and sentiments, that have served, among other functions, to exasperate developmental economists and to reconfirm the cautions of relativistic anthropologists and sociologists.

The historic spread, over the last several centuries, of aspects or by-products of modernization from its fountainhead in northwestern Europe and, later, the United States to the outermost reaches of the world can be viewed as a multifaceted process of cultural diffusion. Diffusion, of course, continues in the contemporary era as exemplified not only in "transfer of technology" but also in eclectic sampling of what might be called "mail-order political ideologies." In one crucial respect, however, diffusion has been so pervasive and universally successful that the theoretical model no longer fits. The ideology or doctrine of modernization has become, in a sense, nationalized. That is, it has become an indigenous component of societies otherwise conspicuously diverse in structure and belief. Another value has also become universal—nationalism expressed as national sovereignity and self-determination. Nationalism is commonly linked to modernization as a rationale for political mobilization and centrally coordinated change. Its emphasis on independence and distinctiveness, however, is a major source of willful diversity among modernizing and indeed among highly modernized societies.

Modernization as a national, collective goal always includes economic development for such perceived collective political benefits as a military establishment, a technically competent civil service, as well as the support of nationally sponsored investments such as irrigation, power, and an international airline. Economic development is also sought for its distributive benefits, to provide for consumer demand that is increasingly insistent from populations that recognize their poverty and do not recognize their condition as either inevitable or just. Modernization, as a politically articulated goal, also includes the expansion of education as a kind of universally accepted prescription for personal improvement and medical and public health facilities, recognizing that health and longevity are also values that know no cultural boundaries.

This brief discussion of goals or values is not meant to discount all value differences, which are real enough, but to put those differences in perspective with respect to long-existing or recently emerging commonalities. And specification of goals is important if we are to view modernization as comprising instrumental activities designed to optimize goals. I have suggested that those instrumental activities be taken as manifestations of *rationalization*, despite the prior use of that term by psychologists to characterize the offering of spurious but self-serving or socially acceptable explanations for basely or irrationally motivated conduct. The cumbersome phrase "institutionalization of rationality" could be used, meaning by that the normative expectation that objective information and a rational calculus of procedures will be applied in pursuit or achievement of any utilitarian goal. Rationalization is the shorthand term for submitting social behavior to that normative standard. It is exemplified but not exhausted by the use of sophisticated technology in construction and production. As defined, it also includes an impressive body of social technology along with applications of physical, chemical, and biological knowledge.

In the chapters that follow I shall explore the various applications of instrumental problem-solving, along with limits to the process—limits that are partly peculiar to particular societies and cultures, partly intrinsic to the human condition as it is biologically endowed and socially required from life in organized social systems.

NOTES

1. Wilbert E. Moore, "Modernization as Rationalization: Processes and Restraints," in Manning Nash, ed., *Essays on Economic Development and Cultural Change in Honor of Bert F. Hoselitz,* Supplement to Vol. 25 of *Economic Development and Cultural Change* (Chicago: University of Chicago Press, 1977), pp. 29–42; quotation from p. 29.
2. *Ibid.* Parentheses in original omitted.
3. Wilbert E. Moore and Arnold S. Feldman, "Preface," in Moore and Feldman, eds., *Labor Commitment and Social Change in Developing Areas* (New York: Social Science Research Council, 1960), p. v.
4. Simon Kuznets, Wilbert E. Moore, and Joseph J. Spengler, eds., *Economic Growth: Brazil, India, Japan* (Durham, NC: Duke University Press, 1955).
5. Moore and Feldman, work cited in note 3.
6. Melville J. Herskovits and Mitchell Harwitz, *Economic Transition in Africa* (Evanston, IL: Northwestern University Press, 1964).
7. Neil J. Smelser and Seymour Martin Lipset, *Social Structure and Mobility in Economic Development* (Chicago: Aldine, 1966).
8. Bert F. Hoselitz and Wilbert E. Moore, eds., *Industrialization and Society* (The Hague: Mouton and UNESCO, 1963).
9. Wilbert E. Moore, *Industrialization and Labor: Social Aspects of Economic Develpoment* (Ithaca and New York: Cornell University Press, 1951; reissued by Russell and Russell, New York, 1965).
10. *Economic Development and Cultural Change,* published by the University of Chicago Press since 1952.
11. Bert F. Hoselitz, "Non-Economic Barriers to Economic Development," *Economic Development and Cultural Change* 1:8–21 (March 1952).
12. Hoselitz, "Patterns of Economic Growth," *Canadian Journal of Economics and Political Science* 21:416–431 (November 1955).
13. Manning Nash, "Industrialization: The Ecumenical and Parochial Aspects of the Process," in Nancy Hammond, ed., *Social Science and the New Societies* (East Lansing: Social Science Research Bureau, Michigan State University, 1973).
14. Karl W. Deutsch, "Social and Political Convergence in Industrializing Countries—Some Concepts and the Evidence," in *ibid.*
15. Wilbert E. Moore, *The Impact of Industry* (Englewood Cliffs, NJ: Prentice-Hall, 1965); Moore, "The Singular and the Plural: The Social Significance of Industrialism Reconsidered," in *Social Science and the New Societies,* cited in note 13.
16. Manning Nash, "Modernization: Cultural Meanings—The Widening Gap Between the Intellectuals and the Process," in Nash, ed., *Essays on Economic Development . . . ,* cited in note 1, pp. 16–28.
17. Benjamin Higgins, "Economic Develpoment and Cultural Change: Seamless Web or Patchwork Quilt?" in *ibid.,* pp. 99–122.
18. *Ibid.,* p. 114.
19. Guy Hunter, *Modernizing Peasant Societies: A Comparative Study in Asia and Africa* (London: Oxford University Press, 1969).
20. For a more extensive discussion, see Moore, *The Impact of Industry,* cited in note 15, Chapter 3, "Conditions for Industrialization."

21. Alex Inkeles and David Horton Smith, *Becoming Modern* (Cambridge, MA: Harvard University Press, 1974).
22. David C. McClelland, *The Achieving Society* (New York: Van Nostrand, 1961); McClelland and D. G. Winter, *Motivating Economic Achievement* (New York: Free Press, 1969); McClelland, "The Psychological Causes and Consequences of Modernization: An Ethiopian Case Study," in Manning Nash, ed., work cited in note 1, pp. 43–66.
23. Clark Kerr, "Changing Social Structures," in Moore and Feldman, eds. *Labor Commitment . . .*, cited in note 3, Chapter 9: quotation from p. 358. See also Kerr et al., *Industrialism and Industrial Man* (Cambridge: Harvard University Press, 1960), especially Part III, "The Road Ahead."
24. See, for example, Moore, *The Impact of Industry*, cited in note 15.
25. See Wilbert E. Moore, "Problems of Timing, Balance, and Priorities in Development Measures," *Economic Development and Cultural Change* 2:239–248 (January 1954).
26. Marion J. Levy, Jr., *Modernization: Latecomers and Survivors* (New York: Basic Books, 1972); Levy, *Modernization and the Structure of Societies* (Princeton, NJ: Princeton University Press, 1966), two volumes.
27. See, for example, Phillips Cutright, "National Political Development: Measurement and Analysis," *American Sociological Review* 28:253–264 (April 1963).
28. Higgins, essay cited in note 17.

3
COMMERCIALIZATION

Every human society has an orderly system of distribution of goods and services necessary for individual and collective survival. Were this not true, no infant could survive, and those temporarily or permanently unable to fend for themselves such as the ill, the wounded, and the unproductive old would be abandoned to die. An occasional social isolate, having survived infancy and childhood through the care of others and having acquired "coping skills" that in the human species are always and exclusively learned from others and never instinctual, may survive as a "hermit" without further recourse to social discourse. For all others, dependency and interdependency relations are normal and necessary.

Through most of human history—in whatever place, in whichever otherwise distinctive culture—dependency relations have been managed through family and kinship organization. Modern socialist and welfare states have substituted charitable or governmental systems of support, first with respect to those lacking responsible kin or in familial situations without adequate resources, and then increasingly as a narrowing of kinship obligations. It can be argued that this trend is a manifestation of rationalization of support systems, and certainly it inevitably entails a high degree of standardization and impersonality, but, of course, it also manifests a value shift from individual to collective responsibility for basic sustenance—also for education, medical services, and a diverse mixture of other social benefits. Public welfare systems mark a distinct departure, as conservative opponents never cease to remind us, from the Social Darwinist doctrine of "survival of the fittest" (which often simply meant the luckiest, such as those whose fitness was demonstrated by the wise decision to be born to well-to-do parents). They also mark a distinct departure from a "pure market" mode of distribution of any sort, but then this figment of economists' imagination never prevailed in the dependency and interdependency relations within families.

My concern here is with interdependency relations, that is, with distribution that involves exchange of goods and services among persons (or families or any other organized social units) who are in some degree specialized in what they produce and therefore likely to be dependent on others for at least part of what they consume. In the limiting case, sometimes assumed as normal in primitive (or non-literate or tribal) societies, the family or household is the self-sufficient unit economically, though not politically or in terms of marriage patterns. In fact, that situation is notably rare, even in hunting and gathering societies, for, as Udy has shown,[1] some activities such as building or boat construction may require both labor and skills beyond that available to every familial unit, and the talents or trained skills for tool-making or hunting and fishing and possibly warfare are likely to be uneven and result in various "achieved" status-and-role assignments—somewhat independent of kinship links.

Thus, some form of exchange outside family units is common, even prior to modern markets and such partial substitutes for markets as socialist schemes of distribution through a centrally controlled administration of prices for goods and services and of prices for labor which become family incomes. The process of rationalization of exchange relationships thus represents a feature of modernization that does not introduce a totally novel social function, creating a radical discontinuity between "traditional" and "modern," but rather introduces behavioral and structural alterations and refinements in a virtually universal characteristic of organized societies. We shall encounter other such features, but they must await their turn.

MONETIZATION OF EXCHANGE

Forms of exchange relationships vary widely in human experience. They range from mutual aid among kinsmen and neighbors, involving reciprocities but not necessarily precisely calculated equality of benefits, through ritualized forms of gift-giving (which still involve reciprocities and may, as Belshaw notes,[2] permit calculations of relative advantage) and "simple" barter with its implied equality of benefits, to highly sophisticated transactions in international money markets. Belshaw, writing from the viewpoint of a comparative anthropologist, says that "there are . . . as many exchange systems as there are types of societies, for they are fundamentally coterminous."[3]

Yet is it interesting to note that the monetized market system, which is the principal indicator of the rationalization of exchange, has not in contemporary "modernized" societies completely displaced more "traditional" forms. Reciprocities based on what sociologists call "particularistic" relations have not disappeared, nor have ritualized gift-giving or simple barter. Indeed, complexity is compounded by the addition of taxation and welfare distributions ("transfer payments" in the language of national income accounting) and somewhat similar functions by private charitable organizations that depend on current contributions and by charitable foundations established by philanthropists, some of them "perpetuities"—as nominally immortal as the national state itself. These latter additions to the forms of distribution (which, incidentally, could not be derived from such simplistic exchange theories as formulated by Homans[4]) have more in common with dependency relations than with interdependence and exchange. They differ from conventional forms of dependency in significant respects, representing forms of rationalization: (1) The assessment of taxes and the distribution of benefits, or the solicitation of charitable gifts and their distribution to worthy causes or needy cases, or the establishment by a donor of a charitable trust and the distribution of the income by a salaried staff to eligible applicants are impersonal transactions. Though individual recipients may be investigated extensively with respect to their personal lives, the inquiry is in terms of formal criteria of eligibility. (2) Although welfare and charitable distributions may be made "in kind" (food, free rent, medical services), much is in the form of money, with or without restrictions on how it may be spent. In any event, the intermediaries between the ultimate donors (taxpayers, contributors to charities, founders of foundations) and the ultimate recipients operate with monetary budgets and accounting systems.

It is monetization, then, that is the most crucial mechanism for rationalization of exchange and distribution, for it lends itself to careful, instrumental calculation in the achievement of individual and collective goals. Whatever the varieties and complications, to some of which I shall briefly attend, the critical definition—and function—of money is as a generalized medium of exchange. Anything that can be used in standardized units with a relatively constant value in exchange for other goods or services will serve as money; in historical and comparative perspective the variety of such "monetary" units has been wide indeed. A frequent basis for monetary units has been coins of precious or semiprecious metals, minted according to standard sizes and metallic purity, permitting fractions and multiples of the unit in coins of sizes approximately proportional to their unitary value. (Whether such coin money has been independently invented or borrowed from earlier precedents, as appears to be the case of the Mediterranean—European world, need not concern us.) Given the presumption of a metallurgical capacity, which many cultures did not develop, coins have the advantage of ready portability and recognizability among parties to exchange relationships, and the additional advantage of "intrinsic" worth that helps assure their exchangeability for other goods or services. Now "intrinsic" value can only mean that the substance from which the coin is made has other uses (for example, as jewelry or other esthetic objects, or as a component of more utilitarian products). Thus coin money has advantages in establishing links between different monetary systems (assuming, say, that gold is universally valued), and for providing confidence in exchangeability when there is substantial distrust of purely symbolic tokens of value such as paper currency.

Metallic coinage has some critical disadvantages as well: in large quantities such money is portable only with great difficulty and great risk; and if the intrinsic value of the coins rests on the relative scarcity of the metals (which have other uses), a metallic coinage is likely to limit severely the amount of money actually available for use as a medium of exchange. In a monetized exchange system, this will invariably lead to the use of purely symbolic tokens of exchange value, carrying varying degrees of exchangeability unless authenticated as "legal tender" by a recognized and moderately stable government. (Legal tender simply means that the token must be accepted for its stated value in monetary units in payment of all debts, public or private.) Coins in all contemporary monetary systems now serve as fractional parts of standard monetary units to accommodate petty transactions and to make exact change. Their metallic value for other uses is less than their stated monetary value, which means that they have become almost as purely tokens as is paper currency.

But we must not become entangled in the varieties of money, whether in comparative and historical perspective or in terms of refinements in contemporary monetary theory in technical economics. That assiduous taxonomist, Max Weber, may be consulted on some of the refinements.[5] What is of interest here is that money as a highly generalized medium of exchange permits and may even be said to encourage a strictly rational calculus in relationships of interdependency that might, both theoretically and experientially, rest on very different grounds.

The concept of money does, however, require some additional specification. As a medium of exchange money also becomes a store of value, for investment or future exchange. This also means that money includes bank deposits, bonds, notes, and other certificates of indebtedness, as well as checks. It is thus foolish to say that money may disappear from use with credit cards and electronic transfer of debts and credits among banks and other financial organizations. This is simply carrying paper currency, the intrinsic value of which is negligible, one step further. As Belshaw properly notes, the critical characteristics of money are liquidity and acceptability over a wide range of transactions—both implied by its characterization as a generalized medium of exchange.[6] Oscar Wilde's famous complaint that Americans knew the price of everything and the value of nothing could surely be generalized to the participants in all highly monetized exchange systems. The estate tax collectors, if no one else, are likely to set a "fair value" or market price on possessions that had for the possessor chiefly expressive, recreational, or esthetic value. Money is useful for whatever it will buy, and an eagerness to acquire money is not necessarily materialistic. Influence and power, recreation and esthetic experience, provision of an estate for heirs, and philanthropy are all possible objects of monetary aquisitiveness.

The monetization of exchange is likely to affect goods before it does services. That is, a commodities market of some sort, perhaps limited initially to only a limited range of "trade goods" not locally available, is likely before persons work for others in exchange for money. In a strictly economic sense, money is useless unless there are goods and services "wanted" by its recipient that money will buy. For example, in a mainly subsistence economy with a modernized and thus monetized sector, individuals may want particular products available only by acquiring money. Some portion of the agricultural product that might be done without may have cash value and the sale permits purchase of the "novel" products. Otherwise, if there is a demand in the modernized sector for unskilled workers, individuals who can be spared (at least for a period) may seek wage labor that permits some savings to be accumulated until sufficient for the price of the products desired. These have been called "target workers," as their commitment to wage labor is temporary and conditional; once the target is hit, the worker is free to return to more conventional activities.[7]

There is, however, an exception to the presumption that labor markets are dependent on the prior existence of commodity markets. In the colonial regimes of sub-Saharan Africa, taxes were imposed on the natives. In the French colonies taxes might be paid by a number of days of labor on roads or other public works—the *corvée*—for the large majority of village dwellers without access to money. The English generally required payment of hut taxes or head taxes in money, and the target of temporary workers initially became simply the required payment to the political authorities.[8] Whether this forced monetization as a consequence of political dependency was intended to be "educational" in the uses of money for ordinary private exchange may be doubted, but that was its inevitable result. Labor was performed in mines or large-scale agriculture or in domestic service in towns and urban areas, where the worker was exposed to exotic products as well as organizations and styles of life. The consumption standards of the dominant group could only be emulated, at however modest a scale, by acquiring money.

Monetization of exchange is commonly viewed in terms of "markets." The classical economists' conception of a "pure" market entailed considerable numbers of buyers and sellers, each with access to all information appropriate to transactions such as the offers being made by various potential buyers and the asking prices set by various potential sellers of a standardized commodity. Competition among the sellers (and possibly among the buyers) will shortly establish a uniform price that will "clear the market," although some participants might be disappointed, since not all buyers may attach the same value to that commodity among alternative uses for their money and not all sellers may be able to supply the commodity at the established price and still make a profit or stay in business. Perhaps the closest approximation to such markets is the market for money itself—that is, international currency exchanges among banks and similar entities—and trading in bonds, stocks, and commodity futures. Most markets display various kinds of "impurities." Let me note a number of significant ones, in a far from exhaustive catalogue.

1. The goods or units of service may not be standardized. All markets depend on a framework of rules with respect to fairness in weights, measures, and descriptions if products are not readily subject to inspection. (These rules inevitably expand as new forms of deceit and dishonesty are tried by purveyors seeking a competitive advantage.) Yet real or claimed quality differences may make competing products or services not strictly comparable.

2. Perfect information is as unlikely as any other form of perfection. Even aside from problems of quality and the inability of the ordinary purchaser to judge the merits of various mechanical or chemical ingredients and combinations, finding the best bargain for comparable products may be difficult and expensive. Spending money to travel to a purveyor with a lower price that would save far less than the cost of getting there scarcely represents rational calculation. Information itself is likely to be expensive, although competition among sellers to announce their prices may aid the moderately industrious buyer. (Of course, purveyors unwilling to meet the lowest advertised prices will emphasize convenience, ambience, or reliability—and even civility. Not all of these fit normal criteria of rationality.)

3. Even in a nominally competitive market, many prices are essentially "administered" rather than set in competition with other purveyors. This is especially notable in the contemporary United States where "oligopoly"—competition among the few—prevails, as in steel and automobiles. Price competition tends to be minimal or missing, as it is likely to be too hazardous, and might well develop into an illegal monopoly. (The natural outcome of any competitive system that does not severely limit competitive strategies is a monopoly: winner takes all. Economists

who remain enthusiastic about pure markets seem never to have understood this elementary principle of social dynamics.) Where collective bargaining in setting wage rates is backed by law, the agreement reached results in an administered price. Managerial and technical positions in both public and private bureaucracies (in mixed economies such as those of Western Europe, Canada, the United States, and elsewhere) have salary levels only partly affected by those of other possible employers.

4. The impersonality of monetized markets is always subject to impairment in the case of units of labor, although standardization of performance criteria and the subjection of interpersonal relations to elaborate and punctilious bureaucratic rules represent forms of rationalization intended to minimize emotion as well as simple variability in human personality. Even commodity transactions, including financial markets that most closely approximate "purity" in other respects, depend upon trust among traders. And any enduring and somewhat limited set of participants in local or specialized markets will be likely to supplement formal exchange transactions with "irrelevant" interaction. Since some of these examples represent limits on rationalization, I shall return to these points later.

But what of distribution in a non-competitive socialist system? Theoretically, in a completely planned and controlled economic system, the planners could "simply" determine the population size, age distribution, and possibly other criteria of consumer needs (such as type of activity and climatic location), determine the feasible or otherwise appropriate level of consumption and thus the requirements for consumer goods. Capital and military goods would be added to this, including transportation, storage, and distribution outlets. (There will be little or nothing to distribute if the planners are firm Marxist believers who accept the ridiculous doctrines of historical materialism by which only physical production is relevant, forgetting the services of planners, managers, teachers, medical and public health workers, not to mention political decision-makers and surveillance and police functions.) To avoid the human propensity to cheat, rationing coupons would have to be issued to, or on behalf of, every member of the population not confined to a "total institution" under constant surveillance. Separate kinds of coupons would need to be issued for each commodity or service available for distribution, or the coupons would become a generalized medium of exchange—that is, money. Even with categorical rationing, unless each coupon carried the proper holder's name or identification number, to be checked against a mandatory identification card with the proper holder's picture, a barter black-market in exchanging shoe-coupons for jacket-coupons would be virtually impossible to prevent. (An identification number prominently tattooed on the forehead, though expedient, might not be highly regarded by a significant part of the population.)

Categorical rationing quickly becomes ridiculously complex when one is beyond food and clothing. A hardware store carries thousands of distinct items in stock, and the American drug store a confusing array. What I am suggesting is that dispensing with money, and what it implies by way of some degree of consumer discretion, would certainly entail inordinate administrative costs. Such cumbersome administrative machinery might aid in providing full employment, but it would add nothing to the "welfare output" of the economy—that is, the supply of goods and services for satisfying the needs or "wants" of the population. Needs—however determined—are of course not uniform across a population, or for any individual at different stages in the life-cycle.

It is diversification of the product-structure of an economy that requires monetized distribution. Product diversification necessarily demands task specialization, but specialized producers of goods and services must have a way to become, along with any dependents, generalized consumers. Someone has noted that in the vast range of work-performing organizations only banks can pay employees out of inventory.

The Soviet system of distribution presents a situation of the state as sole employer and, with the exception of a small free market in fresh produce, sole distributor. The system features administered prices for labor compensation, administrative decisions on what goods and services will be available, and administered prices for their delivery. This system departs so far from the model of capitalist markets that it more closely approximates a money-mediated (and notably inequalitarian) rationing system. Yet operating with money even at the household level provides some consumer choice, and therefore opportunities for some degree of wisdom or foolishness in management of available resources.

For countries seeking rationalization of their economic systems, both commodity and labor markets are essential. And it is scarcely necessary to add that a monetized taxation and fiscal system is necessary, as the state needs money for its own equipment and supplies and for its payroll, as well as for such transfer payments (oriented to welfare recipients or various kinds of subsidies) as public policy requires. Though some types of foreign trade may involve straight barter arrangements, generally both exports and imports are paid in convertible currencies. Similarly, foreign aid may be given in kind, but usually it will include cash or credits; the same is true of foreign loans.

The extent of the monetization of the internal economy, if it can be measured or credibly estimated, is itself a sensitive indicator of economic rationalization. Here, however, some cautions are in order. Goods and particularly services that move through the market are more reliably observed and measured than those that do not. Estimates of production in national income accounts attempt to calculate the value of goods consumed by the producing unit or through non-monetary exchange, such as vegetable gardens and the products of domestic animals. Services are relatively "invisible," being consumed at the time of their production and delivery and not being storable. Thus the monetization of services customarily rendered on the basis of traditional dependency relations or reciprocity may yield a spurious increase in production, adding nothing to the welfare output of the system. Some underestimation of the value of goods production and gross underestimation of the value of services must be involved in estimates of the annual Gross National Product per capita in poor countries of under 100 United States dollars, as there is no way a person of any age or sex could be kept alive for a year in the United States at that level. Given substantial income inequalities, which are especially likely in countries just starting economic rationalization, most of the population would be surviving on even less than the average level. Since most of the population, even in very poor countries, does somehow manage to survive from year to year, the estimates are plainly and seriously wrong. Such calculations represent an unintentional mixture, in unknown proportions, of the production actually measured and valued and, indirectly, of the extent of monetization of exchange. Since both genuine increases in output per capita and monetization of exchange represent forms (or consequences) of rationalization, per capita income figures might, ironically, serve as a kind of approximate indicator of that more general process. This would be true only if the modes of measurement and estimation are uniform from place to place through time.

ACCOUNTING: Credits and Debts

An industrial system of production requires assembling the "factors of production"—in this instance, fixed capital (buildings, machines, transportation access), raw materials, energy, and labor—often from considerable distances and with time delays in filling orders or simply in travel. Whether in a capitalist (or corporate) or socialist system, financial accountability is a principal means of control of the relative soundness or efficiency of productive activities. Such accountability includes credits and debts on exchanges within the system, and thus enforceable agreements on the prices at which transactions are made. Therefore, income and expenditures are subject to strict calculation. Even if profit maximization is not a proper goal of any enterprise or public agency, "living within a budget" is likely to be necessary. Of course, in the corporate version of capitalist enterprise, liquid operating capital (money) represents some variable combination of stockholder investments, bond purchases, retained profits from prior operations, and perhaps short-term bank loans. Investors expect some share of profits as dividends, and commonly hope also for capital gains as the value of the stock goes up. Therefore, the credit-and-debt structure is extensive, with banks and similar organizations making their income from interest on loans, and bond-holders, if private individuals, get interest payments as a supplement to other income until the debt is repaid and the money available for other investment or expenditure.

Money markets were previously noted as among the most highly rationalized parts of contemporary exchange systems. Now we should add that the cost of money, the interest to be paid when it is borrowed, though partly regulated by law and by administrative decisions of the central banks of national states, exhibits considerable volatility in capitalist countries, with many investors (including large "institutional investors" handling other people's money on a fiduciary basis) constantly shifting their funds among sources of dividends, capital gains, or interest. It may be added that although fortunes may be made in the various forms of money markets, they may also be lost, and the rationality of participants is not always self-evident. Although such markets may be highly rationalized in the technological sense of electronic calculators and computerized data storage, retrieval, and transmission systems, their very size and diversity present a formidable barrier to "perfect" information, including, especially, the intentions of other participants in the market.

Max Weber was correct in his high regard for money as the most efficient means for economic accounting, whatever the ultimate goals of economic activity may be.[9] Conversion of all assets from a physical inventory into a single monetary sum permits comparison with the sum of liabilities (which, in a monetized economy, are always likely to be expressed—and payable—in monetary units). The aphorism that one cannot add apples and oranges is nonsense if all can be converted to the common metric of money at a reasonable market price. Of course, in the organization and management of physical production, having ample liquid assets (money) is no substitute for an adequate inventory of tools and machines, raw materials or assembled components of the final product, and so on. That depends on a rational inventory-control system, but costs for the actual units to be kept in adequate supply (as well as the costs of the calculation and control) are subject to precise accountability.

A corporate enterprise in a capitalist economy must attempt to make profits, though not necessarily to maximize short-term profits, or at least to avoid sustained loss. (The credit system of contemporary capitalist economies may, however, permit a corporation to show substantial losses for several years. Sooner or later creditors are likely to insist on a change of policies and probably of management. Stockholders are less likely to revolt than to retreat by selling their equities for investment elsewhere.) In a complex socialist economy, managers of state-owned units face a dual accountability: to produce the number of units specified by the central plan, and to stay within a set budget, showing a "profit" if possible. Planning, in principle an eminently rational process, is subject to manifold sources of error, and thus the factory manager may need to resort to all sorts of essentially illicit devices to comply with the dual accountability.[10] Since physical units may be less subject to discretion than budgets—for example, if the units comprise components for another factory—some form of surreptitious cost-cutting or an actual petition for an increased budget may be necessary. (It is sociological law thar organized sub-units of larger systems will attempt to optimize whatever measurement is most crucially used to judge their success or survival.)

For newly developing economies the problems of commercialization (or monetization, the crucial technical instrument) go well beyond mere exchange relationships in petty trade and distribution to consumers. Fiscal policies of governments, policies with respect to foreign investments and the forms and degrees of their control, and a credit structure permitting the mobilization of private savings for investment as well as transactions among an increasingly diverse array of commercial and industrial units all require trained capacity for managing money. In poor countries short of capital (most poor countries are), there is a powerful temptation for governments simply to print more currency, or—what is essentially the same thing—to extend virtually unlimited credit to ambitious but perhaps inexperienced and naive entrepreneurs. A highly unstable currency impairs the function of money as a unit of value. A steep rate of inflation, of course, encourages the incurrence of debts with the expectation that they can be repaid in a debased currency. For economic development and industrialization, the need for engineers and other technicians concerned with physical production may overshadow the perhaps greater need for bankers, trained actuaries for insurance companies, and a host of accountants not elsewhere classified.

And, for all of the appropriate emphasis on rational calculation and competent instrumental acts, both competence and reliable, *disinterested* performance are essential. The very impersonal utility of money, its portability and liquidity, make it about the most attractive candidate for misappropriation. Accountants, treasurers and controllers, and even bankers, deal mainly with other people's money, and stand in a fiduciary relationship, a position of trust, with respect to the actual owners. If these money-handlers are powerful instruments of surveillance and control within and between organizations, who guards the guardians? From a strictly rational point of view, undetectable theft or bribed connivance at the peculations of others constitute eminently sensible conduct. From the organizational standpoint, or that of the complex system as a whole, such corruption represents a diversion of scarce means from their proper ends. It follows that a collectively rational financial system must provide adequate internal cross-checks on possible fraud, including some persons with authority who can be trusted.

NORMATIVE AND PARTICULARISTIC ELEMENTS

We have just noted the importance of what we may call "conditional trust" when parties to financial transactions must deal through intermediaries, and earlier observed the importance of trust as between traders in money and securities. As Thomas Hobbes long ago observed, in any situation with a plurality of participants and scarce resources, rational self-interested action always would prominently include force and fraud as probably the most effective means for the achievement of individual ends.[11] Since no orderly exchange (or other forms of interdependence) is possible under such conditions, all transactions are subject to rules, to a normative framework of action. From the model of rational action for any individual actor, the collectively sanctioned rules become *conditions*, limiting the choice of means.[12] We might be reminded once more of Durkheim's non-contractual elements in contract, the normative structure that makes a system of voluntary agreements possible.[13] Of course any such system (and indeed *any* social system) operates most effectively—whatever its merits may be from some non-instrumental value consideration—if all participants are conscientious in their compliance with rules. Since that comfortable condition is improbable, sanctions must be available to encourage virtue and discourage sin.

Other than internalized rules of conduct, the next most effective support for a normative order is the good option of *significant* others. Thus, trust rests upon the character as well as competence of the one trusted, and is in turn reciprocated as a way of maintaining his or her own good character. This is of course an impairment of the strictly impersonal transaction, arising only when a small and stable set of participants can make more than technical judgments about each other. As exchange (or any other) patterned relations become more transitory and more often indirect and perhaps physically remote, there is a greater likelihood of highly formalized rules and mechanisms for surveillance and enforcement. If there are strong "cultural" pressures toward rectitude and preservation of personal propriety, with a trust network providing indirect links between strangers, formalization of relations in written contracts and threats of litigation may be virtually unnecessary. The low level of litigation in Japan as compared with most Western countries illustrates the potential range of variation. Extensive and suspicious surveillance, with its high administrative costs, appears to be the Soviet solution.

Of course persons in a mutual trust network need not be friends, having wide-ranging shared interest and emotional attachment. Enduring functionally specific relations have some probability of becoming more diffuse, but this sort of micro-dynamic process is little studied by analysts of interpersonal relations. The question becomes significant at the point that norms and behavioral standards necessary for a rationalized system to work become sufficiently extended and elaborated that they impair rational conduct. Favoritism to relatives and friends, including indulgence of normative violation or emotional rather than rational decisions, constitute commonly recognized departures from cool calculation. And, lest we make the common mistake of assuming that rational action represents the highest virtue, we may remind ourselves that commercialization and monetized exchange and distribution are likely to introduce impersonal, "hardnosed" calculation into relationships otherwise informal and friendly. Money is useful for whatever it will buy, and in a highly monetized system that includes some very non-materialistic ends. Yet there is no credible market for affection or group loyalty. Those, too, are part of our desires.

NOTES

1. Stanley H. Udy, Jr., *Work in Traditional and Modern Society* (Englewood Cliffs, NJ: Prentice-Hall, 1970).
2. Cyril S. Belshaw, *Traditional Exchange and Modern Markets* (Englewood Cliffs, NJ: Prentice-Hall, 1965), pp. 11–52.
3. *Ibid.*, p. 7.
4. George C. Homans, *Social Behavior: Its Elementary Forms* (New York: Harcourt, 1961).
5. Max Weber, *The Theory of Social and Economic Organization*, ed. by Talcott Parsons (New York: Oxford University Press, 1947), pp. 173–181, 280–309.
6. Behshaw, cited in note 2, pp. 9–10.
7. See Wilbert E. Moore, "The Adaptation of African Labor Systems to Social Change," in Melville J. Herskovits and Mitchell Harwitz, eds. *Economic Transition in Africa* (Evanston, IL: Northwestern University Press, 1964), pp. 227–297.
8. *Ibid.*
9. Weber, cited in note 5, pp. 184–191.
10. Joseph S. Berliner, *Factory and Manager in the USSR* (Cambridge: Harvard University Press, 1957).
11. Thomas Hobbes, *Leviathan: Or the Matter, Forme, and Power of a Commonwealth . . .*, ed. by Michael Oakesholt (Oxford: Blackwell, 1946); first published in 1651.
12. See Talcott Parsons, *The Structure of Social Action* (Glencoe, IL: Free Press, 1949); first published in 1937.
13. Emile Durkheim, *The Division of Labor in Society*, trans. by George Simpson (Glencoe, IL: Free Press, 1960); first published in French in 1893. See Book I, Chapter 7.

DIFFERENTIATION

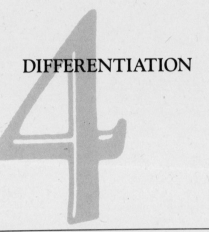

Dwellers in contemporary highly rationalized societies have grown accustomed to increasing specialization. We encounter occupational titles, or specialties within old and established professions, that do not tell the laity, the non-participants, what odd set of tasks are involved, or what range of mysteries the practitioner commands. Units within large corporations or large public bureaucracies have names of frustrating obscurity. Voluntary associations, transitory or enduring, are devoted to promoting goods or defeating evils that, far from engaging the interest of the general public, may leave those outsiders who encounter a member of the group or a news story about it genuinely puzzled about the nature of the problem and why anyone is excited about it.

Increasing differentiation figured prominently in theories of social evolution, both before and after the work of Darwin.[1] The evolutionists tended to take increasing differentiation as a sort of natural law, explainable only in terms of adaptation to diverse environments. It does seem clearly established that in biological evolution there has been increasing differentiation through speciation, that is, the multiplication of classes of distinctive organisms that become reproductive entities. There is, however, no such evidence for an inevitable increase in either increasing differentiation or for increasing complexity (another favorite evolutionary notion) *within* a reproductive group or species. Simple and even somewhat complex types of organisms have survived for millions of years without detectable structural change. If we attempt to adapt evolutionary theory (or metaphor) to social change, it does appear that as human populations expanded into new environments there has been increasing structural and cultural differentiation among distinct societies.

(Convergence theory would hold that modernization is reversing that age-old process by pushing formerly distinct societies toward a common destination.) Increased differentiation within societies, though often taken as a *given* in discussions of social change,[2] is not an invariant process historically, and indeed arises principally as an aspect of modernization.

Population growth, if possible under available conditions for survival and support, clearly makes possible (or even probable) increasing specialization as a way of accommodating variable talents and interests. Population growth, it should be noted, is always a potential development, given the over-reproductivity of nearly all living plant and animal species. Yet human populations surviving literally at a bare subsistence level are unlikely to exhibit appreciable and sustained increase in size. Such increase itself is likely to come from improvement in life-sustaining techniques, in competition with other life forms in the relevant environment. And it is precisely the cumulative growth of useful knowledge, especially to the point that the collective store of such knowledge is beyond the capacity of each (or any) individual to command all of it, that accounts for differentiation.

Durkheim, in his classic work on differentiation, *De la Division du Travail Social,* understood the importance of population size and density, but missed the significance of useful knowledge.[3] Instead, he added the very unsatisfactory concept of "moral density," which is essentially normative complexity—and more likely to be a consequence of differentiation than its cause. Increasing normative complexity is, however, likely in any enduring social system, as "evasive innovation" occurs. Evasive innovation is a novel technique or procedure which, though not in conformity with customary procedure, violates no prohibitive rules.[4] Since knowledge of the rules is presumed in all regular social discourse, the norms become part of useful knowledge and may reach a point of complexity that statement and interpretation of the relevant rules becomes a differentiated task or function.

The significance of increasing differentiation for modernization is that it represents, or may represent, another form of rationalization of social behavior. This is most clearly seen in the division of labor, that is, the specialization of presumably useful tasks. Partly from that specialization and partly from the multiplication of the kinds of rewards societies have to distribute and particularly of the contexts and settings in which ranking and invidious distinctions are probable, the forms of social inequality become highly complex. Organizations, too, are subject to specialization and the links among them that would maintain the semblance of a system may become tenuous or fractured. Finally, as has now become the expository convention in this series of chapters on aspects of rationalization, I shall attend to the restraints and limits on a purely rational system of social placement as well as the limits on heterogeneity among interdependent units, individual or collective.

OCCUPATIONAL SPECIALIZATION

In the year of the American Declaration of Independence, a Scotch moral philosopher, Adam Smith, published a treatise that became one of the early foundations of what later came to be known as "classical economics." Short-titled *The Wealth of Nations*, [5] the book sets forth a view of a productive and exchange economy comprised of rational, self-interested participants in competitive endeavors, alert to the advantages of innovation. Smith started his book not with money (though that is an early chapter) or with the famous (but flawed) threesome of land, labor, and capital as the "factors of production," but with a chapter entitled, "Of the Division of Labour." [6] There he discussed the advantage of subdivision of tasks in production of goods, permitting each task to be performed with a high degree of efficiency, since the ability to make the entire article need not be learned, and time is not lost in shifting from one set of dextrous movements to a very different one.

Smith credits specialized workers (now no longer artisans or handicraftsmen in the proper sense) with introducing improvements in techniques and even in machines as they perceive more efficient procedures. Smith notes, however, that some mechanical improvements are introduced by machine-makers themselves (that too "became the business of a peculiar trade"), and others by "those who are called philosophers [a proper 18th-century use of the term] or men of speculation, whose trade it is not to do anything, but to observe everything. . . ." Philosophy, too, Smith adds, becomes "subdivided."

It was well over a century later that Frederick Winslow Taylor became the founder of a theory of administration that he called "scientific management." [7] He shared with his predecessor an enthusiasm for the subdivision of tasks, but he displayed no confidence in this coming about from the initiative of workers. On the contrary, he made managers responsible for the development of the most efficient bodily movements (through "time and motion studies"), the demonstration of this standard in instructing the worker (whose continued employment depended on his ability and willingness to learn and adopt the standard procedure and pace quickly), and coordinating the entire plan. In this respect Taylor repaired a notable deficiency in Adam Smith's discussion of factory labor, for Smith was insensitive to the authoritative element in what we now recognize as "bureaucratic" employment, and he treated labor markets as though they were entirely like commodity markets. (In the meantime, Karl Marx had discussed the "fetishism of commodities," [8] precisely because the impersonal transactions in commodities concealed what was, to Marx, the exploitative character of the labor necessary to produce them.)

Smith, unlike later and more analytical economists such as David

Ricardo,[9] did not blunder into the error that labor constitutes homogeneous units, which, by constant oversupply, must keep wage levels barely above that requisite for survival. Smith understood at least some of the sources of wage differentials, including skill differentials, degree of trust inherent in performance, and the "agreeableness or the disagreeableness of the employments themselves. . . ."[10] Smith even mentions such non-financial incentives as honor, though more as a substitute than as a complement for higher income.[11] Thus Smith seems to suggest that essentially non-rational motivations, at least in the technical economic sense, may guide some occupational choice as well as performance. Taylor explicitly assumed that only wages mattered to his unskilled steel workers, who could be induced into greatly increased productivity with non-commensurate wage increases.[12] Although decades ago I was strongly critical of Taylor's motivational assumptions,[13] I have since changed my view. Given that the workers were unskilled, often newly arrived peasant immigrants from Europe inexperienced in either a rationalized system of production or a rationalized labor market, and in many instances motivationally "target workers," intent on remaining employed only long enough to escape the industrial system and return to their homelands as farm owners, they could scarcely be interested in anything but payment for their work.[14] A generation later, in the 1920s and 1930s, Elton Mayo and his fellow researchers[15] could find workers in the Hawthorne Western Electric plant in Chicago who were interested in the social setting of the work place, and in the development of informal relations that were, again from a narrowly technical view, non-rational. But this is not good new theory replacing bad old theory. Rather, the Western Electric workers had mainly grown up in a mechanized and commercialized society, in which wage labor in factories had become commonplace, and whatever their dreams and fantasies for becoming independent entrepreneurs, they had a measure of commitment to a modernized economic system. Still another generation later, Rensis Likert could suggest participation of workers in decision-making as the "good new theory," a theory that would make no sense at all if one were establishing a factory in the African bush or a rural village in India.[16]

One must add here, forthwith, that the development of non-financial labor motivations are supplementary to financial rewards, not substitutes. The supplements are possible only if financial rewards are, if not exactly "adequate" (they are rarely perceived as such), at least tolerable—according to changing levels of expectations. Some of the sillier applications of the Western Electric findings in the "human relations" theory of administration would have us believe that employees may be dissuaded from a desire for higher wages or salaries by a kind of manipulation of their non-rational desires to be spoken to kindly and to interact with their peers in ways not technically required for job performance. In a highly commercialized exchange system, anyone, other than someone with extreme wealth, who is not interested in more money is simply insane. That interest, however, is not at any cost in terms of such concerns as "agreeableness" or honor.

I have briefly diverted the discussion from occupational specialization to aspects of labor motivation because the subjects are not truly separable. The *division* of labor calls to mind the subdivision of tasks in completing a finished product, otherwise to be made by a single, broadly-skilled artisan. Adam Smith's illustrations of making pins or nails, as well as Frederick Winslow Taylor's steel workers, confirm that impression, as does much of the long-standing criticism of the industrial system as demeaning to human dignity. Yet Smith's innovative machine-makers and "philosophers," and Taylor's "scientific" managers represent new skill combinations and not old skill divisions. This difference suggests a distinction between the literal *division* of labor and what may be usefully called the *diversification* of labor, the latter referring precisely to the proliferation of new occupations that arise from new products, new services, new "useful knowledge," and possibly new forms of organization rather than merely from greater efficiency in the production of a stable set of goods or services.

The semantic distinction just suggested has both theoretical and ideological implications. Theoretically, it calls attention to the multiplication of occupational positions that do not uniformly lead to a progressive narrowing (and thus "degrading") of the human participant, and thus a progressive subordination of those who do not control the process of rationalization to those that do. Thus, ideologically, it immediately calls in question at least part of Marxian dogma, including not only the doctrine of capitalist self-destruction through polarization and rebellion, but also the doctrine of progressive alienation as the uniform fate of workers separated from the product of their labors. Diversification of labor has led, not to polarization, but to a steady diminution in the proportions of unskilled and semi-skilled workers in the labor force, and a marked increase in professional, managerial, technical, and clerical workers.

The long-term course of rationalization of labor systems has been comprised of four analytically distinguishable processes: (1) sectoral relocation, (2) specialization (strictly speaking), (3) upgrading, and (4) bureaucratization.[17] Sectoral relocation refers to the movement of labor out of agriculture into manufacturing and services. Colin Clark used a simple and now widely used classification of economic production into primary (mainly agriculture), secondary (manufacturing), and tertiary (services).[18] Clark noted that, historically, economic growth has been accompanied—and in a considerable degree caused—by a large proportional shift into secondary production, followed by proportional increases in tertiary production. It should be observed, however, that in many developing countries urbanization is proceeding at a more rapid pace than the expansion of manufacturing employment, resulting in a direct shift out of agriculture and into services—often of a menial or trivial sort.

These aspects of rationalization of labor—I shall return to bureaucratization in a later chapter—are of course interrelated, but analytically distinguishable as I noted previously. All of them rest, directly or indirectly, on *mobility* of labor, not only in the sense of the location of work but probably in the more important sense of location in the economic and political system. Restraints on mobility arising from traditional social bonds or from racial or ethnic or other barriers to competitive access to opportunities impair the optimal utilization of labor resources.

But, of course, mobility has costs, including the notable costs of acquiring the necessary education and specific skills for more amply rewarded positions—another subject to be explored more fully later. And any of the several processes of rationalization of occupational structures just discussed may be carried to irrational extremes. The flight from the land may result in a poorer income for the new urban dweller, perhaps going far enough to reduce the economy's capacity to provide its own food. Specialization of tasks may be carried to ridiculous extremes. It is not only oriental despots of the past who surrounded themselves with hordes of underemployed retainers: overstaffing with administrative assistants is a besetting sin of contemporary bureaucracies. Both situations represent a kind of conspicuous consumption of labor availability. And, as the social critics of industrialism have long emphasized, the presumed efficiency of minute specialization may well destroy the morale of the worker treated as a kind of machine with flawed efficiency. Upgrading may go so far as to denigrate any manual skills and total lack of interest in physical labor not readily mechanized. (Of course, in developing areas, too, physical labor may be viewed as unfitting for those with even very modest educational attainments if in the recent past mere literacy was enough to assure "white-collar" employment.) Bureaucratization, as has long been perceived by its victims, may be carried to the point that overly careful definition of responsibilities may make the solution of an evenly slightly unusual problem virtually impossible.

The extent of occupational specialization appears to be still increasing in all highly rationalized economies, as well as in those with more or less modest beginnings in modernization. The trend is difficult to substantiate unequivocally from existing statistical data, as national statistical services display a strong propensity to group occupations into a relatively small set of categories in approximate order of socioeconomic status. Even the successive editions of the American *Dictionary of Occupational Titles* have destroyed comparability in gross numbers by changing criteria of identification.[19] Yet a net total some years ago of over 22,000 distinct occupations—that is, excluding redundant titles that represent different terms for essentially the same kind of work—probably has substantially increased. My hypothesis is that the birth rate of occupations substantially exceeds the death rate (from product or skill obsolescence).

For what I earlier called the *division* of labor, strictly speaking, Adam Smith had the correct perception that its limit was "the extent of the market."[20] This essentially picks up the importance of population size and growth for increasing differentiation, modified only by the economist's notion of effective demand. Recently, Peter M. Blau has put this relationship in very general terms in relating size of social systems to heterogeneity.[21] The increasing *diversification* of labor, on the other hand, is most likely to arise from the growth of useful knowledge, as implementation of such innovations are almost certain to require new skills and/or new skill combinations. Although these new occupations are most likely to be filled by new or recent entrants into the labor force, the hazards of occupational obsolescence from mechanization or from new knowledge are real, and from either source career shifts and adult retraining become a part of the continuing rationalization of occupational placement. Mobility, then, takes on a continuing quality for many individual lives, with the costs earlier noted. Some of those costs are not readily, or not at all, convertible to monetary or market terms.

NEW AND MULTIPLIED FORMS OF INEQUALITY

Inequality is a universal feature of human societies. Over three decades ago Kingsley Davis and I stated as a general theory that social inequality (we improperly used the term "stratification") is to be explained by the differential functional importance of social positions and differential scarcity of qualified persons to fill them.[22] The lasting controversy over this theory has made clear that it remains essentially neither verified nor disproved, in large part because its very general and abstract form would require much greater specification of the critical variables of functional importance and scarcity of personnel than has so far been accomplished.[23] The high degree of correspondence in occupational prestige rankings across a considerable number and range of countries adds some support to the theory,[24] but does not entirely refute the possibility of mere imitation of precedents and does not directly speak to the question of inequality in (rapidly disappearing) non-literate societies that have experienced only minimal differentiation stemming from a rationalized division of labor.

What is true of such *relatively* undifferentiated societies, but also of moderately complex but essentially agrarian-based societies, is a high degree of diversity among them in the forms and degrees of inequality. The "estates" of premodern Europe, the caste system (ideal and actual) of India, the feudal order of Japan until late in 19th century are only illustrations of a much wider range of social structures. Although the impact of Westernization may take a variety of initial and partly enduring forms, let us take the typological case of commercialization, urbanization, and industrialization. Recruits seeking new economic opportunities (real or imagined) find themselves in a situation with monetized labor and commodity markets, with rewards for training and skills not available in peasant villages, with an authority system that is novel and highly restricted rather than diffuse, based on ownership or management of rationalized enterprises rather than on age or kinship position, and with an individualized mode of social placement and differential rewards. In short, there are competing systems of social inequality.[25]

Since migrants to cities and seekers after new economic activities are preponderantly youths and young adults, the hiatus between systems of status and authority often turns out, in the concrete instance, to be also a conflict between generations, although not all of the younger peasants or villagers may abandon the old ways. Within the rationalized sector of the economy, few and sharp distinctions in social status emerge. During the early stages of commercialization and industrialization, the differences in social origin, education, and power of managers and workers are likely to be profound—even in countries where the status of managers is not that of owners, as in socialist economies. Welfare considerations in those socialist economies may protect the workers from exceptionally harsh conditions of employment, but the lack of competition among employers may give the workers no opportunities for improving their situation. However, the fundamental fact of radical disparity in social positions remains. This is what Marx observed in early capitalism. He made two blatant errors in interpretation: (1) he blamed the disparity on the capitalist system of property ownership rather than on differences in sponsorship and skill levels; and (2) he assumed that, as archaic forms of social placement were displaced through rationalized production, polarization would increase in both magnitude and extent.

Actually, the revolutionary potential is highest at early stages of rationalization of the economy, and though Marx was absolutely wrong about the future of capitalism in this respect, his perception of early polarzation is confirmed as successive parts of the world get drawn into the universal process of modernization. The circumstance that the resulting turmoil (often confounded by very un-Marxist ethnic divisiveness) commonly leads to repressive militaristic regimes imposed by powerful "modernizing elites" simply says that revolutions or threatened revolutions need not lead to democratic socialism as the outcome. None has so far, including not only the Soviet Union and China but also the growing number of "people's democracies" (What an outrage to semantic sense!) among the new nations.

As rationalization of the economy advances, the skills of manual workers become more differentiated, and clerical, managerial, technical, and professional occupations proliferate. As noted earlier, the net balance in terms of occupational distributions is thus not progressive "emiseration" of workers but upgrading of skill and income levels. The steady rise of education and skill levels for employment does indeed lead to a new division: between the great majority of the fully or mostly employed and the "hard-core" unemployed who have no skills that employers seek. The movement toward the middle of distributions of the population in terms of gradations of money income, occupational prestige, or relative authority has led the sociologist Harold Wilensky to suggest the concept of the "middle mass."[26] The term is certainly superior to the much-abused concept of the "middle class"—a point to which I shall return shortly—but still has the defect of implying far greater homogeneity or uniformity than the factual situation warrants.

The movement toward the middle along the various measures of socioeconomic status (the commonly used ones being income, education, and occupational rank) has been more nearly from the bottom up than from the top down. Thus, with the growing total wealth available for distribution in highly rationalized economies, income inequalities have generally increased, partly by widening the range of rewards distributed. Wilensky finds no substantial difference in this respect between nominally capitalist and nominally socialist economies.[27] It would of course be hard to demonstrate that the amount of inequality, or the relative advantage of those most highly paid, represents a kind of collective social judgment that the rewards are precisely proportional to the functional importance of the tasks performed. Indeed, the salaries and other sources of income of corporate executives in Europe and America or of high officials in socialist states are more nearly "administered prices" than market prices, and to a high degree the power of the executives simply permits them to set their own pay, with resulting remarkable differences in how far avarice is indulged.[28]

The multiplication of occupations and the fact that, except in terms of income (and, less reliably, training time or broad prestige categories), they are comparable only to a low degree, may heighten the importance of occupational distinctions within particular work contexts while reducing precise occupational position as an indicator of general social status. In other words, if "difference" means generalized social rank, then a rationalized system of occupational allocation results in many distinctions without a difference.

The question of equality or inequality of participants is never irrelevant in any social context, although the answer may be that a single benign or despotic leader holds all followers in a uniform state of subservience, or that a nominally equalitarian group making all decisions without any leadership actually does so—an almost unknown occurrence in actual practice. The proliferation of groups and associations, of categories and "identities" (such as ethnicity, regional accent in speaking, optional lifestyle) means that individuals may be subject to ranking of some sort in very diverse contexts. Matters would be tidier for sociological theorists using "integration" models of societies if one prime source of relative status—say economic position—determined all others as dependent (or simply reflected) variables, or (an even more improbable situation) the relative qualities of the individual resulted in precisely the same ranking in highly diverse social situations. Although a spill-over effect may indeed occur (perhaps most likely where full professional or bureaucratic titles are used in every social context except the most intimate, a bizarre German propensity), criteria of performance are bound to differ in rationalized organizations with entirely different objectives, and some social groupings are highly resistant to rationalization.

Differentiation, then, produces great complexity in the forms and circumstances—indeed, in the degrees of social inequality. It is perhaps a quest for simplification that has led sociologists and other social scientists to adopt the concept of "class" as a cross-cutting set of categories that will rank an entire population into a few general strata. The fundamental difficulty with this expository convention is that the demarcations are essentially arbitrary and conceal much diversity within each category. Since the usual criteria for determining general social position—education, income, and occupational rank—represent scales of essentially continuous variables, there are no factual bases for determining where and how many lines are to be drawn across the distributions. The boundaries of a class thus remain entirely at the whim of anyone arrogant or foolish enough to make a decision. In American social theory, until recently little influenced by the Marxist tradition, the "rule of three" has become conventional: upper, middle, lower. That this is simply a way of distinguishing the two extremes and the middle of any scale is evident from suggestions that the discriminations are too coarse and one should have nine categories: upper upper, middle upper, lower upper, and so on. Since no two individuals, or more properly family or household units, are likely to have precisely the same scale scores if they are measured with exquisite accuracy, the absurd extreme would be a situation with each unit literally "in a class by itself."

If class be given somewhat greater resemblance to its historic meaning of hereditary social strata, the extensive mobility of contemporary highly rationalized societies denude the concept of much of its relevance. In American society, for example, we do find a small population of the hereditary rich, who comprise only a part of the wealthy (many of whom are literally *les nouveaux riches*) and a small population of the hereditary poor, who comprise a modest fraction of the poor (most of whom are simply the aged and the handicapped).

The Marxist division of capitalists and the proletariat has suffered a fatal blow through the corporate form of diffused ownership. (An extremely high-salaried corporate executive with trivial, if any, equity ownership in the employing company is of course a proletarian owning only his—or more rarely her—own labor, which is sold dearly.) The powerful will to believe in the reality of social classes on the part of neo-Marxists displays an obdurate refusal to follow Marx's own insistence on the relativity of historical circumstances.

These critical comments on the illusory character of social class relate of course only to that outworn mode of simplification. Increasing differentiation has multiplied the forms of inequality. It has also increased the degree of inequality in terms of ranges of rewards, but generally decreased inequality in the sense of rigid barriers and boundaries marking off strata. On neither score could it be argued that the consequences represent a completed process of rationalization or, for that matter, that those consequences are completely consistent with the professed standards of equity in the relevant societies. Some are illicitly rich and others undeservedly poor. The equality of opportunity essential for a merit-based competitive placement to be "fair" is impeded by such non-rational structural arrangement as entrusting families with recruitment of infants and their initial socialization (with continuing differential advantages until adulthood and possibly beyond).

FUNCTIONAL SPECIALIZATION OF ORGANIZATIONS

Increasing differentiation in the course of modernization is evident not only in the specialization of individual positions but also in the proliferation of organizations. The multitude of organizations devoted to the production and distribution of goods and services in a highly rationalized economy is especially pronounced in large countries with a competitive market system. Socialist systems and corporate conglomerates "simplify" this diversity only in terms of some centralization of administrative controls, but are still characterized by a high degree of internal specialization at the operating level. The degree of administrative control—or put conversely, the degree of autonomy—of specialized units is highly variable in both publicly owned and privately owned economic, or work-performing, organizations. This variability arises in part from the consequences of ideological or value differences between public or non-profit and profit-oriented enterprises—always with the probable restraint of cost accountability in either—and in part because there is no perfectly rational solution to the conflict between centralization and decentralization as administrative policies: each has its own distinctive costs and benefits.

Rationalization of collective efforts is not limited to economic or officially political structures. More-or-less formally organized voluntary associations also abound. Among such associations a distinction commonly made is that between interest-oriented organizations and those that fulfill primarily expressive functions. Thus, the labor union, professional association, or trade association serve to promote the economic interests that members share. Political parties or other organizations designed to achieve some particular worthy objective or to prevent a particular evil perceived by members display common "interests," perhaps not readily convertible into merely monetary terms. Expressive associations—athletic groups, collectors' societies, associations of amateur players of chamber music—seem least reflective of rationalization, except as one recognizes that they bespeak a differentiation of preferred forms of recreational and esthetic expression and that the formation of a formal organization with officers, dues, scheduled meetings, newsletters, and so on, provides a rationalized scheme for achievement of essentially emotional goals. Rationality, we remind ourselves, provides no criteria for choice of goals but only the means for achieving them. And by narrow delimitation of what the members of voluntary associations have in common, the joint activity may be pursued outside the range of common interests characteristic of such multi-functional organizations as families or neighborhoods. Yet in the dynamics of social interaction an enduring association is likely to develop into a single "friendship group" if it is small, or into several such groups if it is large. This leads to the paradox that the association itself becomes the goal, the original shared interest the means (or excuse) for its continuation.

The early impact of modernization on premodern forms of social organization is erosive or destructive. Extended kin networks and village communities "lose functions" or cease to operate as effective decision-making and security systems.[29] In early transitional situations there is either a gross inconsistency between the principles governing duties and reciprocities in such relatively unspecialized social units and those appropriate to rationalized organizations or a kind of a gap or vacancy between the individual or nuclear family and the increasingly bureaucratic national state. Impersonality marks the employment situation, the market, and community functions. Even those associations we have been discussing, by the very narrowness of their collective purposes, may only partially fill the space between the individual or small family and the great society.

The persistence of tribalism or other forms of ethnicity such as maintenance of ties with rural communities is thus scarcely surprising as a form of resistance to rapid rationalization of social systems. I previously argued with respect to kinship organization that the early impact of rationalization is the most severe, as both geographical and social mobility essentially dismember extensive and traditionally obligatory networks.[30] As modernization finally extends to those not initially caught up in the process, that particular division loses its significance and kinship is restored to considerable, but reduced and altered, significance. Kinship is alive and well in modern Western societies, having survived the almost certain differentiation and highly probable inequality of its nuclear family units. Japan, where the dismembering of extended kinship has been rather recent, seems certain to follow the same course. The conflict between traditional Chinese familism and the Communist regime is an ongoing one. The organization of "communes" may provide a functional substitute for relationships partly based on affective ties provided by kinship. The Israeli *kibbutz* does so only in part.

Given the evidence for what is sometimes called the "recrudescence of ethnicity" in Western societies,[31] I should now extend the same argument respecting kinship to broader forms of somewhat sentimental affiliation. Though Orlando Patterson's characterization of modern ethnicity as "reactionary" would thus be narrowly and literally true,[32] I should dispute his explicit argument that by being a barrier to rationalization ethnicity is perforce pathological. On the contrary, that or some other form of broadbased identification in a society with highly specialized organizations may be essential.

OVERSPECIALIZATION AND ALIENATION

There are rational limits to increasing differentiation, as well as the limits to rationalization itself. Economists and theorists of administration write confidently of the "economies of scale," which remind one strongly of Adam Smith's enthusiasm for increasing division of labor with expansion of the market for particular goods and services. Smith, we have noted, failed to distinguish between the impersonal coordination presumably provided by a competitive market for craft-produced commodities and the coordination provided by the employing bosses of workers performing distinct operations in the production of common pins. It is administrative coordination that is mainly relied upon in highly rationalized economic production. For routinized tasks mainly paced by machines—the assembly line is the prime example—supervision can be minimal and mainly for surveillance except in emergency situations. With diversified and not simply divided labor, coordination and decision-making increase in importance. The consequence is that increased diversification leads to disproportional increases in administrative costs, represented not just in the decreased "span of control" (number of immediate subordinates) of coordinators but also in the costs of information ("staff" functions necessary for informed decision-making).[33] Although the value of exercising controls over increasingly extensive domains is judged clearly to be worthwhile, as witnessed by centralized socialist regimes and conglomerate corporations, the cost of realizing those values is inevitably either diseconomies of scale (probable in socialist regimes) or control only in terms of profit accountability without extensive coordination (probable in corporate conglomerates).

At the more general, societal level increasing differentiation also has its costs and perils. We have noted that in the newly modernizing society there will be a number of disjunctions between traditional modes of social placement and reward and those of the modernizing sector. In that modernizing sector—there are commonly several, such as the economy, the civil service, the military, education, and public health, not necessarily closely coordinated—there is a substantial risk that the avid, rational pursuit of specialized interests will lead to uprooted individuals and families without meaningful affiliation to the community and society. One must also expect a considerable display of unchecked avarice and unprincipled exploitation of privileged positions. Differentiation, in short, is not necessarily self-limiting and in accordance with larger social purposes. For these reasons, political ideologies, including nationalism in its various vehement forms, become important not only for articulating collective goals but also as the value-oriented rationale for strong (most commonly authoritarian) political regimes as the mode of providing some level of coordination and control. And political participation—not necessarily democratic—may provide a kind of functional substitute for those "intermediate" attachments between the individual and society-at-large likely to be undermined in the course of rationalization. Such forms of organized activity will normally bear a thicker veneer of rational instrumentalism than some multifunctional units such as the village community, but their important "latent" functions may be more nearly "expressive" than instrumental.

One cannot leave the discussion of differentiation without reference to its most glaring pathology as historically perceived in the development of capitalist industrialism. Alienation, although now most commonly studied and measured as a personality characteristic—apathy, feelings of incompetence, feelings of powerlessness—in the Marxist tradition was treated as a *structural* consequence of expropriation from the means and instruments of production. Or, more precisely, alienation was the pathology that resulted from the separation of the worker from the product of his labor, which in turn was blamed on capitalist modes of economic organization.[34] Since at the time of Marx's writings only capitalist enterprise had created the factory system of goods production, his confusion of specialization (the literal division of labor) with a particularly property system is perhaps understandable if fundamentally wrong. Considerably later his colleague Friedrich Engels correctly identified the culprit as the division of labor,[35] but still blamed that evil on capitalism, on the rather fanciful grounds that mechanization had already (in 1878) made routinized labor unnecessary, as would be recognized in a socialist regime. Taking into account both the Marxist perspective, stripped of its largely irrelevant rhetoric regarding property ownership but retaining the notion of separation of the worker from the product of labor, and the social-psychological perspective, Blauner found substantial diversity in American industry.[36] The kind of technology, managerial policies, extent of individual or work-group control of work processes are among the variables that account for differences in how individual workers regard their jobs.

It would be foolish indeed to deny the degradation of human personality and its innovative, problem-solving potential that results from treating the worker as a rather inefficient machine through routinized machine-paced work assignments. It would be equally foolish to suppose that the form of property ownership makes any difference where the rationalization of production leads to this "inhuman" use of human beings. From a somewhat detached viewpoint, it is noteworthy that the administrative decision to carry the division of labor to that extreme is a major source of subsequent mechanization, for the task has been sufficiently simplified that even the engineers can perceive how a machine could perform the operation.[37] This, incidentally, was exactly understood by Adam Smith in his discussion of the division of labor more than two centuries ago.[38] That detached perspective scarcely remedies the situation of the overspecialized worker until the mechanics arrive, or assures him or her of gainful and exhilirating employment when actually displayed by a machine. Informal groups at the workplace (which might be characterized as play at work), "job enrichment," and participatory decision-making uniformly testify to the limits of rationalization asserted by its victims or recognized by administrators as a relevant fact at a superior level of rationality that goes beyond mechanical models of efficient systems. Much depends, of course, on the qualities and expectations of participants in work organizations. One inevitable consequence of the long-term upgrading of the educational and skill distributions among workers is that rationality and wisdom cease to be a presumptive monopoly of managers, and a probable further consequence is that "meaningful" work—including the non-rational components of that fortunate state—comes to be expected by the lowly as well as assumed by the exalted.

NOTES

1. See Robert A. Nisbet, *Social Change and History* (New York: Oxford University Press, 1972).
2. For example, see Talcott Parsons, *Societies: Evolutionary and Comparative Perspectives* (Englewood Cliffs, NJ: Prentice-Hall, 1966); Parsons, *The System of Modern Societies* (Englewood Cliffs, NJ: Prentice-Hall, 1971).
3. Émile Durkheim, *The Division of Labor in Society*, trans. by George Simpson (Glencoe, IL: Free Press, 1960); first published in French in 1893.
4. See Wilbert E. Moore, *Social Change*, 2nd ed. (Englewood Cliffs, NJ: Prentice-Hall, 1974), pp. 19–22.

5. Adam Smith, *An Inquiry into the Nature and Causes of the Wealth of Nations*, ed. by Edward Cannan (London: Methuen, 1950); first published in 1776; numerous editions exist.

6. *Ibid.*, Book I, Chapter 1.

7. Frederick Winslow Taylor, *The Principles of Scientific Management* (New York: Harper and Brothers, 1911); Taylor, *Shop Management* (New York: Harper and Brothers, 1911).

8. Karl Marx, *Capital* (New York: Modern Library, n.d.) pp. 81–96.

9. David Ricardo, *Works and Correspondence*, ed. by Piero Strafa (Cambridge: Cambridge University Press, 1951–1955), ten volumes, especially Vol. 1, *On the Principles of Political Economy and Taxation*; first published in 1817.

10. Smith, work cited in note 5, Book I, Chapter X, Part I.

11. *Ibid.*

12. Taylor, *The Principles of Scientific Management*, cited in note 7.

13. Wilbert E. Moore, *Industrial Relations and the Social Order* (New York: Macmillan, 1946), Chapter IX.

14. See Gerald W. Rosenblum, *Immigrant Workers* (New York: Basic Books, 1973).

15. See Elton Mayo, *Human Problems of an Industrial Civilization* (New York: Macmillan, 1973); F. J. Roethlisberger and William J. Dickson, *Management and the Worker* (Cambridge: Harvard University Press, 1939); T. N. Whitehead, *The Industrial Worker* (Cambridge: Harvard University Press, 1938), two volumes.

16. Rensis Likert, *The Human Organization* (New York: McGraw-Hill, 1967).

17. See Wilbert E. Moore, "Changes in Occupational Structures," in Neil J. Smelser and Seymour Martin Lipset, eds., *Social Structure and Mobility in Economic Development* (Chicago: Aldine, 1966), Chapter 6.

18. Colin Clark, *The Conditions of Economic Progress*, 2nd ed. (London: Macmillan, 1951), pp. 395–439.

19. See, for example, U.S. Department of Labor, *Dictionary of Occupational Titles*, 3rd ed. (Washington: U.S. Government Printing Office, 1966, Vol. I, *Definitions of Titles.*

20. Smith, work cited in note 5, Book I, Chapter II.

21. Peter M. Blau, *Inequality and Heterogeneity: A Primitive Theory of Social Structure* (New York: Free Press, 1977).

22. Kingsley Davis and Wilbert E. Moore, "Some Principles of Stratification," *American Sociological Review* 10:243–249 (April 1945).

23. For a recent review of the status of the theory, see Wilbert E. Moore, "Functionalism," in Tom Bottomore and Robert A. Nisbet, *History of Sociological Analysis* (New York: Basic Books, 1978).

24. See Donald J. Treiman, *Occupational Prestige in Comparative Perspective* (New York: Academic Press, 1977).

25. See Melvin M. Tumin, "Competing Status Systems," in Wilbert E. Moore and Arnold S. Feldman, eds., *Labor Commitment and Social Change in Developing Areas* (New York: Social Science Research Council, 1960).

26. Harold L. Wilensky, "Orderly Careers and Social Participation: The Impact of Work History on Social Integration in the Middle Mass," *American Sociological Review* 26:521–539 (August 1961).

27. Harold L. Wilensky, "The Political Economy of Income Distribution: Issues in the Analysis of Government Approaches to the Reduction of Inequality," in J. Milton Yinger and S. J. Cutler, eds., *Major Social Issues: A Multidisciplinary View* (New York: Free Press, 1978).

28. See Leonard Broom and Robert G. Cushing, "A Modest Test of an Immodest Theory: The Functional Theory of Stratification," *American Sociological Review* 42:157–169 (February 1977).

29. See Wilbert E. Moore, *The Impact of Industry* (Englewood Cliffs, NJ: Prentice-Hall, 1965), pp.85–92.

30. *Ibid.*
31. See, for example, Nathan Glazer and Daniel P. Moynihan, eds., *Ethnicity: Theory and Experience* (Cambridge: Harvard University Press, 1975); Andrew Greeley, *Ethnicity in the United States* (New York: Wiley, 1975).
32. Orlando Patterson, *Ethnic Chauvinism: The Reactionary Impulse* (New York: Stein and Day, 1977).
33. See Wilbert E. Moore, *The Conduct of the Corporation* (New York: Random House, 1962).
34. See Karl Marx, *Economic and Philosophical Manuscripts of 1844* (Moscow: Foreign Languages Publishing House, 1961). An essay, from these manuscripts, "Estranged Labour" has been reprinted in Robert C. Tucker, ed., *The Marx-Engels Reader* (New York: Norton, 1972), pp. 56–67.
35. See the essay by Friedrich Engels translated as "On the Division of Labour in Production," reprinted in Tucker, work cited in note 34, pp. 321–327.
36. Robert Blauner, *Alienation and Freedom: The Factory Worker and His Industry* (Chicago: University of Chicago Press, 1964).
37. See Wilbert E. Moore, ed., *Technology and Social Change* (Chicago: Quadrangle Books, 1972), editor's "Introduction."
38. Adam Smith, work cited in note 5, Book I, Chapter I.

TECHNIFICATION

Technification is a term that, with some regret, I use as a one-word concept for the more cumbersome "deliberate technological change." Its utility may compensate for its novelty and lack of euphony; it compares favorably with the names for those polysyllabic chemicals that improve (or adulterate) every conceivable variety of processed foods. And those chemicals—never mind their unintelligible names—precisely illustrate the process of technification, carried perhaps well beyond any sensible benefits other than to justify the salaries of organic chemists hired by food processors.

Technology, perhaps even more than monetary calculation, is commonly assumed to be the quintessence of rationalization. But then, technology, properly defined as "useful knowledge," comprises economic transactions as well as much other instrumental information that has little or nothing to do with applied physics, chemistry, or biology. The mechanical marvels that, along with their discarded debris, stand as the most visible symbol of highly rationalized societies, have led to what Lewis Mumford calls "the myth of the machine," which both vulgarizes the range of useful knowledge and asserts a causal primacy to technological change that is simply wrong. [1]

Before technology is embodied in machines or chemicals or heavy-breasted turkeys it exists as ideas, information, plans, experimental designs. Technology is thus as cultural as music, language, legal codes, or theology. And, as I have noted in a previous writing:

> Technology may be, and usually is, shared, and thus to some degree is collectivized and depersonalized, but it is neither a disembodied nor a nonhuman force. It is the product of human ingenuity, and without human purpose behind it, it is not the cause of anything. [2]

It is true that useful knowledge is generally cumulative, and as additions are made to the stock, new combinations of principles and practices become additional sources of novelty. This occurs only if time and energy—not to mention wits—are devoted to adding new knowledge and to finding new combinations.

Like other aspects of rationalization, technology is not peculiarly "modern." To avoid the mechanical bias inherent in the characterization of our species as *homo faber*, the tool-using animal, a more apt designation is the problem-solving animal. No society has a trouble-free relation to its non-human environment, and the seeming progress from environmental adaptation to environmental mastery turns out to be both incomplete and increasingly costly and hazardous. Additionally, no society fully attains its own professed goals and ideals or enjoys full compliance with its normative codes. Both of these gaps between the "ideal" and the "actual" provide a hospitable setting for innovations that promise to narrow the gap.[3]

What is distinctive, if not unique, to the modern era is the organization and institutionalization of rationality. That is, resources such as money and skilled personnel are devoted to the deliberate creation of both problems and technical solutions, and a common, though not invariant, rule of human conduct is to act in a calculated and dispassionate fashion in terms of reliable information and effective means for achievement of human purposes. In rationalized economies with an increasing proportion of productive activity devoted to services, the sociologist Daniel Bell has argued that the "knowledge industry" is a prime component of such "post-industrial societies,"[4] and the economist Fritz Machlup has traced out the extensity of that industry in American society.[5] Thus, most of contemporary technical innovation is deliberate, although accidental inventions do occur, mainly as a by-product of quests for solutions to other problems. It follows that highly rationalized societies have about as much technology as they deserve, or at least the kind of technology that various decision-makers have chosen to pursue.

Here I shall accede to conventionality by discussing mainly the technology of production and distribution of goods and services, deferring consideration of education and bureaucratization, as other notable manifestations of technification, to the two ensuing chapters. As usual, this chapter will conclude with a consideration of costs and limits.

RATIONALIZATION OF PRODUCTION AND DISTRIBUTION

It has been the factory system of industrial production that permitted and, in a sense, required other technical features of rationalized fabrication of goods.[6] With the invention of the steam engine powered by the burning of coal, more powerful and reliable energy could be used that did not depend on the uncertainties of wind and water power. With transportable natural power, factories could be located conveniently to transportation routes and markets. Processes, difficult or impossible with human or animal power, became increasingly commonplace—with speed an additional benefit. Both sheer force and speed encouraged the development, through metallurgy, of more durable machines. Raw materials and labor were assembled where machines were established, the workers becoming more nearly the servants of the machines than the masters of tools as had been the skilled craftsmen. Marx, apparently viewing the technological change as inevitable (none is) blamed this demeaning of the worker on the property system that "expropriated" the worker from ownership of the tools of production. Had Marx been more consistent with his own professed historical materialism, he would have identified correctly the mechanical technology as the culprit in the subordination of the worker, although of course private property as the source of the authority of the owner or manager was not irrelevant in such other respects as the setting of wages or the decision to adopt a particular technology.

It was, further, the concentration of workers "under one roof" and, especially, under direct supervision of managers, that encouraged the specialization of tasks—the literal division of labor—and thus destroyed the (hunger-limited) freedom of the craftsman.

The acme of machine-dominated specialization is represented in the assembly line, resting on the mass production of standardized parts put together in sub-assemblies and finally put together in an orderly process of sequential operations for a product as relatively simple as an electric toaster or as relatively complex as an automobile. In this mode of technification various tasks are truly interdependent in the total design of the process, but the individual worker is relatively isolated from others in the process and the interdependence is more nearly "serial service" (pass it on) rather than direct cooperation. Informal job exchanges on the line and formal experiments with group assembly rather than the moving conveyor indicate that alternatives exist in both the mechanics and the social structure.

Other types of industrial processes exist. For unstandardized or only partly standardized products (electrical generators, complex weapon systems) "job shop" production requires more craft skills in actual work. (Assembly-line production conceals the extensive dependence on problem-solving skills in the fabrication, installation, and technical repair of the machines that actually do much of the work.) In chemicals, metallurgy, and petroleum refining, one encounters a somewhat comparable contrast between "batch" and "continous flow" processes, the latter presumably permitting a greater substitution of machines for human skills and wits.

Mechanization has two overt and damaging consequences for the manual worker: the degradation of skills through the subdivision of tasks and the risk of outright displacement as machines are substituted for manual operations. Both of these consequences have occurred over the history of industrial technification, but some other considerations require attention. As just noted, the routinization (and thus quasi-mechanization) of labor in apparent subservience to machine pacing is the consequence of decisions by managers implemented by engineers, technicians, and maintenance craftsmen, and that labor, except occasionally for the diagnosticians and therapists, is concealed in actual productive processes. Although the machines are used for much work that would otherwise have to be done by hand or could not be done at all, the machines do not invent, install, or repair themselves, or decide whether, where, and when they will operate. Labor-saving as a consequence of mechanization is thus always in part and sometimes totally spurious. A new form of highly skilled, technical labor (plus managerial time) has been substituted for more archaic craft skills, or, if that substitution has already occurred and the process of nearly total displacement of direct production workers is accomplished through "automation," the substitution (some of which of course is a one-time expense) is that of dispensing with hourly rated workers at modest wages, at the cost of dependence on high-salaried employees. It is a managerial and accounting convention, with the approving connivance of labor economists and statisticians in ministries of labor, that accounts for industrial productivity being measured only in terms of units of output per units of labor time among those in direct production. The additional labor needed in order to reduce the amount of direct manual work becomes buried as "equipment costs" or as management, staff services, or maintenance—all conventionally viewed as "overhead" and not as labor, properly speaking. That consequence of mechanization does not represent the pursuit of rationality but of obfuscation.

It should be added that for those workers remaining in direct contact with productive processes in highly automated systems, the relationship to the machine is more nearly mastery than servitude. Productive processes are manipulated by buttons and powered levers, or they are monitored at an instrumented control panel. Judgment and responsibility are essential, not strength or dexterity.

Technological displacement of workers does occur, for those replaced rarely have the training to undertake one of the new occupations that were, in whole or in part, their undoing. In a truly (and truly mythical) self-regulating economy, if the cost reduction by increased technification is genuine, the displaced worker should be readily re-employable through one route or another to increased demand and increased investment. If reduced costs are entirely passed along to the consumer, the consumer can buy more of that or other products. If reduced costs simply are treated as higher profits, a corporation retaining them has capital for perhaps diversified investment, or if passed along to actual investors they may be reinvested or lead to higher consumption. If, as a last resort, the savings are passed along to the remaining workers as higher regular wages or bonuses, increased demand is again provided. Now, in the course of Western industrialization all of these benefits from technification have occurred, in various mixtures determined by variable strategies of decision-makers and differing bargaining strengths of claimants.

Since the labor that is saved by more efficient processes becomes thereby what the British charmingly call redundant, it is not surprising that resistance to technological change has been most overt on the part of labor unions representing the affected workers. And, such opposition has a considerable history in the long course of industrialization. The Luddites in Northern England early in the 19th century smashed textile machines that threatened the livelihood of home weavers. Modern unions may insist on overstaffing or "feather-bedding"—or at least with employment security for the existing work force, permitting reduction of numbers only by normal attrition through death, retirement, or resignation without replacements being hired. Even though commonly viewed by those not involved as a resistance to "progress" and therefore somehow anti-social, the cost of a worker's livelihood, of possible re-training for re-employment, and of support for the worker and his or her dependents between jobs are as equitably attributable to the price of new technology as are the capital and technical-labor costs involved in the change. The only questions are who bears the costs and whether, once taken into account, the benefits still make the change rational. Otherwise, labor-saving technification is a form of income redistribution, including perhaps public subsidies for private investors or managers that may or may not correspond with perceived public policy.

Changes in technical processes have adverse effects on other interests also. Some firms, as well as some laborers, may become technologically obsolete. In recent years there has been the suspicion that American industry has failed to keep pace in international markets with the technological advances made in Japanese and German manufacturing, thereby joining the British in over-compensating the managers and underinvesting in research and development (R & D)—thence in new plants and machinery.

The rationalization of production is most readily apprehended in terms of new processes, as this represents the selection or development of new means for stable goals. Yet, the products of industry do not represent a stable set. If standardization has been the key to mass production for a mass market, technification has also yielded a tremendous multiplication of products. With respect to some consumer goods in competitive markets the attempts at product differentiation may lead to spurious distinctions in brand names, packaging, or irrelevant ingredients. To take an extreme example, the best aspirin one can buy is the cheapest, as all aspirin is made by an absolutely uniform chemical recipe. But genuine product differentiation occurs in sensible terms such as quality, effectiveness, or durability, and in essentially expressive ways such as style. Differentiation in terms of use, even for consumer goods, is extensive. Consider the inventory of a retail hardware dealer. The number of different kinds of screws available will surely exceed 100, of various lengths, thicknesses for the same length, kinds of metal used, shapes of the head. Comparable profusion (and, for the uninitiated, confusion) prevails in nails, nuts and bolts, finishes for preservation and decoration, screw-drivers and wrenches, and tools for the home repairman or amateur or employed artisan. Even Adam Smith's common pin becomes uncommon when provided with an enlarged head for excessive use in folding a man's shirt for retail sale, or lengthened and provided with a fake-pearl head to accompany a corsage sold by a florist.

The multiplication of specific products increases as machines become more complex. The storekeeper (probably called an "inventory control officer") in a large manufacturing plant must have at hand the multitude of parts for the automobiles or food processors being produced, tools for the workers, and probably standard replacement parts for the machines that make the machines. And here it is lack of standardization that introduces complications. Technical improvements, or merely cosmetic changes, may require a significantly altered system, with changes in parts not directly and originally involved in the presumed improvement. Model changes thus greatly increase the range of replacement parts needed as previous models still function. Competing product lines exacerbate the problem. Consider automobile "fan belts," which now propel not only fans to dissipate the heat of radiators in water-cooled cars but also alternators for the electrical system, power steering and power brakes. The service station operator who tries to accommodate customers needing a new belt needs a very extensive inventory of belts, and a manual to check which belt is right for the year, make, and model of the car requiring repair. In short, the principle of "interchangeable parts," originally a fundamental tenet of standardization for mass production, has been steadily eroded by product differentiation. Only in a very large total market could such an otherwise irrational diversity prevail.

Lack of standardization indeed complicates the problem of rational choice, whether one is buying machinery as capital goods or consumer durables. The availability of parts and service becomes an important component of choice, for at the worst the machine may be useless when a single part fails, or— perhaps little better—one becomes "locked into" a particular technical system with no recourse for maintenance other than the original supplier.

Both in production and distribution, matters are presumably simpler in a centralized socialist system. The planners determine what goods are to be manufactured, how they are to be distributed among manufacturing units as components of other products and to "retail" outlets for household consumers, and the prices to be charged for each transaction. The lack of formal competition provides strong encouragement to standardization, although slight concessions may be made to differences in consumer taste. All decisions on volume of production and its distributive allocation are made on the basis of "need," as determined by the planners, reflecting "demand" only as the plan may be subject to some change in the face of complaints by intermediate users (for example, managers of factories dependent on availability of components) or ultimate consumers.

Both communication and transportation are closely interdependent with physical production, although each has other uses and dimensions. Technification here has generally taken the direction of increased speed, with reliability a constant concern. Space travel and the possible importation of extraterrestial raw materials might be cutely characterized as still "far out." Air travel and transport are increasingly commonplace; generally speaking, there is a direct relation between speed and transport costs, and decisions on alternative modes of transportation, where available, thus involve placing a monetary value on time itself.[7] Communication at a distance has moved from smoke signals, talking drums, and messengers, through postal systems, telegraph, telephone, radio, and television, to the telex and wire or wireless links between computers who talk (or, more properly, exchange signals) with each other.

The computer revolution—the world abounds with real and metaphorical revolutions these days—makes possible not only complex numerical calculations at high speeds but also information storage and retrieval that, once in operation, makes all other filing systems seem hopelessly inefficient. The vulgar but correct aphorism, "garbage in, garbage out" reminds us that accuracy of information and programs is especially essential if all subsequent operations are automatic. (The large number of victims of "computer errors" in bank accounts, credit accounts, and insurance policies may rest assured that the culprits are human and their defenders are liars. Computers do not make mistakes, but those who operate them frequently do.)

Computer technology greatly extends the tools of rational decision, for the machine may be asked to make fine calculations well beyond the available time (and perhaps wits) of decision-makers. Problem-solving need not be limited to "current state" information. Hypothetical variables may be fed into the computer along with decision rules and assumptions, and simulated solutions may be sought for possible future courses of action. It is thus scarcely surprising that schools of business administration, while not totally abandoning the "case-study" method of learning how to make administrative decisions, increasingly emphasize mathematical rational-decision models, aided by computer simulation to arrive at decisions that are formally rational, under the assumptions given. Pricing policies, inventory control, the costs and benefits of a change in product or process may all be brought under this kind of careful calculation—always with the warning that the solutions are limited by the amount and quality of information supplied and the reasonableness of the assumptions made concerning their relevance to the problem at hand.

The technification of distribution has involved not only the development of jobbers, wholesalers, and retailers, each with inventory and price decisions to be made, but also transportation, communication, and the development of mechanical aids in accounting and record-keeping.

In the discussion of technification so far, I have adopted the conventional but incomplete equation of that process with "embodied technology" or mechanization. With regard to distribution it is appropriate to broaden the meaning to include essentially social (though mechanically assisted) technologies: advertising and self-service retail distribution.

Proponents of advertising argue that it is a form of information that aids the consumer in making intelligent choices in a competitive market, and that "it pays for itself" by expanding the market and thus permitting economies in scale that are reflected in lower prices. Commercial radio and television are said to provide free news and entertainment to listeners and viewers, and the cost of newspapers and magazines would be much higher were it not for the major contribution of paid advertising to the costs of production and distribution. Opponents argue that advertising has little effect on the overall volume of demand, particularly for fairly standardized products, and may simply add to the costs of distribution with benefits to advertising agencies, other advertising writers, and the media that charge for their dissemination, but with few if any benefits to the consumer. For example, cigarette advertising, which represents a large fraction of the retail cost of cigarettes, probably has little effect on the volume of demand among confirmed smokers, and thus serves at most to reallocate demand among competing brands. No manufacturer has yet seen fit to limit advertising to inexpensive announcements of a price reduction (made possible by reduced advertising costs) as a competitive strategy. The producers in short may be caught up in a shared and costly myth, which no one dares to dispel.

I am not about to attempt a convincing resolution of the question of the rational role of advertising in distribution. A few further comments are in order, however. Legal rules against false and misleading advertising exemplify once more the rational efficacy of fraud in any competitive situation unless prevented by rule. Similarly, advertising may rely on essentially irrational appeals, such as sexual exploitation in selling everything from shampoos to automobiles. In the Western world, if a manual worker wears anything around his neck at all, it is a "tie." Men who aspire to higher social status buy and wear "cravats," while for those of assured social position the merchants sedately advertise "neckwear." Costs escalate with the elegance of the term, although qualities may vary little. The same merchants who sell neckwear also advertise "suitings" and "shirtings," though the garments are not tailored to order; the ungrammatical term is apparently thought to reflect greater elegance than mere suits and shirts. These tactics reflect the strategy of rational manipulation of others' irrationalities. They remind one of the "human relations" approach to administration, whereby the morale and productivity of subordinates is encouraged by feigned informality and friendship as a possible substitute for higher compensation.

Self-service retail distribution, particularly as exemplified by supermarkets, provides convenience to consumers by the sheer array of partially competing products available for choice, with a single financial accounting when "checking out." This innovation in distribution results in considerable savings in labor costs by the simple expedient of passing the labor along to the consumer. The innovation works most effectively for highly standardized products. The small and specialized merchant can compete (at higher prices) only by offering superior quality, giving attention to "odd" requests, providing advice for customers with problems, and providing other services not available in mass-distribution outlets.

Even the impersonally sterile ambience of the self-service store has not removed all of the traditional features of markets as partly informal social settings, as the aisle-blocking assembly of shopping carts in the custody of gossiping shoppers on a common marketing schedule amply testifies. The general sociological principle here is that repeated social encounters by the same small number of participants are almost certain to produce non-rational and technically irrelevant bases of social relationships.

ALTERNATIVE TECHNOLOGIES

We have been attending to the causes and consquences of technological change in what have become "high-technology" economies. The evolutionary formula of progress from simple to complex fits the historical path of technology very well, although the evolutionary assumption of mindless adaptation does not fit at all: nearly all technical change is purposive and intentional, with some accidental innovations, some unforeseen additional uses of new processes and products, and many unforeseen costs.

A poor country with no manufacturing and primitive transportation and communication facilities must alter somehow those conditions in emulation of the technological change that has led to the economic rationalization underlying the wealth of the rich countries, if the poor countries seek modernization—and all so profess. Yet, although the head-start of many rich countries is long and its consequences large, it does not follow that "latecomers" must repeat either the pace or the sequence of historic developments.

(However, as the sociologist Marion Levy has correctly argued, closing the gap in per capita incomes in rich and poor countries will take a long time indeed, even if the rate of economic growth in poor countries is several times that in rich countries.[8] Of course, greater equalization of income internationally would be hastened if the rate of growth of "mature economies" were to approach zero and rapid growth were to continue apace in newly modernizing economies. The world is sufficiently interdependent economically that stability—or "stagnation"—in already relatively prosperous countries would almost certainly make rapid growth in most poor countries impossible.)

Nowhere is the presumed autonomy of societies or of nominally sovereign national states less tenable than with reference to the stock of useful knowledge. To a remarkable extent there is now a world pool of technology ready for selection and use, despite valiant attempts at secrecy or exclusive proprietorship. That pool of knowledge is available—at variable costs and under various, but always stringent, conditions—without regard to the order in which items or systems entered the inventory. Consequently, one may have airlines before railroads, perhaps skipping rail transport altogether and choosing compact electronic calculators without giving a second thought to bulky hand-cranked or merely electrical calculating machines.

The presumption of progress thinly concealed in evolutionary models of social change leads to the almost unchallenged conventional wisdom that "newer is better" (except for the perhaps equally fallacious nostalgic distortion of the "good old days"). The most general characteristic of the technification of production in highly rationalized economies has been increasing capital intensity through the embodied technology of mechanization—labor-saving in physical production. In most of the newly modernizing countries of the world, capital is acutely small and labor is super-abundant, although mainly lacking in the skills appropriate for a rationalized economy. The latest, capital-intensive technology may thus be inappropriate, and an earlier, more labor-intensive system is the rationally correct choice. Political considerations, which may operate according to a different set of rational calculations for officials who prefer to stay in power, may well lead to the economically irrational decision to settle for nothing less than the "best." Who wants to claim credit for a new factory with outmoded machinery? Here we encounter a possible competition among rational systems of calculation, apart from probable intrusion of non-rational values and sentiments. The engineer's conception of efficiency may differ from an economist's cost−benefit analysis of alternative courses of action, and both differ from the practicing politician's calculation of feasibility (which has the highest probability of sensitivity to symbolism and emotion, at least as attributed to constituents, the engineers and economists having been carefully trained to ignore such considerations).

Earlier I mentioned the stringency of conditions under which technology may be transferred. Those conditions will of course vary in significant detail according to the chosen goals and sequential strategies in their pursuit (since "everything at once" is not a practical possibility), and according to many other circumstances of time and place. In the most general terms, the successful adoption of novel technology will require a stable political order, a market system, domestically produced or imported skills, and geographical and social mobility on the part of workers independent of kinship ties. These conditions are not impossible to meet, as the air-polluting smoke from countless new factories testifies in towns previously tainted only by time-honored poverty. These conditions reflect the correct but incomplete conventional wisdom of the social sciences, that the components of social systems are interdependent. The ordering and timing of induced changes has received less attention, but is critical for modernization strategies. Causal linkages through time must be correctly perceived, as well as simply consideration of "lead-time," that is, the time required to bring a planned result to fruition. An ordering of goals to be achieved according to a scale of value preferences is unlikely to correspond to a temporal ordering of places for investment of effort and capital.

Technology itself commonly presents itself in systems. The extreme case is the "turn-key" complete manufacturing installation, which still requires a broader support system ranging from the "hardware" of power and transportation and replacement parts for the machinery to the "software" of appropriately trained personnel. And since there are alternative systems, partly lacking standardization of components for substitution between them—a defect of technological diversity previously noted—the rational purchaser or recipient of a system needs to worry about the hazards of being "locked into" dependence on the original supplier.

THE PRICE OF PROGRESS

In a complex social system, any social change is likely to affect some interests adversely. Just as the division of labor in manufacturing threatens or destroys the economic position of the broadly trained artisan, and a merit-based civil service takes away the livelihood of loyal incompetents in a public patronage system, rationalization in general threatens social structures that operate through shared myths and interpersonal obligations. To avoid equating any change with progress—a strong propensity with respect to technification—the negative consequences must be perceived and evaluated. The contemporary enthusiasm for cost–benefit analyses and "environmental impact statements" reflects the recognition of negative effects. Those approaches, a sociologist is required to assert, are best pursued by including "costs" that may not be readily convertible to monetary units, in the vain quest for a singular, decisive balance sheet. For example, it may be economically cheaper to import skilled workers for technically sophisticated production or monetary management than to invest in a formal educational system of the level and quality to produce them locally. Yet such a policy is likely to be regarded by unemployed nationals as a further evidence of dependency and neo-colonialism, with resulting tension, conflicts, and political dissidence that a precarious political regime can ill afford.

Raw materials depletion and environmental pollution are the most widely recognized costs of the technification of physical production. In the increasingly shrill arguments between the "haves" and the "have-nots," sometimes now called the North—South conflict, these problems figure in rather ironic ways. Rich countries are accused of exploiting the raw materials of poor countries, taking them by theft under colonialism or by artificially rigged low prices under "economic neo-colonialism," not only to the detriment of the past and current state of the "dependent" areas, but also to the peril of adequate future supplies as they seek modernization. Now it has been historically true that "unfavorable terms of trade" for producers of raw materials as compared with manufacturers have generally prevailed, both internationally and within national economies. It would be naive indeed to suppose that manufacturers would have been too honorable to rig prices when they could, and at times no doubt they did when less than free and multilateral national trade permitted essentially "captive" markets. An international conspiracy among manufacturers to hold down prices of raw materials is less credible, as the chief countries in international trade have been fiercely competitive on the whole. The currently successful price-fixing cartel formed by the Organization of Petroleum Exporting Countries (OPEC) was formed to redress the balance, and other less notable cartels are in being or in prospect.

The problem of resource depletion is a different matter. The case is clearest with respect to fossil fuels, which are finite, and being used up at an accelerating rate. Demands for energy continue to grow everywhere in the world as newly developing countries seek energy for manufacturing and transportation while high-technology countries continue to use steadily increasing amounts. The economic costs of power are bound to increase, with clear implications for rates of technification.

The depletion of minerals is different. Metallic ores, which are also finite, but which in the cases of iron and aluminum remain extensive indeed, are not destroyed in the process of extraction and fabrication. Copper for inks and silver for photography are not really recoverable, but with these relatively minor exceptions the earth has about the same supply of minerals as it started with. That may not be enough, in every instance, to go around at the same level and kind of use now enjoyed by the most affluent countries, but the "technology of substitution" is a thriving sub-set of the knowledge industry. The undoubted waste of metallic raw materials has been expensive but not fatal. The metal mines of the future may be the junk yards and land fills of today.

A very different complaint of the poor against the rich is made with respect to pollution. Highly industrialized societies have discovered tardily that they have thoughtlessly used the air (which is also, in effect, finite) as a dumping ground for smoke and noxious chemicals, and water for similar deleterious purposes. Having seen the light, in a manner of speaking, industrial countries have increasingly made environmental protection (natural ecological systems along with air and water) a matter of public policy. They now even seek international controls of environmental exploitation, and thereupon rests the complaint. Countries that are beginning industrialization are being admonished not to repeat the past errors of the "successful" nations, though, they observe, part of the success rested precisely on the practices now regarded as regrettable. Some spokesmen for developing countries would no doubt be willing, wryly, to promise to be sorry after they have had their turn in spoiling and despoiling the environment.

What we may call the "ecology movement" does not proceed on strictly rational grounds, and indeed symbolizes the limits of rationality. Pleas for environmental protection abound with references to natural beauty, the "rights" of other living things, and the interests of generations yet unborn. With respect to the claims of posterity, the perfectly correct reply in terms of economic rationality is, "Why should I bother with posterity; what has posterity done for me?" Although Thomas Jefferson insisted that "the earth belongs to the living," he was more of a dedicated rationalist than are most persons living now, however much pride they may take in their rationality. Adults are sentimental about their own children and, in a more attenuated way, about children in general. A vision of the future that one will not live to see is non-rational but, like love, not necessarily pathological.

I have not attended to other well-known risks and horrors of technification, such as weapons of terror, sophisticated instruments for surveillance and invasions of privacy, computerized dossiers for use as means of blackmail. As this is written, we are a scant five years from 1984, and a re-reading of George Orwell's modern classic, Nineteen Eighty-Four, may provide a suitable caution for those who regard the uses of useful knowledge as requiring no restraints. Orwell's rational society comes too close to some actual ones, and aspects of his society are too widely adopted in many societies to give any comfort to rationalists pure and unsullied by sentiments and values.

NOTES

1. Lewis Mumford, The Pentagon of Power, Vol. II, The Myth of the Machine (New York: Harcourt, 1970).
2. Editor's "Introduction" to Wilbert E. Moore, ed., Technology and Social Change (Chicago: Quadrangle Books, 1972), p. 7.

3. On the significance of the gap between the "ideal" and the "actual," see Wilbert E. Moore, *Social Change,* 2nd ed. (Englewood Cliffs, NJ: Prentice-Hall, 1974), pp. 19–22.
4. Daniel Bell, *The Coming of Post Industrial Society: A Venture in Social Forecasting* (New York: Basic Books, 1973).
5. Fritz Machlup, *The Production and Distribution of Knowledge in the United States* (Princeton, NJ: Princeton University Press, 1962).
6. See Wilbert E. Moore, *Industrial Relations and the Social Order,* rev. ed. (New York: Macmillan, 1951; reprinted New York: Arno Press, 1977), Chapter II, "The Factory System and Its Forerunners."
7. See Wilbert E. Moore, *Man, Time, and Society* (New York: Wiley, 1963).
8. Marion J. Levy, Jr., *Modernization: Latecomers and Survivors* (New York: Basic Books, 1972), pp. 11–21.

EDUCATION

Education is the closest rival to industrialization as a universally sought solution to the problems of backwardness or underdevelopment. Though lively argument may surround such questions as whether more elementary schools or a hydroelectric development will yield a higher return on investment, or whether public schools or private employers should provide training in particular vocational skills, the demand for increased educational opportunities is a political reality that makes merely economic or technical arguments of secondary importance. No political regime, no matter how authoritarian and repressive, is likely to risk the popular outrage that would follow any attempt to stop educational expansion, to say nothing of reducing commitments already made.

Of course, in the proper sense of the term, education is a social or cultural universal in the human species and a requisite for survival. Human beings have no instincts worthy of the name. That is, we have no genetically determined, precisely programmed, complex behavior patterns oriented to sexual behavior, environmental coping, aggression, or anything else. The current mini-fad for "sociobiology" represents a revival of instinctivism long since discredited.[1] No persuasive leap can be made from insect societies or even from primates to human culture.[2] Sociobiologists do not argue for special instincts for each society or culture, but seek behavioral universals in a species correctly perceived as singular. Amply documented cultural variability defeats any proposed instinctive pattern. Proponents of sociobiology must therefore stand convicted of willful ignorance or of stupidity: the classic condemnation, either knaves or fools.

Everything from coping mechanisms for mere survival to the values that inform rules of social conduct must be learned—all depend on education at the hands of those already "socialized." Parents, older siblings, and other kin are almost always involved in this education, although children of the wealthy and powerful may have much of their tutelage from servants. In most societies, for most of human history, this education has had the mission of preparing the child for a socially preordained adult social position.

Even formal schools are not a peculiarly modern invention. In ancient Egypt, physicians, priest-magicians, and scribes received formal training;[3] in classical Greece academies trained the sons of citizens in literature and philosophy (but not resident aliens or slaves); in Tokugawa Japan (1614–1868) a considerable hierarchy of schools existed, approximately graded and differentiated by the social ranks of the students' parents.[4] Until recent centuries, the clergy monopolized literacy in Europe; later, children of the nobility and landed gentry had tutors or attended schools limited to those of proper birth and wealth. The expansion of the curricula of schools and universities to include more "worldly" subjects, and the extension of at least elementary education (reading, writing, and arithmetic, along with religious and moral precepts) to a growing proportion of commoners preceded industrialization, though not commercialization and occupational specialization.[5]

Whence came the universal commitment to education? In the contemporary condemnation of colonialism, some of its possibly positive consequences may be overlooked. Had colonial authorities withheld all formal educational opportunities from the natives, the literacy (in an alien tongue) and other mysteries commanded by those in power might have remained simple symbols of superiority. But once at least partial access to the exotic mysteries was given to some of the local population, education became an instrument for achieving higher social position and not simply a reflection of superiority otherwise established. (After all, in most of the great cultures with a written language, literacy, or, later, higher education, were more nearly perquisites of an hereditary elite than a means of climbing a pyramid of prestige. Not that education was irrelevant to power; it could be used as a way of maintaining superiority as well as a status symbol unattainable by the low-born.) The subjects of colonial rule could scarcely avoid noticing that the continued and regular exercise of authority rested far more on a formal bureaucratic structure than on any crude display of police power and weaponry.

Oddly, in British colonial administration, the governors were more likely to have had traditional rather than utilitarian or pragmatic educations. A kind of highly cultivated amateurism long prevailed in English educational policy: training in Greek and Latin, ancient and English history, and a fine sensitivity to English itself as a language of discourse and expression. The Scots, with their strong Calvinist tradition, were more likely to have skills in accounting and engineering, and even in military technology. Lower levels of the civil service could be staffed by those with less exalted educational attainments, and here selected natives could be given an opportunity to join the administration of their less privileged compatriots. In the latter days of colonialism, particularly in this century, a considerable number of subjects of European colonial powers achieved university educations in the homelands of their rulers and, in due course, became the leaders of the independence movements. Education, for them, became an instrument of collective as well as individual status-striving, and that of course colored their own policies and set an example for the citizens of new nations.

Countries such as Japan[6] and Czarist Russia,[7] exempt from colonialism but not from Westernization in its many other guises, moved both toward "secularization" of education—that is, at minimum, admission of "practical" courses—and toward relaxation of the rank-ordered access to formal schooling.

Thus, whether through imitation and explicit borrowing, or through the meager but significant opportunities for status enhancement under colonialism and their much wider emulation as examples, formal education has achieved the standing of a universal human right (and therefore goal of public policy). Putting the matter that way, however, obscures the issue as to whether education serves primarily as an instrument of rationalization (and of individual achievement) or as a symbol and goal sought for its own sake. Since complete equalization of educational opportunities *and* results would provide no differential advantages in status seeking, it would appear that some level of formal education—e.g., functional literacy and common arithmetic—becomes both an instrumental requisite and an accepted symbol of social participation; differential advantages flow from the level and kind of education beyond that common base. I suggest, however, that the issue remains cloudy, both in the motivations of those seeking (or whose parents are seeking) educational opportunities and in the formulation of public policy. The ambiguity and ambivalence are intrinsic.

Now I shall consider the uses of literacy and technical skills, and then some of the problems of the broader uses of education, of various levels and qualities. Finally, I shall comment on some of the irrationalities evident in educational systems and their uses, and of course the non-rational limits and virtues of knowing a great deal.

FUNCTIONAL LITERACY AND TECHNICAL SKILLS

A written language has all sorts of advantages over merely oral communication: reliable communication at a distance without the hazard of distortion by intermediaries, precision in the formulation of instructions and rules, record-keeping for reliable recall of the past. It is to written records that we owe much of our knowledge of human history, along with the religious, philosophical, and expressive literature that forms part of the "cultural heritage" of modern man.

For the spread of literacy beyond a small, privileged sector of the population (priests, university "philosophers," mandarin administrators in Confucian China, nobles and samurai warrior-governors in Japan, Brahmins as priests and experts on sacred texts in India, similar authorities in other cultures), there were many reasons. In the recent Western world, Protestantism sought universal literacy among congregations of the faithful, with its emphasis on the "priesthood of all believers" and the importance of access to the Bible and religious literature expounding and applying doctrine. When combined in America with the Enlightenment view that a self-governing society requires an informed electorate, the foundation was laid for universal public education. That public policy was well established (early in the 19th century) before anyone hinted that the cost of education was a capital investment in the future economic productivity of the labor force. Later, with large-scale immigration from Europe, the education of immigrants was sought primarily in terms of their "Americanization," not in terms of their greater economic value to themselves or their employers.[8]

Besides religious and recreational reading, which safely elude criteria of rationality, literacy gives access to current printed information on a wide range of subjects, from prices of advertised goods and services to the state of the economy and polity, and these may meet the criteria of "information relevant to rational decisions." Condensed and highly selective information of this sort is now also available by radio and television, but those are scarcely a substitute for the fuller information available from printed sources, which can be consulted again when memory lapses.

Though repeated studies demonstrate the high relationship between education and income everywhere in the contemporary world,[9] Carney, in a careful review of the evidence, finds little proof of the value of education in increasing productivity.[10] He does, however, indicate a stronger relationship in countries in the early stages of economic and educational expansion than in countries with highly educated populations.

The situation is complicated by questions of "current state" and temporal trends. In a society in which the traditional culture or cultures did not hit upon the marvelous social invention of writing, those few residents who acquire literacy in the language of the colonial administrators or foreign traders are almost certain to be exempt from manual labor. Later, as the country approaches nearly universal literacy, that differential advantage disappears. If compulsory education continues to be pushed to higher and higher levels (or ages of students), differential advantage requires levels beyond that common base. For others, the common level tends to be assumed for any employment: a necessary but not sufficient condition. At the point (now reached in the United States) where the highest formal degree or certificate granted by the educational system is no assurance of privileged employment, the purely instrumental view of extended education, from the individual viewpoint, becomes seriously strained.

The case for education as a part of a rationalized *economic* system, especially in terms of capital investment, thus remains mixed and uncertain. The meaning of literacy for awareness of the world outside the immediate social setting of the reader, for living in a society dense with communications ranging from tax notices to solicitations for charitable enterprises, is more difficult to measure but apparently widely accepted as positive and valuable. Levy argues that the expansion of education, in addition to the "democratizing" influence of sharing a common curriculum before specialization sets in, suggests a sort of convergence among societies: "Beyond the basic common curriculum of learning to walk and to talk and to eat and to sleep and control bodily functions and interact with other human beings, the common curriculum for all mankind has never been so great as it becomes with modernization."[11]

Levy adds that this common curriculum is steadily becoming greater, presumably as a consequence of the steady expanding literacy in developing areas. Now, as Levy properly indicates, the notion of literacy does include common arithmetic, which may be fairly readily freed from linguistic entanglements, but ". . . some of the general facts and myths of the history and civics of the peoples concerned" will be learned in the particular language of the texts studied, and in any case will be local lore.[12] Since linguistic differences are a fundamental fact of a world becoming similar in many other respects through common processes of rationalization, the "common curriculum" would appear to be grossly exaggerated.

There can be little dispute concerning the economic and technological importance of specific occupational skills for an increasingly rationalized economy. Here the issue concerns costs and auspices. Is training in particular skills in anticipation of employment the proper function of schools— whatever their auspices or support—or a necessary and proper responsibility of employers through on-the-job training? As I have written earlier:

> The short supply and often poor quality of the output of schools in developing areas make on-the-job training . . . essential. It is also . . . difficult, since the supply of qualified managerial personnel is severely enough limited before training is added to supervisory functions.[13]

Some training by managers or experienced workers is a probability in any stage of educational and economic development, because of the near impossibility of getting a precise match between school curricula and the demand for skills, sometimes at a somewhat remote future. Philip J. Foster, arguing that general and vocational education are not substitutes for each other but complementary, has serious reservations concerning school-based vocational training in developing areas:

> It is widely believed that schools can readily be modified to meet new economic needs and, more particularly, to accord with the intentions of social and economic planners. I shall argue, on the contrary, that schools are remarkably clumsy instruments for inducing prompt large-scale changes in underdeveloped areas. [14]

Foster suggests, in addition to a variety of possible short-term training courses for readily identifiable employment opportunities, more extensive formal training sponsored by employers. [15] It should be emphasized in this connection that, whatever the impact of a military establishment on internal political organization and external relations of national states, the military is often the best organized system for providing training in modern mechanics, as well as familiarization with a formal bureaucratic organization, both with varying transferability to civilian employments.

KNOWLEDGE AND CHARACTER

Education, even in the constricted sense of formal schooling, may represent only modest additions to rationalization. Learning to read and recite sacred texts by rote, or learning secular language only to serve as a scribe-secretary for an illiterate governor, adds an instrumental tool that has limited utility. Literacy of course does give access to novel ideas and information if those have—somewhere, sometime—been committed to writing.

Perhaps the most important immediately "practical" consequence of elementary education, apart from literacy and common arithmetic, is not a specific body of stored information but the skill that might be called "learning to learn." Whether that skill is adequately learned is likely to be a sensitive test of the contribution of education to the rationalization of social systems.

Any generalization about the organization and curricula of schools is hazardous, given the manifest differences in educational "philosophies," the preconditioning of children to school attendance and learning, the qualities of materials and teachers, and so on. Yet a number of features are sufficiently common to warrant a few somewhat speculative generalizations. (1) The curriculum and study plan, as such, involve not only major, progressive steps in accomplishments—the "grade" or "form"—but also within the term, the week, and even the day, the child is required to adjust to change in both subject and level of proficiency. (2) The school provides the setting for competitive performance, with presumably commensurate rewards. (3) The introduction of problem-solving into the curriculum (usually beyond the two or three most elementary grades, and sometimes scarcely at all except for work in arithmetic and mathematics) presumably encourages both an adjustment to uncertainty and some measure of creative mastery of that uncertainty.

The encouragement of both achievement orientations and a problem-solving habit of mind are different from the training for a stable future and a predictable individual place in it characteristic of most traditional societies. Levy discusses "education for an unknown future" and notes in passing that it is inconceivable that "general" education can keep pace with the rate at which additions to knowledge are being made in the contemporary world. [16]

I shall return momentarily to the troublesome question of attitudes; however, what the current vernacular calls "information overload" warrants a brief digression. The rapid expansion of knowledge provides problems for educational policy. The child in the highly rationalized societies, where much of this information has been developed and where the largest investments are currently made in knowledge production, has thereby no substantial advantages over the child of the illiterate peasant in a society newly dedicated to education. Since cultural accumulations are not genetically transmitted, in either case the student has "too much" to learn. This requires decisions by policy-makers on both the criteria of selection of "what everybody should know" and the point or points at which specialization should begin. The strong "humanistic" traditions in Western education have helped prolong "general education" well into college and university curricula for the first (baccalaureate) academic degree. Yet lively controversy prevails among the faculties of liberal arts colleges or units within universities over what furniture of the mind a "well-educated person" should possess. "Premature" specialization risks both occupational obsolescence without adequate general education to provide the basis for a new specialty and a poorly furnished mind for the multitude of social contacts outside the occupational setting. Postponed specialization entails costs that poor countries in desperate need of practical skills may be unable to afford.

What is needed in developing countries that become borrowers or beneficiaries of the world pool of technology is some cadre of local people sufficiently well-informed to know what to borrow, including informed judgments of the relative merits of alternative technical systems. The tactic of sending local talent abroad for training encounters the obvious hazard that they may not return, thus becoming part of the "brain drain" to technically sophisticated and prosperous countries. A somewhat subtler hazard is that technology learned aboard may be too advanced, relying on a more extensive support system than can be readily transferred to the very much less highly rationalized social structure of countries that seek modernization.

The problem of what is to be taught (and presumably learned) is complicated by the historic and contemporary function of universities as producers and not merely as transmitters of knowledge. If all else fails as a subject for argument, one can always get a division of opinion between most university students, on the one hand, and most faculty members, on the other, concerning the relative weight that should be attached to teaching and research in judging the qualities of the faculty. Since time and energy are finite, the answer "both" or "both and administrative duties also" glosses over the issue. Yet if "learning to learn" is the critically important product of a rationalized education system, some experience in producing knowledge might claim some superiority over formal instruction as the proper mission of a university education.

The question of attitudes assumes considerable importance in view of uncertainties about the relation between education and the future, and the certainty that motivation is a major determinant of performance. Mere dissatisfaction with present conditions does not clearly predispose to any particular course of change, or at least to any program after the "establishment" is dismantled or destroyed. Inkeles and Smith, on the basis of a methodologically highly sophisticated comparative study of factory workers in six countries, demonstrate rather conclusively that "modern" attitudes are acquired by young adults in the work situation.[17] The one notable flaw in that study is that it does not account for the initial provocation for some young men to leave their villages and seek factory employment and others—sufficiently similar in background characteristics to constitute "control groups"—not to do so. When formal education is made compulsory, the coercion may possibly outweigh the rather uncertain benefits.

Despite considerable attention to "indoctrination" with respect to social values and approved rules of conduct in educational curricula, knowing what teachers and others expect as correct answers to relevant questions has slight if any significance for internalization of those values and norms as part of individual character and personality. As I have noted elsewhere, ". . . normative internalization takes place only in situations marked by strong affectivity in relationships, and some part of that affect must be positive; fear of disapproval or punishment is not to be discounted, however."[18] The more impersonal, and in that sense rational, the relations of teachers and students, and the more segregated schools become from other social settings,[19] and in that sense a product of rationalization, the less effectively will they serve as mechanisms of what Durkheim called "moral education."[20] In most societies the family and play groups are the principal sources of character formation. Teachers, occupational peers, and recreational groups may supplement those more conventional sources, but only if those "others" are emotionally significant for the individual. In societies marked by substantial social disorganization, the influence of peers and other friends may be consistent neither with traditional values nor with those favorable to building some form of better world.

HAZARDS AND VIRTUES OF IRRELEVANCE

In all highly rationalized societies formal education has become the principal mechanism for inter-generational mobility—that is, of children pursuing occupations and enjoying social rewards superior to that of their parents. Mobility may of course be downward, and that does occur, possibly for lack of adequate basic intelligence and more probably because of lack of study-oriented motivation. Again, it is well to emphasize that in newly developing areas the status of parents in traditional pursuits and that of children in the modernizing sector may be difficult to compare in terms of rank, but they are indisputably different and schools are a principal avenue of access to the new order.

We have become increasingly aware that the formal equalization of educational opportunities does not assure true equality of opportunity to learn, for much of school (and other task-oriented) performance depends on attitude and motivation.[21] The child born into a culturally deprived family starts with substantial deficits in both preschool learning and, especially, in the requisite achievement orientation. Thus it is not simply that some parents can afford better educational opportunities for their children; publicly supported education at all levels has substantially attenuated that advantage. Affluent parents (and particularly those who were upwardly mobile themselves) strongly encourage superior performance by their children.

However, as I briefly discussed earlier, the advantages accruing to those with more formal education are highly relative to the shifting situation of supply and demand. As formal education expands in proportions of children and youths in school, and the average or median years of school completed also steadily increase, the expectations of differential career advantages to be derived from education are likely to be out of date and overly optimistic. The "unemployed intellectual" in India, who may have had some secondary school education, finds that white-collar jobs have not expanded as fast as the output of the schools. The American college graduate now working as a service-station attendant or taxi driver or as a construction worker is a victim of the same lack of synchronization in structural change that frustrates his Indian counterpart. The educational attainment in both cases has become irrelevant, if relevance consists solely of education as an investment in differential employment and career opportunities.

In the aggregate, education has not lost its significance for social placement, for it is uniformly highly correlated with income and occupational prestige.[22] For some individuals those aggregative relationships are not comforting; on the contrary, they may deepen the frustration.

The blame for education that is out of phase with changes in demand for particular skills and skill combinations, changes that are often rapid and poorly predictable, rests in part on the "cumbersome" quality of school systems of which Foster complained with respect to vocational education and in part on intrinsic lead-time considerations.[23] The only way to measure skill levels is in terms of the time required—genuinely and not spuriously prolonged to limit competition—in specialized training. If it requires eight years beyond undergraduate college education to produce adequately skilled specialists in medicine, three years in law, five years for college teaching, any relatively rapid change in demand for those skills is bound to result in surpluses or shortages.

Some individuals seeking to make somewhat rational career choices may be wise enough to look at trends rather than merely the most recent statistical information (which, however recent, is merely historical and not binding on the future), perhaps aided by governmental "occupational outlook" estimates. But, short of tight educational and career management by a central planning authority, individual preferences may still be asserted despite gloomy prospects, and school systems are genuinely cumbersome both with regard to curricular change and with regard to admission criteria for those schools that enjoy substantial discretion on numbers and qualities sought. In principle, totally planned systems such as the Soviet Union or mainland China can determine the "manning tables" requisite for various future goals in production of goods and services, and then instruct the appropriate units of the educational system to deliver the needed personnel on schedule. In practice those regimes have frequently made sharp changes in policies and plans, either because of perceived changes in international relations or because of internal political considerations or doctrinal disputes.

The hazards of educational preparation that is "irrelevant" to occupational placement are compounded by continued structural change. Changes in markets, in governmental policies, and particularly in technology as useful knowledge constitute constant or intermittent threats of occupational obsolescence. Educational levels and types are of course a major determinant of first employment, and first employment strongly affects subsequent careers.[24] Yet, over 40 years or more of full occupational careers, mere increasing proficiency from practice may not be an adequate protection against external structural changes. Adult re-training and "continuing education" represent partial adaptations to those hazards, but assume a continuous ability and willingness to learn, which a premature and continuing specialization may have successfully stultified.

With increases in educational attainment outstripping the genuine upgrading of skill distributions in the labor force, discussed in Chapter 4, many new employees may be "overqualified" for the positions offered. Such a judgment assumes a more precisely measured relationship between educational qualifications and job requirements than generally exists, but still has crude validity. If a college graduate occupies a position that a suitably educated high-school graduate (not an illiterate given a succession of "social" promotions and a diploma to avoid embarrassment) could perform at least as well, then the college graduate is overqualified. If possession of the college degree was a condition for employment, then "credentialism" is operating. Credentialism of this sort might be characterized as another example of conspicuous consumption of labor resources, along with overstaffing.

Yet before making a hasty judgment that overqualification is automatic evidence of irrationality, let us put the situation in the perspective of careers rather than first employments. Apart from mere question of specific knowledge gained and retained, if—and the uncertainty is important—the college graduate has a greater capacity for and interest in continuous learning, the educational investment may pay off in terms of longer-term career opportunities.

The rationalism of the Enlightenment as manifested in its support for learning was not narrowly confined to matters of production and trade. Late 18th century rationalism, as represented in America by a Franklin or a Jefferson, contained a strong component of classical revival. In addition to the *true*, they would add the *good* and the *beautiful*. The views of the Calvinists and related dissenters were hostile to frivolous enterprises of all sorts, including "irrelevant" (or positively harmful) learning. Education was supported to learn the divine will through scriptural study and to build the kingdom of God on earth by rational mastery of it. In England, the product of a proper upper-class education could discuss Virgil and Aristophanes, whereas an educated Scott could build a bridge, invent a machine, or keep a company's accounts in order.

These two divergent approaches to education may be viewed as standing for a persistent antinomy in the philosophical foundations of modern education in the Western world. With the progressive rationalization of the social structure in general and the progressive democratization of access to formal education, the more pragmatic view of learning has steadily gained ascendancy, but not total victory. In higher education the liberal arts do not flourish in comparison with engineering and business administration—both probably representing premature specialization—but they survive, partly by demeaning exercises in demonstration of relevance. In America, many elementary schools have special teachers for music education and art education, although the extra expenses involved are most likely to be considered dispensable frills when budgets are cut. (Physical education, the practical utility of which is commonly asserted but never demonstrated, is probably subconsciously supported more for its competive sports by-product than for its contributions to health. That would be hard to admit overtly. In the pragmatic watered-down Puritan tradition, recreation is only permissible if it aids productivity.)

What I am suggesting is that there are values in education and in learning, "for their own sake," that the civilized or cultivated mind relfects more favorably on human dignity that the grubby practicality of education merely to build things and make money. The practical goals are of course essential and not really despicable. But the rationalization of education has been predicated almost solely on learning as an investment, a form of capital. Learning may also be considered as a product of a prosperous economy, a consumer's good. Western education owes much to its aristocratic origins. To a high degree in England (which still has a strong residual influence in what was the British empire) and to a less marked degree on the European continent, education beyond minimal literacy and arithmetic was a privilege enjoyed by essentially parasitic portions of the population: the clergy, university professors who occupied endowed chairs, and landlords who lived off the rents of the tenants. No wonder that in the democratic or populist environment of the modern world such "useless" knowledge has a poor reputation.

Yet the affluent modernized societies cannot find total "practical" employment for the educational output that they are amply capable of producing. Some of this seeming overproduction of learning simply reflects irrationalities in the allocation of talents, but some surely reflects a high degree of efficiency in economic production and distribution. This state of affairs is consistent with the Marxist vision of well over a century ago, premature at the time, of humanity sufficiently freed from the drudgery of labor that time and energy can now be spent simply in cultivating culture. Certainly the growth of leisure and of a sort of dedicated mass recreation is evidence of the possibility. One only needs to admit that education may be an alternative form of recreation, without insisting that it be useful.

The utilitarian view of education is bound to be paramount in newly developing economies. Yet, as an additional benefit of colonialism, or simply as a remaining autochthonous tradition, many poor countries have a small and precarious commitment to "higher learning." It will, I believe, be sad if in the allocation of grievously scarce resources that commitment is completely abandoned. The lot of the desperately poor is mean enough without removing small glimpses of humanity in a higher state of grace.

NOTES

1. See E. O. Wilson, *Sociobiology* (Cambridge: Harvard University Press, 1975).
2. See S. L. Washburn, "What We Can't Learn About People from Apes," *Human Nature* 1(11):70–75 (November 1978).

3. See Henry E. Sigerist, A History of Medicine, Vol. I, Primitive and Archaic Medicine (New York: Oxford University Press, 1951), pp. 323–324.

4. See Herbert Passin, "Portents of Modernity and the Meiji Emergence," in C. Arnold Anderson and Mary Jean Bowman, Education and Economic Development (Chicago: Aldine, 1965), pp. 394–421.

5. See C. Arnold Anderson, "Literacy and Schooling on the Development Threshold: Some Historical Cases," in ibid., pp. 347–362.

6. See Passin, essay cited in note 4.

7. See Arcadius Kahan, "Russian Scholars and Statesmen on Education as an Investment," in Anderson and Bowman, eds., work cited in note 4, pp. 3–10.

8. See Gerald Rosenblum, Immigrant Workers; Their Impact on American Labor Radicalism (New York: Basic Books, 1973).

9. See Peter Blau and Otis Dudley Duncan, The American Occupational Structure (New York: Wiley, 1967); Donald J. Treiman, Occupational Prestige in Comparative Perspective (New York: Academic Press, 1977).

10. See Martin Carney, "Education and Economic Development: The First Generation," in Manning Nash, ed., Essays on Economic Development and Cultural Change in Honor of Bert F. Hoselitz, Supplement to Vol. 25, Economic Development and Cultural Change (Chicago: University of Chicago Press, 1977), pp. 428–448.

11. Marion J. Levy, Jr., Modernization: Latecomers and Survivors (New York: Basic Books, 1972), p. 100.

12. Ibid., p. 99.

13. Wilbert E. Moore, The Impact of Industry (Englewood Cliffs, NJ: Prentice-Hall, 1965), p. 99.

14. Philip J. Foster, "The Vocational School Fallacy in Development Planning," in Anderson and Bowman, eds., work cited in note 4, pp. 142–166; quotation from pp. 143–144.

15. Ibid., pp. 154–159.

16. Levy, work cited in note 11, pp. 42–51.

17. Alex Inkeles and David H. Smith, Becoming Modern: Individual Change in Six Developing Countries (Cambridge: Harvard University Press, 1974).

18. Wilbert E. Moore, "Occupational Socialization," in David A. Goslin, Handbook of Socialization Theory and Research (Chicago: Rand McNally, 1969), pp. 861–883; quotation from p. 869.

19. The noted "developmental" psychologist Urie Bronfenbrenner discussed this point in a public lecture, reported in The Denver Post p. 33 (October 26, 1978).

20. Émile Durkheim, Moral Education: A Study in the Theory and Application of the Sociology of Education (New York: Free Press, 1961); first published in French 1902–1906.

21. See James S. Coleman et al., Equality of Educational Opportunity, U. S. Department of Health, Education, and Welfare (Washington: U.S. Government Printing Office, 1966).

22. See Treiman, work cited in note 9.

23. Foster, essay cited in note 14.

24. See Blau and Duncan, work cited in note 9.

BUREAUCRATIZATION

Bureaucratization is the process of rationalizing work organizations. The impersonal administration of specialized tasks for the achievement of clear-cut goals such as producing automobiles, delivery of health services, or instructing the young rests on a form of complex organization with features sufficiently common to justify the standard designation: bureaucracy. The circumstance that the term is often used almost as an expletive will engage our attention, along with the manifest advantages that such organizations have over other ways of getting complex tasks performed.

Like other forms of rationalization that we have been discussing, bureaucracy is not a strictly modern social invention. The hierarchical principle of authority delegated (and progressively narrowed) through a "chain of command" was understood in ancient empires, and probably owed much to the problems posed by coordinating large military operations. The principle of selection by competence for performance of specialized tasks has occurred in nonliterate tribal societies,[1] despite the general practice in such societies of "ascriptive" status, that is, position (and therefore duties) assigned on the basis of age, sex, and kinship position—circumstances over which the individual has no effective control. Some collaborative tasks, we observed in Chapter 3, do not readily fit those traditional reciprocities embedded in kinship systems, and thus specialized work organizations also appear as supplements to more functionally diffuse social organizations. Such organizational specialization, it was argued in Chapter 4, derives from the same sources as individual occupational specialization, namely, the increasing size of encompassing social systems (societies), and the increases in useful knowledge (technology) available to the system as a whole but not to every unit within it. Since, as argued in Chapter 5, there is now a "world pool of technology," accessible to meagerly rationalized societies if they have the capital and skills to make use of it, mere size is now less critical for rationalizing work organizations (though by no means irrelevant) than the specialization required if the available technololgy is to be adopted and possibly adapted where it was not invented. It is in the coordination of specialized tasks that bureaucracy excels.

As a prelude to the discussion of the (sometimes depressingly) common features of bureaucratic organization, some rational sources of variability need to be noted. Let me first attend to questions of size, now not in the context of societal size as predictive of organizational specialization, but rather in the context of those specialized organizations. Clearly, large numbers permit (and might even be said to encourage) specialization. And, because the number of direct subordinates (technically called the span of control) of any supervisor is always limited, large numbers will require several levels of authority to coordinate. Yet size alone is an inadequate basis for predicting organizational complexity. Large numbers of agricultural workers performing similar tasks in planting, cultivating, or harvesting foodstuffs or cotton will not occasion organizational complexity, except the possibility that a number of foremen or supervisors are subordinate to a general manager. And even for such seemingly simple tasks, the totally inexperienced worker will require some initial instruction in proper procedures.

A small number—say four to eight—medical specialists practicing as a group will have a surprisingly complex organization. In addition to the fully professional practitioners, there are likely to be one or more nurses or laboratory technicians, a receptionist who may also be the appointments clerk, and a business manager or bookkeeper who is responsible for purchasing necessary supplies, arranging to have offices cleaned and in good repair, and, not least, collecting the fees charged by the professionals. Even among the professionals, their specialization implies a fairly elaborate set of rules or understandings concerning who is in charge of which portion of medical practice, how referrals are made within or possibly outside the group, and procedures for keeping records or charts for subsequent reference by any member of the group. In the particular case of the medical group, the rules for relations among the members may not be committed to writing as statutes or contracts, for the professionals are likely to have had common prior experience in medical schools and teaching hospitals, where the rules for relations among specialists have been learned. Other formal rules will be specified, however. These will include the "tax" to be paid by each practitioner for support of common costs and services.

Size, then, is positively related to the number of levels of authority. Internal specialization increases this relationship, as coordinating dissimilar tasks is more difficult than supervising standardized activities. Additionally, higher skill levels of subordinates will decrease the tolerable span of control and thus add "peakedness" to organizational structure. But, I have also suggested that multiplicity of rules is an additional indicator of complexity, and that the same variables of size, specialization, and skill level are correlated with that organizational characteristic.

Work-performing organizations differ in other significant ways, of which three are especially significant: goals or missions, physical setting, and social setting.

Since work is purposive activity, the first question about any work organization is, "What is it designed to do?" That is, what physical products or what services are supposed to result from the activities of participants? Individuals have goals or ends; strictly speaking, organizations do not. Yet organizations evolve to serve the common goals of participants, or are created to serve a specified purpose and participants are somehow induced to play their parts. (I use the neutral term *mission* for the intended outcomes of work organizations, as it leaves open the questions as to who has determined the purposes and whether they are shared by participants.)

The mission of a work organization has immediate implications for the instrumental activities appropriate to its accomplishment: What component tasks are to be done, by whom? What relevant technologies are available, including the social technology of administrative organization?

The "geography of work" is most apparent in food production and various extractive activities such as lumbering and mining. The location of work is determined by where the crop lands or trees, or minerals and coal are. Underground mining would appear to be about as narrowly constrained a physical setting as could exist, until we recall life aboard a submarine or the confined space in an airplane. Deep-sea fishing puts the fishing crew in fairly confining space, often for considerable periods of time. Some of these activities are intermittent or periodic, because of weather and the seasons; some, such as agriculture and forestry, are appealing or appalling because they must be done in the open; some are exceptionally hazardous, and participants thus especially dependent on the competence and conscientiousness of others in the work group.

The great majority of contemporary work settings are man-made, and "nature" intrudes only at the extremes of heat or cold, snow or floods, earthquakes or volcanic eruptions. Yet those settings are highly variable, being themselves the combined product of work missions, the technology of production, and considerations of social status. We may contrast the clean, quiet, and opulently furnished executive suite with the noisy, smelly, and dirty environment of many factory jobs.

It is useful to distinguish aspects of the physical environment along several dimensions: (1) degree of physical constraint or confinement as compared with relative liberty of movement; (2) noise; (3) physical and health hazards—including not only dangerous machines (some are found in offices as well as in shops) but also radiation, chemical fumes, air-borne particulates such as cotton lint, asbestos, sawdust; (4) physical and esthetic comforts and amenities, ranging from temperature control to art work.

The social setting of work organization comprises a considerable array of inter-organizational relationships, ranging from the families and communities of the workers to the pervasive influence of the state and its legal system. Of course, public bureaucracies are ultimately accountable to political authorities from which they derive their revenues, their authority, and their mission or excuse for existence. Private business corporations are subject to controls or at least constraints from all levels of government along with such interest groups as labor unions, professional associations, stockholders and creditors, and perhaps even organized consumers. In the simplified model of rational action, these aspects of the social setting become conditions that limit the choice among courses of action. In a somewhat more complex reality, they will often be treated as negotiable or perhaps even convertible into resources for instrumental use.

Despite these sources of variability in rationalized work organizations, the structural consequences of rationalization are sufficiently common to lend further credibility to the increasing structural similarity among societies. Especially notable is the machine-like impersonality with which bureaucracies carry out their collective missions. It is to the interdependent components of that social machine that I next turn our attention. Like any metaphor, the mechanical one has defects. The complex interdependence leads to the presumption of stability, and bureaucracies are commonly cumbersome. Yet that form of organization is also used to plan and implement change (though perhaps less on itself than on its setting), and I shall later discuss that seeming anomaly. Finally, suitable note will be taken of the resistance of participants to purely machine-like performance, a resistance that may literally subvert the organization or force its adaptation to a closer fit with "human nature." And the ultimate rationales for bureaucracies, the missions that they are supposed to be accomplishing, warrant scrutiny, for those after all derive from beliefs and values and not from a rational calculus.

THE SOCIAL MACHINE

A bureaucracy may be initially defined as an organization with these features: (1) purposes (or missions) are specific, limited, and ordered in terms of importance; (2) membership constitutes a livelihood for participants; (3) specialized activities are governed by explicit rules of conduct; (4) those rules of conduct include coordination on the basis of differential authority. Other bureaucratic features may be derived from these essential components, and will be noted as the discussion proceeds. One further feature of most bureaucracies deserves initial comment, and that is that these work organizations are commonly designed to be immortal. Thus the organization exists prior to all participants except those "present at the creation." The organization is also expected to endure beyond the working life of current members, those quitting or getting fired, dying, or retiring being replaced by others. From this important characteristic we derive the common organizational problems of *recruitment* and *succession* in positions. In principle, the organization endures, despite the somewhat transitory character of its inhabitants. In fact, turnover and succession are bound to make at least some noticeable difference in how the organization operates.

The comparison between "in principle" and "in fact" is one that will recur frequently in analyzing work organizations. Exposition of the features of bureaucracy is commonly credited to the German sociologist Max Weber,[2] with numerous modifications and amendments by later scholars.[3] In Weber's terms, the essential features of bureaucracy constituted an "ideal type," consistent within itself and useful as a standard for comparison with actual cases. In contemporary usage, the term "model" is often used in the same sense. The important analytical point is that a model may not be a precise representation of actual situations, but it is not thereby useless or irrelevant. Whenever a model serves not only as a standard for comparison but as a standard for approximation, the tension between the "ideal" and the "actual" is productive of efforts to close the gap or accommodate to its existence.

More than any other variety of organization, bureaucracy rests upon a selection and distribution of personnel according to specialized abilities and particular duties. It is thus in marked contrast to social units like the family or community that recruit their members chiefly by natural reproduction, and in which the division of labor is limited by the quality of the human resources available.

Bureaucratic specialization depends not only upon an adequate recruitment process, but upon an effective classification and coordination process as well. Specifically, the high degree of division of labor characteristic of modern bureaucratic organization rests upon three types of differences in the personnel available for productive labor. (1) It assumes and utilizes differences in native ability. One important distinction between bureaucratic principles of organization and those operating in other types of cooperative social systems is that the former frankly take into account both qualitative and quantitative differences in ability. (2) The differences in native ability, however, are in general meaningless or useless without specific training along the lines of existent or possible future occupational demands. In fact, bureaucratic specialization goes so far beyond any "natural" (untrained) differences in ability that it calls for high degrees of skill often requiring long preliminary training or apprenticeship. (3) Since position in a bureaucratic organization demands at least nominal loyalty to the system as a whole (sometimes called *esprit de corps*) and to the duties required by the individual's particular place in that system, it may be said to depend upon differences in occupational interests. This expectation sometimes poses problems, for the individual in modern society is in general assumed to be dissatisfied with his particular place in society, yet proud of his importance to his occupation, business organization, industrial plant, or independent profession. It is precisely in the bureaucratic organization that this pull-hauling upon the individual's occupational sentiments is reduced to a minimum by various devices now to be discussed.

Ideally, the three types of differences in the available personnel are expected to operate together. Thus, the methods of selection and training are expected to provide a general sifting process on the basis of ability (as defined by the particular standards of selection considered important), and to induce the appropriate sentiments in regard to the specialized task and the system as a whole. Where *choice* of occupational interests exists to an unusually high degree, the recruitment of the necessary qualified personnel for specialized work positions depends to a marked extent upon the advantages that such positions seem to offer to the individual. It is thus not simply necessary that the quantity and quality of the laboring population should have the necessary native ability, but that ability must be translated into usable skills through training, mediated by interest.

A shortcoming in any one of the three prerequisites to bureaucratic specialization may reduce the possible diversification of activities. Given a reasonably satisfactory solution to the general problem of personnel supply, however, the organizational problems resulting from specialization are not all taken care of.

Whether in society as a whole or in a bureaucracy, *the higher the degree of specialization, the greater the problem of coordination.* The integration of almost countless activities toward the achievement of the goals of the organization as a whole is one of the most persistent sources of difficulty in bureaucratic management. This would be true even if labor were simply *divided*. It is all the more true since the division takes place in the form of functional specialization, which I have previously termed diversification.

The executive, technical specialist, junior manager, line supervisor, and to some degree the productive laborer have special *spheres of competence* based upon particular abilities of functional importance to the organization as a whole. Within these broad or narrow spheres of competence the individual specialist reigns supreme. Thus a given riveter or welder may know considerable more about his job than does the foreman who supervises his work. The equivalent situation is most certainly true in the relation of the research chemist to the president or general manager. Authority is divided as well as delegated. Of this I shall have more to say presently, but it should be observed at once that this does not settle the issue of coordination: it simply documents its importance.

A good deal of the coordination of diversified activities is ensured by the character of the formal organization itself. Thus, every person's (or at least every "manager's") status in the organization is, formally considered, a well-defined position or office. This means that the rights and duties of the person occupying the office are largely determined by the relation of the *position* to others (and only incidentally, or even accidentally, by the relation between concrete persons). Under the triple assumption that the system is already established, that it is perfectly integrated, and that the occupants of the various positions will in fact fulfill precisely those official expectations demanded by the positions (no more, no less), the coordination might properly be viewed as automatic. That this result is rarely, if ever, achieved implies that ordinarily one or more of these assumptions are not in fact borne out. Nevertheless, the organizational advantages of the typical bureaucratic formalization merit some further consideration.

One of the most consistent criticisms of bureaucratic organization, and one that usually makes of the term *bureaucracy* an epithet, is its emphasis upon routine and form. However, from the point of view of maintaining a smoothly operating social system with a complex structure and diversified personnel, the criticism loses some of its merit. The elaborate ritual associated with interpersonal relations in a bureaucratic structure is well designed to maintain the division of spheres of competence, and to a certain degree the coordination of these. To the layman, or the person seeking help or information, the characteristic "passing the buck" is a sign of inefficiency. To the bureaucratic officeholder in government or industry, this is simply a process of referring a problem to the person or department within whose sphere its solution lies. Failure to follow this pattern would destroy the efficacy of the organizational specialization and cause general confusion of well-defined roles in the total system.

A major function of "rules and regulations" in any social organization is that of ensuring predictability of behavior within the organization. Thus the formal pattern of relations fixes responsibility for various decisions and standard activities. In this way it prevents overlapping authority, gaps in responsibility for important duties, and the arbitrary exercise of authority. To the extent that the rules are formal and the expected activities attach to the office and not to the particular occupant, the organization can maintain a high degree of stability with a changing personnel. (This principle is most strikingly illustrated, of course, in the organization of the army, where the most general rule is that a subordinate reacts to the uniform, and not to its wearer.)

A further corollary of the function of rules in ensuring predictability is their function in reducing or eliminating friction. The importance of this function is directly related to the highly diversified personnel making up the organization. The abilities, training, and interests represented are ordinarily such as to make impossible a friendly informal cooperation throughout the organization. Formal rules make it possible even for potential enemies to maintain cooperative relations, and also for those who would under informal conditions remain indifferent toward one another. To the extent that the person's significance for the system is determined by his position, and his relations with others follow predetermined routines, the significance of the total personaility is minimized. What is of primary importance in a highly formal structure is rather the "organizational personality." Again this principle is of much more general application than its usefulness in a governmental bureau or a business main office. The elaboration of rules of etiquette in "polite society," for example, allows strangers who are familiar with the rule book to act properly toward one another, and minimizes the necessity of making personal adjustments. Its relevance to operation of an elaborate, large-scale bureaucratic organization is enhanced, moreover, by the diversity of the personnel, the specialization of activity, and the necessity of coordination if the goals of the entire organization are to be achieved. It is in bureaucracy that a social system most closely approximates the coordinated complexity of the modern machine.

The distinctions among personnel in any social organization are not all representable on a "horizontal" plane, for authority is never distributed evenly throughout a social system. Even if the source of the authority is a "popular mandate" expressed through some democratic procedure, the importance of responsibility and unified direction are such as to require a demarcation of persons on a "vertical" plane. The wide extension of functional specialization does not remove the necessity for centralized administration and control, but rather increases it. Thus bureaucratic organization, wherever its field of operation, is typified by definite gradations in relative rank.

Part of the necessity of a rather elaborate hierarchy is to be found simply in the size of many work organizations, since convenience and effective organization requires that the number of persons directly supervised by a single administrator should not be large. This means that general policies or goals are passed down from one rank to the next, becoming more definite at each step, until they become explicit directions for the performance of those activities that will produce the general results desired.

The importance of "functional authority," that is, authority within special spheres of competence, has increased in most modern work organizations because of the growth in use of technical bodies of knowledge and skills. One striking result of this "technification" of work is that the chief executive thereby ceases to be the most skilled workman or even the most competent "authority" in the organization. But this does not mean that the necessity for hierarchical organization is removed. On the contrary, addition of the problem of coordination to the general necessity of sub-delegation of authority in a large organization increases, rather than decreases, the necessity of hierarchical arrangement of ranks and corresponding authority and responsibility. In fact, the wider the horizontal extension of functional specialization, the greater the necessity for vertical sub-delegation of authority. This may be called the *pyramidal principle of bureaucratic organization*. That pyramidal principle, however, does not mean that autocracy prevails, or that the chief coordinator can pretend to be the sole fount of knowledge and wisdom. The mysteries commanded by subordinates are likely to be exaggerated in their relevance and importance by their possessors, but they must be accommodated when they are both right and apt. A country or a company facing a thin and uneven supply of highly trained talent will require managers and executives with a greater command over practicalities and abstruse information than those who "merely" need to be concerned with goal-setting and the coordination of specialists.

ORGANIZATION OF CHANGE

The finely calculated interdependence of tasks in bureaucracies, together with an elaborate set of specific procedural rules governing behavior, indicate a considerable resistance to change. Yet at the very least an organization can survive and remain effective in performing its mission only if it has adaptive capacity in the face of uncontrolled change in the relevant environment. Thus one of the strategies that executives in such organizations pursue is to attempt increased control of the environment. Thus, a manufacturing corporation may seek ownership of its raw materials and parts suppliers, to become as "autonomous" as possible. And, rather than merely "adapting" to what legislatures and administrative agencies decide by way of rules, attempts are made to influence the political and administrative process in ways favorable to the corporation's interests. Principal agencies of the government do the same with respect to the legislature and the executive. But if all else fails, "coping mechanisms" are developed to cushion the impact of environmental change. What cannot be controlled may at least be predicted, so that adjustment time is available for avoiding sharply disruptive changes.

Change is intrinsic to rationalized systems, not stability. Failure to perceive that reality is fundamental defect of purely mechanical models of bureaucracies as rationalized work-performing organizations. Stability could only occur under two unlikely conditions: (1) that goals or missions are being accomplished to perfection, with no shortcomings or partial failures; and (2) that all relevant knowledge conceivably knowable is known, including every imaginable procedure for achieving desired goals. Thus although many bureaucratic organizations may have achieved secure niches based upon adequate if not ideal performance, that security may still be threatened by external change. And the quest for improving efficiency and for more nearly approximating ideal goals prompts many bureaucracies to initiate change and not simply evade or accommodate.

The most conspicuous evidence of organized change in bureaucracies is in the resources devoted to technification, discussed in Chapter 5. Research and development (R & D) units within manufacturing corporations and those in governmental agencies, universities, and private "consulting" research organizations are devoted to deliberate change. When, as in the case of the corporation, the change is to be implemented by the sponsoring organization itself, predictable tensions and conflicts occur. Novel products and novel processes upset routines and may even threaten livelihoods. Conflict between coordinators and information-suppliers (line and staff in the language of administration) is endemic in bureaucracies, and a principal reason is precisely that new information is likely to be troublesome because challenging to established assumptions and procedures. Since innovation is costly in time and energy and probably in money, opponents may challenge on those grounds though conceding the improvement "in principle." Executives have veto power, which may be exercised on grounds that are rational on narrowly personal grounds but not defensible in terms of organizational welfare. (I shall return shortly to the difference between individual and collective goals.) Some years ago I suggested that although the absolute and probably the relative amounts invested in R & D budgets are correlated with corporate size, actual innovations come disproportionately from small enterprisers as a strategy for getting a foothold in the market.[4] I suggested that the relatively low innovation rate by large producers arises from the multiplication of veto powers with increased organizational size. If the decision to change is made, junior managers have no legitimate veto, but do have discretionary non-cooperation, that is, strictly speaking, sabotage.

Planning staffs within bureaucracies—public or private—face problems similar to those more immediately concerned with near-term innovations. The mere postponement of the time for fruition of needed innovative or adaptive strategies does not effectively disarm opposition, for if planning is a sensible undertaking at all, its consequences properly result in current actions in order to assure future outcomes. Opposition may in fact be strengthened by suggesting that the assumed future conditions are dubious, or that scarce resources are best devoted to more immediate benefits. (One of the advantages of the "immortality" of bureaucracies is that plans may be made for futures well beyond the retirement ages or life expectancies of decision-makers. Again, this "collective rationality" may not correspond with the personal interests of those involved.)

Indeed, planning more closely exemplifies rationalization of social systems than does the metaphor of the machine—whether literal and physical devices or figurative and social constructs. Time is always implicit in the calculated manipulations of means to achieve specific ends, though in the simplest case the time for the causal nexus to be completed may be very short. Planning simply makes explicit some more perceptible delay from the start of a course of action until its completion or at least advancement. Both the mechanical installations of a factory and the bureaucratic organization designed to operate the machines and market the product represent the fruition of plans, and both are subject to errors of estimation.

Planning is almost a synonym for rational action. It is introduced here under the general rubric of bureaucratization because in the contemporary highly rationalized world planning is subject to organization, and partly carried out by, and for, collectivities.

The ends of planning are as variable as the goals of human activity. It is subject to the criteria of rationality only if those goals are this-worldly. Planning by individuals and families has long been viewed as commendably prudent in Western societies, and planning by private business, even in its corporate form, has been given comparable approval. American unease and opposition with respect to centralized socio-economic planning by the national government stems from association of planning with socialism. The association is not completely wrong, for effective implementation of plans does require control by the state of the processes and intermediate goals leading to the final goals. (Since centralized planning may be done by authoritarian as well as democratic governments, and the distribution of benefits may reward the rulers and scarcely those ruled, the equation with socialism may be superficial. "Statism" might be the better designation.) A society rationalized to that degree seriously impairs freedom, a goal that some would cherish for its own sake. But in principle freedom has costs as well as benefits (one of which may be innovations not part of the official plan). The meaning of freedom is choice, and a cost of choice is uncertainty.

Urban, regional, and national planning by specialized staffs encounters, in a somewhat different context, the equivalent of line-staff conflicts, for politicians will have the final decision, and may veto plans in view of other values or simply by reflecting personal interests and prejudices.

The principal issues involved in any organized planning, then, relate to the extent or comprehensiveness of the system to be brought under control and the temporal horizon in view. In general, the more extensive the plan and the number of changes to be implemented, the longer the temporal horizon must be. The lengthened time arises from two sources, analytically and often concretely distinct. One is the complex causal linkage that may be necessary to get from present state to the desired future. To move from mass illiteracy to universal adult literacy, one must train additional teachers to train teachers to teach the illiterate. To move from hand-operated pumps or waterwheels for irrigation to electric pumps, one must locate or import a suitable source of power for generating electricity, build the transmission lines, and manufacture or import the appropriate pumps. Even in these examples there is embedded a second source of delay, which we may call lead-time. This is simply the time necessary to complete a process: to train a teacher or to learn functional literacy or to build a dam for a hydroelectric installation. As I noted earlier, the things that need to be done first are not necessarily the most valued goals but are either first links in a causal chain or something that simply takes time to complete.

"Total" planning would imply total control, or at least a constancy of conditions not subject to control. Though that might be the aim of a "completely" rationalized system, it is unlikely of achievement. However, if the uncontrolled conditions are subject to orderly and not simply erratic change, planning may be improved by forecasting. Here there is a convenient conceptual distinction between *teleology*—the purposive orientation to future goals—and *teleonomy*—the forecasting of future conditions and taking anticipatory measures to take advantage of them or to cushion their negative impact.

Two further points are of interest. First, for planning that is partial and restricted—for example, the desirable technology, product mix, and share of the market for a manufacturing corporation ten years hence—aspects of the significant future that are not subject to control still retain teleonomic significance and require forecasting. Second, it has been the aim of much of our technification to extend rational controls—that is, to convert teleonomic conditions into teleological instruments. Weather modification comes quickly to mind as a simple illustration.

The complexity of the future, the system properties that must be taken into account for even restricted planning, constitute the reasons that the process is likely to be bureaucratized. The chain-of-command model scarcely fits the organization of a planning team, particularly in the pure form of wisdom proceeding solely from the chief executive. Rather, the "think tank" organization is more typical and more appropriate, but the critical problem of integration, the coordination of the contributions of specialists, remains. The necessity of coordination and the utility of various "support staff" services produce a type of quasi-bureaucratic structure that more nearly resembles the operations of the joint chiefs of staffs for military units than it does maneuvers in war games or actual battles.

PATHOLOGIES, AMENDMENTS, AND PURPOSES

All administrative organizations are beset with various human frailties that cause chronic disorders in the ideal organizational structures.[5] Some of these disorders are in fact common to most organizations, as they arise from the lack of exact correspondence between collective and individual interests— the uncertain commitment of individuals to cooperative endeavors. Other pathological states are either peculiar to complex work organizations or flourish there to an unusually high degree.

Favoritism essentially represents the intrusion of particularistic relations into organizations predicated on universalism, of competence as the sole criterion of appointment. Nepotic practices, honorable in most traditional orders, are usually contrary to the rule of competence. Even if kinship ties lose their strength in large and visible organizations, other forms of social bonds do not. Naturally, favoritism flourishes most vigorously in filling positions that are fairly unexposed, that is, where neither personal qualifications nor the value of the performance can be specified easily. For example, "assistant managers" may be line officers and heirs-apparent to higher office, but "assistants to the manager" have more ambiguous duties. Such positions indeed may represent part of the rather modest patronage that newcomers to the seats of power are accorded.

Lethargy and *sabotage* reflect lack of enthusiasm that may remain passive or manifest itself in undetected acts of subversion. Lethargic performance may arise from an employee's own sense of futility and lack of recognition or from a properly sensitive response to the dampening pressure of colleagues. (Restraints on productivity are probable at all levels of bureaucracies. Some restraints are essential to avoid disruptive excesses that may invade the jurisdictions of others, but some may simply protect the lazy and incompetent.) Since every position is likely to entail a range of acceptable performance, "getting by" may be more common than pressing the upper limits. Sabotage, in its strict and original meaning of treading with wooden shoes or, in Veblen's language, the "conscientious withdrawal of efficiency," may actually take more effort than conscientious performance. Yet to the disgruntled employee anxious to fight the system, the trouble may be worthwhile. The tactics of delay and evasion may be as effectively disruptive as the flurry of apparently well-meaning errors.

Corruption involves the substitution of individual for organizational interests. It is an omnipresent possibility in view of the "bribed" character of much organizational cooperation. Embezzlement is a crime available only to those entrusted with other people's money, but the requirements shade off into padded expense accounts, the conduct of personal business on the employer's time, "liberating" office supplies or shop tools and materials, the use of official cars for weekend travel. Persons with the highest standards of personal honesty in their dealings with real people may have no hesitation in converting the property of that legal person, the corporation, or the public agency to their own use. The view appears to be that collective property may be appropriated by those to whose custody it is assigned.

Technicism or ritualism is perhaps the principal fault that gives "bureaucracy" a bad name.[6] The mindless adherence to rules and procedures without realistic reference to the goals to be accomplished or problems to be solved makes of the rules ends in themselves. Safety for office holders often lies in applying some rule, not in rational disposal of the issues. Penalties, for the most part, are prescribed not for failure to achieve organizational ends or even for failure to believe in them, but for violation of the procedural rules designed at some time to achieve the desired outcomes. Those rules may have long since lost their original sense, or may be encumbered with so many modifications and exceptions as to encourage a pettifogging legalism in interpretation. The bureaucrat's sense of personal security may rest only on being expert in his knowledge of rules, not in making reasonable judgments.

These pathologies testify to the human resistance, at times passionate and at times craven, both to total subordination to the collectivity and to the standards of rationality.

Other evidence of such resistance comes from what I have called in this section's title "amendments." The most common amendment to the formal structure of bureaucracy is that of "informal organization." That concept, I have previously complained, comprises a "basket of unwritten scraps"—that is, a residual category.[7] Anything that takes place at work that is not provided for in the formal plan thus becomes "informal," and that can range from by-pass routes evading formal channels of communication to ethnic cliques or simply some form of deviance just discussed. The central and useful reality, however, is that persons who encounter one another over considerable periods of time in the work setting are likely to elaborate or "ornament" their required relations with informal patterns of interaction and perhaps even form a distinctive group identity. As documented in the literature of industrial sociology, such patterned relationships develop their own rules of conduct and their own sentiments and goals. Although how salient these informal groups are for their members in non-work settings cannot be determined from the research literature, they represent an intrusion of sentiment into a nominally impersonal and rationally sterile organizational environment. Yet institutionalized rationality is also difficult to suppress. The discovery of informal organization and its virtual immunity to total eradication led to the "human relations" theory of administration, whereby these sentimental practices are recognized and made a part of the incentive system to encourage morale and attachment to the employing organization.

I insist that rationality is concerned with instrumentation for achieving goals that are not themselves derived from a rational calculus. The public bureaucratic agency is established to foment economic growth, or education, or "distributive justice"; to protect national sovereignty and to keep the peace internally; to collect taxes and to manage public budgets; to regulate where it does not control, as in the conduct of privately owned businesses or the formation of labor unions and political parties. The final accountability of public bureaucracies is to political authorities, and their claim to legitimacy in exercising that authority rests, from one time or place to another, on a wide variety of grounds. Goal-setting is determined by political processes, which may have a high or low degree of popular support. Simply staying in power is a manifest goal of political regimes, and terror is among the rational means for doing so, unless the laws prohibiting such means are truly and effectively recognized as having a higher value than the mere survival of politicians.

Corporate bureaucracies have as their avowed mission the production and sale of a specific range of goods and services at a profit, mainly (except for rate-regulated public utilities) in a competitive market. In fact, for large corporations, profits (not necessarily every year) become a condition for survival but not a sole or perhaps even a primary goal. The giant Western-style corporation has achieved sufficient independence from stockholders and a multitude of other interests, to have a large measure of autonomy. Among the various interests that must be accommodated in modest degree, the organization itself becomes a principal and successful claimant. Such a corporation may be described by a slightly pretentious term, "autocephalous." It is self-headed, strictly accountable only to itself. It is by no means self-evident truth that public ownership improves efficiency or results in equivalent innovation and expansion. It does clarify, in principle, the question of accountability and thus of the goal-setting responsibility. Meanwhile, the true rationality of corporate bureaucracies, of policies and procedures, is impossible to judge as long as corporate goals remain unclear. And, I maintain, they are.

NOTES

1. See Stanley H. Udy, Jr., *Work in Traditional and Modern Society* (Englewood Cliffs, NJ: Prentice-Hall, 1970).
2. See *From Max Weber: Essays in Sociology*, trans. and ed. by H. H. Gerth and C. Wright Mills (New York: Oxford University Press, 1946); see also Carl J. Friedrich, "Some Observations on Weber's Analysis of Bureaucracy," and Alvin W. Gouldner, "On Weber's Analysis of Bureaucracy Rules," both in Robert K. Merton et al., eds., *Reader in Bureaucracy* (Glencoe, IL: Free Press, 1952), pp. 27–33 and 48–51.

3. For example, see Stanley H. Udy, Jr., " 'Bureaucracy' and 'Rationality' " in Weber's "Organization Theory: An Empiricial Study" *American Sociological Review* 24:791–795 (December, 1959); Helen Constas, "Max Weber's Two Conceptions of Bureaucracy," *American Journal of Sociology* 52:400–409 (January 1958).

4. Wilbert E. Moore, *The Conduct of the Corporation* (New York: Random House, 1962), pp. 212–214.

5. This discussion of pathologies is mainly derived from *ibid.*, pp. 160–163.

6. On ritualism as a form of deviance, see Robert K. Merton, "Social Structure and Anomie" in his *Social Theory and Social Structure* (Glencoe, IL: Free Press, 1957), pp. 131–160.

7. Moore, work cited in note 4, pp. 94–109.

RATIONALIZING BIRTH, LIFE, AND DEATH

We are members of a biological species that reproduces itself sexually; depends almost exclusively on learning for achieving coping capacities for sustaining life and participating in social systems that are our universal condition; is subject to malnutrition, debility and disease, accidents and aggressions; has individuals who grow older with varying degrees of adjustment to changing social circumstances and individual capacity and sooner or later die. We have the further common biological characteristics of cognition, consciousness, and capacity for deliberate goal-seeking, which provide the basis for treating the first set of biological givens or universals as subject to manipulation and at least partial control.

The life-cycle approach, which, along with the actual course of modernization and many other aspects of social dynamics has been neglected in social scientific analysis through failure to develop sequential models, is reflected in the title of this chapter. [1] Because our central theme is rationalization and its limits, however, I shall start with health and longevity, goals that are widely cherished and sufficiently mundane to offer prospects of attempts at rational, instrumental action aimed at their attainment. Then I shall discuss fertility control, which prompts no such universal enthusiasm, and indeed over which much value controversy prevails.

The time-lag between increased rational control of mortality and declining fertility as a consequence of conscious control produces what has come to be called "transitional" growth. That is the situation of large parts of the contemporary world, and raises questions not only of the positive or negative consequences of such growth for other aspects of modernization but also of the detailed validity of the generalization concerning the sequence of changes from high death and birth rates to a situation that might be called a more efficient system of population maintenance. The chapter will conclude, as usual, with attention to the limits of rationalization in all of these literally vital concerns.

HEALTH AND LONGEVITY AS UNIVERSAL VALUES

In their proper concern for recording and analyzing behavioral and cultural differences among the world's peoples, comparative anthropologists and sociologists sometimes improperly exaggerate distinctiveness by scanting commonalities. On the evidence, human beings everywhere prefer food to hunger, good health to illness, and life to death. Now that is essentially a statistical generalization, and does not extend to every individual or what we may call sub-cultures. In the historical and contemporary Western world, religious deviants have practiced "mortification of the flesh," and suicides may occur (with varying numerical rates) on the part of those with severe emotional disturbances to which economic or physiological defects may be contributory causes. Even where fate (or God's will) is believed to hold supremacy, as in some prominent strains in Christian and Moslem theology, or where a single lifetime is viewed as a relatively unimportant event in a long series culminating in Brahma or Nirvana (the Hindu and Buddhist eternities, respectively), true and total adherence to other-worldliness is always, and has always been, characteristic of small minorities of the nominally believing populations. For most mere mortals, the final reply of Voltaire's Candide to the philosopher Dr. Pangloss, "It is well said, but we must cultivate our gardens," represents self-evident practicality.

Just as justice may be conveniently defined negatively as the absence of perceived injustice, health may be defined as the absence of serious pain or debility. Iwao Moriyama of the U.S. Public Health Service has proposed that illness or morbidity be defined as sufficient impairment of health to make impossible the maintenance of normal social functions (work or housekeeping, school attendance, and the like.)[2] That, of course, does not set absolute standards of "good health," which may, as I have indicated, elude direct definition. Additionally, what constitutes "normal" vigor may vary among individuals and even among whole populations. Thus, a population where malnutrition is the common lot of the poor or malaria is endemic (perhaps not discriminating by economic status), normal expectations may be substantially lower than in a more fortunate or more affluent and technically sophisticated population. Generally speaking, measures that decrease morbidity should also decrease (that is, postpone) mortality, for the obvious reason that some illnesses may be rather quickly fatal and even chronic illness may shorten the life-span. The relationship is not perfect, as some chronically ill persons may, through exceptional care, survive as long as their "healthy" age-peers, and a high rate of accidents or violence may reduce the life expectancy of otherwise healthy populations.

The bare minimum for survival—the qualifier "bare" may be apt in the tropics—includes food, water, shelter, and warmth in frigid climates, plus protection against predators and marauders. Technically unsophisticated populations have always been prey to unseen enemies represented by microbes and viruses; enduring groups offset high mortality, especially among infants and children, with fertility that would be excessive if all survived and the means for their support limited. Yet, in most recorded cultures rules and taboos have "evolved" (to use the term loosely) with regard to food preparation and human waste disposal, and some folk medical remedies have had technical efficacy along with magical substances and acts. The premodern Chinese, for example, though presumably not understanding the hazards of water-borne diseases, punctiliously boiled water to make tea. On the other hand, medieval Europeans did not associate devastating plagues with rats and their fleas and had developed no conscious or unconscious tactics for effective control.

The historic decline in mortality in Europe, dating from around 1700, owed much simply to improved adequacy of food supplies, partly from increased output of domestic agriculture, aided by overseas expansion which added foods, textile fibers, and other commodities (and incidentally an outlet for surplus population), and by the expansion of transportation from surplus to deficit areas.[3] Improved housing, especially with respect to sanitation, and improved and moderately safe water supplies reduced the incidence of infectious diseases, abetted only within the last century by innoculations and vaccinations. These are essentially public health measures, readily available for diffusion to high-mortality populations, with only moderate cost, moderate need for highly trained personnel, and minimum administrative machinery. Mortality control in the 18th century and most of the 19th century owed little, if anything, to the private delivery of medical services by "professional" physicians. Indeed, until well into the present century it is doubtful whether the tender mercies of professional medicine postponed death for more patients than those whose demise was hastened.

Man-made hazards as a consequence of "high technology" now provide new challenges to public health measures. Water and air pollution, atomic radiation, fabrication of dangerous substances such as asbestos, and a torrent of new chemical compounds—some of now-known harmful effects on health and many others with their integrity impugned by critics—may be more difficult to constrain than poisonous snakes and man-eating tigers. And we must not forget the dangers from the machines themselves, the most lethal of which by far is that adult toy, the automobile.

Many peoples of the world, and of course those in poor countries and the poor everywhere, have inadequate nutrition by modern standards. However, the substitution of tasty processed foods for bland native diets, of processed infant-feeding formulas for breast-feeding, of imported stimulants (coffee, tea, alcoholic spirits) for traditional ones may actually cause nutritionally poorer fare than the premodern diet afforded.

Partly because of "miracle drugs," some of which like the broad-spectrum antibiotics are indeed highly effective, and partly because of super-specialization and elaborate hospital-based machines for diagnosis and therapy, medicine and surgery rather than public health measures are commonly perceived as representing the most advanced form of rationalization of health services. Undoubtedly, highly rationalized (and very costly) medical services have marginally improved survival rates and more substantially improved speed of recovery from accidents and illnesses and reduced the discomfort of the ill and convalescent.

The treatment of external wounds and bruises lent itself more readily to treatment with rational technology than did internal medicine, for the cause of illness and internal pain was not correctly understood until the "germ theory" was discovered and slowly accepted by learned physicians. (Of course, a patient's survival of surgery was greatly improved by an understanding of infection, just as the excruciating pain was alleviated by the development of anasthetics.) Ironically, in Western Europe, surgeons, as mere craftsmen, were regarded as inferior to physicians who spent long training in acquiring a (mainly erroneous) body of theory.

Again, however, we must be wary of too readily accepting a contrast between bad old and good new theory and practice. The gradual and still incomplete understanding of psychosomatic elements in illness and health, and thus the rejection of a radical duality between the mind and the body, indicates that some physiologically neutral of even somewhat deleterious remedies may have worked for the "wrong" reasons. Just as the "placebo effect" has been repeatedly confirmed in the use of "useless" drugs, belief in the efficacy of essentially magical remedies may, perversely, make them work. Taking the patient seriously as an individual, which is increasingly difficult with extreme specialization of medical practice and the bureaucratic regimen of hospitals, may be more effective than what may be excessive rationalization—so argues Arthur Kleinman, comparing Western medicine unfavorably with Taiwanese folk healers.[4] Another author in the same issue of a "popular science" magazine says that medical technology has become so complicated that the search for a definitive diagnosis may endanger the patient's life (reminding one of the ancient witticism that the operation was a success though unfortunately the patient died.)[5]

Certainly, these considerations along with the time and money costs of training specialists and the costs of a highly technified "health delivery system" caution against the assumption that the latest is best in transferring health care techniques to areas with high morbidity and mortality rates. Although the goals of improved health and longevity are scarcely in doubt anywhere, there remain sufficient uncertainties concerning the most efficacious means for their attainment and sufficient variabilities in national and local circumstances that a standardized and prepackaged health-delivery system would represent the kind of silliness that donors and merchants often practice.

FERTILITY CONTROL

Unlike the attempted control of disease and death, rational planning of reproduction immediately encounters problems of values. Most societies for most of world history have encouraged high fertility as a compensation for high mortality, particularly among infants and the young. To supplement this essentially non-rational appeal to group survival, which has the weakness of many "functionalist" interpretations of social behavior in assuming a kind of collective will or deliberate collective planning that may be hard to verify, we should note that families may benefit from the additional labor provided by children when they are old enough to be useful and, later, rely on support from children when parents (should they be fortunate enough to survive so long) are no longer able to be completely self-reliant.

As Kingsley Davis pointed out some decades ago,[6] high fertility in pre-modern societies cannot be explained as simply instinctive—"doing what comes naturally"—for, apart from the extent that heterosexuality, as distinct from other forms of sexual gratification, is learned behavior in the human species, there are notable cultural and structural differences in the ways fertility is encouraged and the ways it is limited. Were fertility at its maximum, every fertile female would be almost continuously pregnant from puberty to menopause, and no society of which we have any knowledge has either values or behaviors that confirm such reproductive behavior. Unlimited promiscuity as a norm or as generalized behavior is a figment of fiction writers' imaginations. Every society has pro-fertility values and indirect structural inducements (such as status privileges accorded to married couples not accorded to other adults), and every society has both indirect limits on reproductive behavior (rules on marriage and sexual access) and possibilities of direct controls. Since it appears unlikely (contrary to some ethnographic reports) that any society fails to understand the relation between sexual intercourse and the possibility of conception, coitus interruptus is always an available contraceptive, although perhaps impairing gratification and risking error in timing.[7] Abortion, entailing some risks to the female's health if crudely performed, provides a "second line of defense," and infanticide a "last resort." Thus, in purely rational terms, without regard to morals and values, high fertility cannot be the product of mere ignorance and error, but either the result of positive motivation or of social prohibitions on prevention of pregnancy or early remedies for failure.

Pre-industrial Europe differed from Oriental and most non-literate societies by having achieved substantial reductions in mortality (mainly through improved nutrition and public health measures as just noted) and in fertility (mainly through age and other restrictions on marriage).[8] "Industrialization and urbanization" are often credited with prompting the long downward trend in birth rates in Western Europe from early in the 19th century (later in the United States, where labor was scarce and land relatively cheap until late in the century). However, fertility decline in rural France—where the fact that the legal code required equal division of property among heirs was probably significant—cautions against too mechanical an interpretation. Surely it was the fairly rapid declines in mortality, particularly of infants, making large families burdensome in an economy with decreased demand (or legal permission) for child labor that provided a negative restraint on fertility. Also, the expanding economy provided increased opportunity for inter-generational upward mobility, particularly for those with educational advantages beyond elementary schooling. Fewer children could be given greater advantages by their parents than those available to large families where the mere burden of support pressed the limits of economic resources.

In general, the well-to-do and particularly the better educated led the movement to fertility control, adding some form of deliberate contraception to marital restraints and other indirect controls. The consequence of this pattern of social change was that for about 150 years, birth rates were inversely proportional to socio-economic status, and thus the anomaly that those who could best afford children had the fewest and those who could least afford them had "too many."

It was only with the steady spread, not only of reliable contraceptive information but also of attitudes favorable to rational control that the marked fertility differentials diminished and have, in the most highly rationalized societies, virtually disappeared.[9] Both the informational and the attitudinal diffusion probably owed much to the steady expansion of education, and particularly the education of females.

A good part of the remaining fertility differentials reflects attitudinal differences rather than any presumption of mere ignorance and error. Orthodox Jews, who represent a declining minority of ethnically Jewish populations, are on religious grounds forbidden to practice contraception, though undoubtedly some of the "modern orthodox" do.[10] Roman Catholics are officially permitted sexual abstinence only during the presumed most-fertile period of wives, linked to the menstrual cycle. This control method is technically highly unreliable. Mechanical and chemical contraceptives are forbidden on grounds that, being artificial, they violate "natural law." Since Catholic doctrine does not forbid mechanical and chemical aids in health-restoring and life-saving, this skeptic finds the argument inconsistent and illogical. Declining Catholic birth rates in the highly rationalized societies in which Catholics represent majorities or significant minorities indicate considerable rejection of the rulings of celibate religious authorities by non-celibate parishioners; that the rates still remain higher than for the non-Catholic populations indicates some influence of the religious doctrine.

Among preventive measures to avoid unwanted pregnancies, contraceptive practices have the greatest rational appeal. Changes in the technology of contraception have been proceeding rapidly in recent years. Among mechanical devices, the "intra-uterine device" (I.U.D.) has supplemented the female diaphragm and the male condom, without a clear physiological explanation of its demonstrated effectiveness. Oral contraceptives ("the pill") have negative side-effects for some users, but are now probably the most widely used method in most Western countries. Sterilization has the advantage of taking care of the problem once and for all, with the principal defect that the surgical operation cannot be reversed if a child is later desired. Abortion requires relatively simple surgery if clinically sterile conditions prevail, but it is certainly more costly than prevention of conception and appears to stir up more ideological opposition (primarily, though not exclusively, by Roman Catholics) than contraception. Opponents argue, with some semantic justification, that abortion involves taking a "life," whereas contraception involves the possibly lesser evil of condoning sexual gratification without the responsibility of reproduction. Infanticide, which still occurs surreptitiously here and there, would be unlikely to be socially condoned anywhere in the contemporary world, which, incidentally, is evidence that values other than merely practical ones (such as economic development) may also be diffused across cultural boundaries. But, we already knew this in view of the relative success of the world's great missionary religions: Buddhism, Christianity, and Islam.

The critical question for newly developing countries is whether fertility may be brought under rational control more quickly than the rather gradual adoption of contraception in the Western world. As sociologist Normal B. Ryder observes, "It is a well-established sociological doctrine that institutions of long standing and deeply internalized bases, like the normative pressure for high fertility, are very slow to change."[11] Yet, as he also notes, the circumstances are now very different from those of Europe in the 19th century. Prior to industrialization, European populations were less dense, having expanded to the east and into thinly populated America and Oceania; most of the population was already above a bare subsistence level, and mortality fell slowly. Asian countries (though not all of the rest of the "less-developed" world) have dense and impoverished populations with essentially no expansion room, while modern public health technology can and does reduce mortality quickly.

Japan is perhaps the outstanding example of rapid reduction in fertility, mainly through general adoption of contraception, although with some aid of abortion, having had traditional use with slight ideological opposition.[12] The Republic of China (Taiwan) represents a less complete but apparently rapid decline in birth rates and, although less information is available, a rapid fall in fertility may have occurred also in the much more numerically significant (mainland) People's Republic of China.[13]

Elsewhere, officials of many countries have recognized that high fertility resulting in rapid growth in view of declining mortality represents a problem, although for some that recognition is not untainted by the Marxist position that there is no overpopulation but only defective economic and political structures resulting in maldistribution.[14] And that leads to an examination of what is called "transition theory" among demographers, derived essentially from Western historical experience in modernization.

DEMOGRAPHIC TRANSITION

The generalization concerning the historic trends in control of mortality and fertility represents essentially a three-stage process. Premodern populations were comparatively stable. High and relatively constant fertility rates were offset by high and variable mortality rates. With modernization (that is, increased rationalization of behavior and social organization), death rates were reduced, and fertility rates were reduced considerably later, with the result that there was rapid transitional growth. The transition is presumably completed when low and constant mortality is matched by low and variable fertility. Figure 1 shows a schematic representation of this generalization.

The three-stage formulation was first made explicit by Warren Thompson[15] and Frank Notestein,[16] both of whom presented a tripartite classification of populations: (1) high birth and death rates, (2) high birth rates with declining death rates, and (3) low birth and death rates. Notestein made explicit the "transitional" character of his second category, which he called "transitional growth."[17] Another, and somewhat more figurative, designation for the process is the "vital revolution."[18]

To the extent that the generalization holds not only for the Western world but for other populations as they extend the rationalization of social systems, the demographic transition represents perhaps the only valid example of an

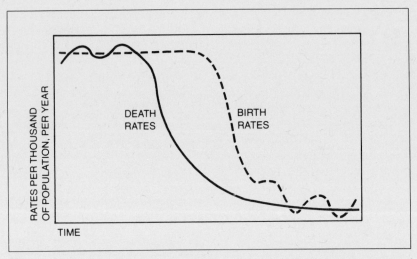

FIGURE 1. Generalized course of the "demographic transition" under the impact of
rationalization. Reproduced from Wilbert E. Moore, *Social Change*, 2nd
ed. (Englewood Cliffs, NJ: Prentice-Hall, 1974). [*Reprinted by permission of
Prentice-Hall, Inc.*]

analytical and expository scheme very commonly (if often implicitly) used in
the literature on modernization.

> By exclusive attention to societies "in transition" students of economic de-
> velopment implied a preceding, traditional stage and a succeeding, industrial or
> advanced stage. The premodern stage was taken to be essentially static, the
> social structure persisting through a balance of interdependent forces and ac-
> tions. Even more unrealistically, the fully modernized society was also taken to
> be static, though this assumption had to remain implicit because of its patent
> falsity.[19]

Transition theory does not go unchallenged, even if limited to historical
generalization concerning the course of change in countries now highly
rationalized. Judah Matras, in a formidably comprehensive text in demography, is cautious to the point of abstinence with respect to transition theory,
arguing essentially against its high level of generalization at the sacrifice of
detailed differences.[20] The demographer Donald Bogue, in a similarly comprehensive text rich in statistical data, is more favorably impressed by the
generalization, but also expresses cautions about variations in time and space,
and, most importantly, its lack of precise predictability of when, and even
whether, populations with current high fertility and high population growth
rates may be expected to start (and complete) the transition.[21]

In a much shorter book primarily concerned with demographic policy in developing areas, José Hernández rejects transition theory as applicable to such areas, finding little evidence for *any* fertility declines, and doubting that "development" is an adequate cause for achieving such declines.[22] The author espouses essentially a scandal or conspiracy theory of the relations between developed and developing countries, and argues (here I oversimplify by abbreviation) that only widely shared participation in national power will be consistent with attitudes favorable to fertility control. He does, however, note the role of education in declining fertility, and, of course, favors equalization of educational opportunities—especially the education of females, which is consistent with scattered evidence from developing countries.

Bernard Berelson and his associates at the Population Council find the evidence mixed with respect to the applicability of transition theory in developing areas. Rather than abandon all hope of generalization, they suggest two different patterns of mortality and fertility control. The one (called Case A) shows a steep decline in mortality and a later significant and continuing decline in fertility. Parts of east and southeast Asia (additional to Japan, which is fully "Western" in its demographic trends), the Caribbean, and South America seem to fit this pattern. The other (called Case B) shows an initial period of rapid decline in mortality, but ". . . the further decline of death rates appears to run into the resistance of low levels of living and slow down significantly, but the persistence of high birth rates still generates rapid growth."[23] India and much of Africa seem to fit this more depressed state. Noting that at least a dozen developing countries during the 1960s recorded a strong and well-documented decline in fertility, and others probably did so judging from indirect evidence, the Population Council report concludes that ". . . it is likely that the 1960s marked the beginning of a worldwide fall in the fertility of developing countries—likely, but not yet certain."[24] That report was issued at the beginning of 1974. By late 1978, the United States Bureau of the Census reported that the rate of world population growth had declined for the first time, and the decline affected all major areas except Africa (noted above as a Case B situation).[25]

I have already commented briefly on the Marxist view denying that "overpopulation" ever exists, and arguing that only a radical change in social institutions is necessary to assure equitable distribution. It is noteworthy, however, that the Soviet Union and communist-ruled countries of Eastern Europe have followed the "Western" demographic transition pattern, and in mainland China postponed marriage is fostered and contraception may be practiced by some.

Some economists, not Marxists, have doubted the gloomy urgency of reducing "excessive" growth. Noting that in the Western experience population growth and economic growth went on concurrently, and that population growth creates new demands and an expanding labor force, Julian Simon, for example, argues that the alarm over expanding numbers is misplaced.[26] The expansion room available to Europe does not exist for densely settled Oriental populations, though parts of South America and Africa are not densely settled. The fundamental fact, which Simon and others appear to ignore, has been well stated by Berelson:

> Whichever is the cause and whichever the effect—and the influence seems to run in both directions—high birth rates are the companion of poverty. Countries with the highest birth rates are usually those with the least productive economies, the lowest urbanization, the highest illiteracy, the lowest percentage of children in school, and the lowest availability of medical personnel.[27]

Ryder, a demographer trained in both economics and sociology, adds a perhaps excessively gloomy view, although highlighting the advantages of rationalized fertility control. He writes, ". . . [A] dilemma is posed for the underdeveloped world: attempts to raise the scale of living will be frustrated by the inertia of high fertility, and attempts to lower fertility will be frustrated by the consequent inertia of socioeconomic development."[28]

LIMITS AND RESISTANCES TO RATIONALIZATION

Highly rationalized systems of mortality control and provision of health services rest upon a combination of public health, medical technologies, and essentially bureaucratic forms of coordinated specialization. In many traditional societies, various "folk remedies" have been part of the general culture, and treatment of grave illnesses by specialists often combined pharmaceutically effective aids to restore health with substantial uses of ritual and magic. As discussed earlier, following the argument of Kleinman,[29] the seemingly less rationalized procedures do not always compare unfavorably with highly specialized medical services. Certainly the persistence of resort to traditional curers (*curanderos* in Latin America) may owe something to cost, availability, and at least partial efficacy as well as mere irrational resistance to novelty.

We do not have to go so far afield to find resistance to rationalization of health services. That resistance is represented by the American failure to provide universal health services and sickness insurance programs, common in other affluent Western countries. Here the resistance comes in a curious form, the adherence to the nominally rational principles of market-oriented distribution of medical services, making those services a function of ability to pay rather than need (except for the provision of frequently substandard services for those below some arbitrary "poverty line"). The consequence, as Matras notes, is that the United States compares unfavorably with other economically advanced countries on equality of access, cost, and availability.[30] Although commonly expressed in ideological terms, particularly by spokesmen for organized medical practitioners, of freedom to choose personal physicians and the supposed evils of "socialized medicine," what Matras calls the ". . . archaic institutions and systems for provision of medical care" has enriched professional practitioners and some private insurance companies while providing highly uneven health care.[31] Of course, there is a value question involved: whether health services are a common right of citizens or a differential privilege associated with income or other invidious status distinctions.

Another value question intrudes with respect to the supposed universal values of health and longevity. I have commented previously on the supposed "otherworldliness" of some Oriental cultures, particularly in Hindu or Buddhist religious beliefs. The evidence appears overwhelming that if options are available, survival and creature comforts are everywhere sought. But what then of the "cheapness of life," particularly where death is an almost daily possibility? I suggest that the living may become in some degree calloused, inured to death even of family and friends in those circumstances, but I have seen no evidence that it is viewed indifferently, to say nothing of joyfully. Despots with a superabundance of subjects living on the edge of starvation may indeed regard *those* lives as cheap but presumably not their own. This is not to deny that a strong belief in fate or a divine plan for everything that occurs may provide little positive incentive to prevent or control adversity. Initiatives of that sort have been notably scarce in predominantly and profoundly Buddhist cultures, but it would be improper to assume that if a more secular segment of the society were to tempt fate by preventing or mitigating natural disasters and human foolishness, the innovation would be resoundingly rejected. We are moving into largely unexplored and cloudy area here, for neat quasi-experimental situations have not clearly presented themselves.

Other ideological or value issues revolve around the very beginning and the very end of life. I have earlier alluded briefly to the abortion issue, now being passionately debated in the United States. Does the unborn fetus have a "right to life" that others are bound to respect and protect despite the desire of a woman to terminate an unwanted and perhaps involuntary pregnancy? What of the virtual certainty of serious birth defects? Of extremely high risks to the mother's life if the pregnancy is permitted to come to full term? Is life, however defined, a higher value than avoidance of physical and emotional suffering, the impairment of human dignity? Clearly these questions will not be answered on solely rational grounds, for the answers will depend on non-rational beliefs (such as what constitutes the natural law or divine will) and values (the rights of a woman to her own body as opposed to the rights of a non-sentient organism to which she is the unwilling host; the right of an infant to survive at the cost of the death of its mother). That these issues are argued passionately is an indication that they are outside the arena of rational discourse. Similar issues are presented by the debate over sustaining life by all known means even though the personality has been irremediably destroyed as against "death with dignity" for the incurable and non-sentient patient. Of further interest with respect to both the "right to life" and the "right to die" is the circumstance that the decision is not and cannot be made by those for whom the right is claimed, but by others who may have a personal, emotional stake in the outcome—the usual situation with regard to life-support systems for patients in an irreversible coma—or may have only a "principled" position, the usual situation with respect to those opposing abortion. The frequency with which males, and often celibate males at that, take strong stands against legalized abortion cannot escape notice.

Finally, I return to the perennially fascinating subject of sexual behavior and its relation to birth control. In the biological evolution of the human species, the relatively infrequent recurrence of sexual attraction (estrus) typical of most mammals was replaced with the practically constant potentiality of sexuality for all those beyond puberty. To be sure, human sexuality has a large component of learned behavior, but "nature" provides few if any restraints. Controversy still clouds the explanation of the universality of the incest taboo, which does not appear in other mammalian species. It is sufficiently variable in its precise applicability among different cultures to rule out merely instinctive interpretations; and certainly all other restraints on unlimited sexuality are purely cultural inventions.

It is the constant sexual potential that has prompted stringent limitations or prohibitions on unchaperoned heterosexual contacts between unmarried and unrelated men and women by Orthodox Jews, conservative Moslems, and the early Calvinistic protestant sects. From a contemporary secularized perspective, this nervous sexual segregation appears more nearly a neurotic preoccupation with sexuality in the total range of human interests than a successful suppression. Yet no society, we have observed, is without at least indirect controls on maximum reproductivity, through the "principle of legitimacy" with respect to child-bearing and age and other restrictions on eligibility for marriage, and a variety of others.[32]

Like all behavior, sexual intercourse is motivated. But that does not necessarily mean that it is calculated behavior, particularly with regard to its consequences in possible pregnancy. Were this class of actions to be interpreted solely in terms of the model of rational behavior, unplanned pregnancies could only result from ignorance and error (and some pregnancies do, of course). Sexual behavior is a prime example of emotionally motivated action, and it has strong recreational rather than carefully pragmatic elements. As Alice Rossi notes with regard to family behavior generally—a subject on which I shall add a few comments in a later chapter:

Because social science theories are themselves rational structures, they may encourage a tendency to assume that the behavior they analyze is also rational. It is with considerable discomfort that I read the economist's cost—benefit calculus applied to such family decisions as whether to have a child or whether to get a divorce.[33]

The emotional, recreational, and expressive aspects of sexuality precisely account for the resistance to rationalizing fertility control. For birth-control methods to be acceptable the goal of preventing pregnancy must be strong and the means for its achievement not so difficult, distracting, and unesthetic as to seriously impair or destroy the physical and emotional gratification. And this leads to the further observation that although the most economically disadvantaged sectors of a population may be most victimized by ignorance and error, one must also note that the unavailability of other intellectual, social, and recreational interests and activities may lead them to both strong familial relationships and a high degree of sexuality. That the consequences of excessive child support serve to reinforce their poverty is scarcely an adequate motivational basis for adopting restraints that will not assure escape.

NOTES

1. See Wilbert E. Moore, "Toward a System of Sequences," in John C. McKinney and Edward A. Tiryakian, eds., *Theoretical Sociology: Perspectives and Developments* (New York: Appleton-Century-Crofts, 1970), pp. 155—166.
2. Iwao M. Moriyama, "Problems in the Measurement of Health Status," in Eleanor Bernert Sheldon and Wilbert E. Moore, eds., *Indicators of Social Change* (New York: Russell Sage Foundation, 1968), pp. 573—600.
3. See Harold F. Dorn, "Mortality," in Philip M. Hauser and Otis Dudley Duncan, eds., *The Study of Population* (Chicago: University of Chicago Press, 1959), pp. 437—471, especially pp. 454—455.
4. Arthur Kleinman, "The Failure of Western Medicine," *Human Nature* 1(11:63—69 (November 1978).
5. See Franz J. Ingelfinger, "Can You Survive a Medical Diagnosis?" in *ibid.*, pp. 38—39.
6. Kingsley Davis, *Human Society* (New York: Macmillan, 1949), pp. 553—564.
7. See Clellan S. Ford, A *Comparative Study of Human Reproduction,* Yale University Publications in Anthropology No. 32 (New Haven: Yale University Press, 1945).
8. See Normal B. Ryder, "Fertility," in Hauser and Duncan, work cited in note 3, pp. 400—436.
9. *Ibid.*
10. See Samuel C. Heilman, *Synagogue Life* (Chicago: University of Chicago Press, 1976).
11. Ryder, essay cited in note 8, at p. 433.
12. See Irene B. Taeuber, *The Population of Japan* (Princeton: Princeton University Press, 1958).
13. See Bernard Berelson, "World Population: Status Report 1974," Population Council Reports on Population/Family Planning, No. 15, (January 1974).
14. *Ibid.*

15. Warren S. Thompson, *Plenty of People* (Lancaster, PA: Jacques Cattell, 1944); also his earlier "Population," *American Journal of Sociology* 34:959–975 (May 1929).
16. Frank W. Notestein, "Population—The Long View," in Theodore W. Schultz, ed., *Food for the World* (Chicago: University of Chicago Press, 1945), pp. 36–57.
17. *Ibid.*
18. See Ryder, essay cited in note 8, at pp. 432–435.
19. Wilbert E. Moore, *The Impact of Industry* (Englewood Cliffs, NJ: Prentice-Hall, 1965), p. 14.
20. Judah Matras, *Populations and Societies* (Englewood Cliffs, NJ: Prentice-Hall, 1973), pp. 24–28, 471–477.
21. Donald J. Bogue, *Principles of Demography* (New York: Wiley, 1969), pp. 55–61.
22. José Hernández, *People, Power, and Policy: A New View on Population* (Palo Alto, CA: National Press Books, 1974).
23. Berelson, report cited in note 13, at p. 6.
24. *Ibid.*, p. 7.
25. Advance report on "World Population 1977" by the U.S. Bureau of the Census, reported in *Rocky Mountain News*, Denver p. 12, (Monday, November 20, 1978).
26. Julian L. Simon, *The Economics of Population* (Princeton, NJ: Princeton University Press, 1977).
27. Berelson, report cited in note 13, at p. 9.
28. Ryder, essay cited in note 8, at p. 433.
29. Kleinman, essay cited in note 4.
30. Matras, work cited in note 20, at p. 232.
31. *Ibid.*
32. See Davis, work cited in note 6.
33. Alice S. Rossi, "Epilogue to The Family: A Sociologist's Perspective," *Bulletin of the American Academy of Arts and Sciences* 31(6):14–22 (March 1978); quotation from pp. 21–22.

SECULARIZATION

The rational turn of mind, when properly engaged, has the strong propensity to question, to challenge, to explore alternatives. When the possessor of that mind is narrowly goal-oriented, the questioning may be limited to "thinking through" or actually trying alternative courses of action, as in maximizing the monetary return on an economic transaction or minimizing friction within a complex machine. Matters become more complicated, more unsettling, when the way society is organized is subject to question, when doubt is cast on the assumptions underlying the authority of the state or lesser organizations such as corporations, when the very meaning of human existence is uncertain. Mythical distortions of history may be challenged, heroes brought down to human size, and even religious doctrines on cosmology and human destiny may fall from unchallenged verities by increased knowledge of other belief systems and pragmatic demands for (intrinsically impossible) demonstration and proof.

This invasion of the realm of the sacred, the questioning of beliefs and of (often unstated) assumptions, we may call secularization. Strictly speaking, secularization means the reduction or elimination of strictly religious influence on worldly thinking and behavior, but by extension may be applied to myths and unexamined assumptions. Gino Germani seems to view secularization as any undermining of traditional beliefs and practices through rationalization, and thus virtually an equivalent concept.[1] My concern here is narrower: with the relative shift of human attention from other-worldly to this-worldly concerns, and the reduction in the obligatory nature of beliefs and exactly prescribed actions set by ancient or even contemporary authority viewed as sacrosanct.

By extension, thus, secularization means a functional separation between "church" and "state," between the affairs of "Caesar" and those of "God," and in this process a diminution of authority based on claimed divine sanction or even on tradition, and the substitution of popularly sanctioned legality as the source of political legitimacy.

Since secularization represents an extension of rationalization well beyond practical, mundane matters like science and technology, economic transactions, the organization of work, or reproduction and longevity, we may expect it to be in contested territory immediately. The arenas of conflict are numerous and the situations are often unstable, but a generalized view of the limits of this most presumptious form of rationalization will, as usual, conclude the chapter.

QUESTIONING BELIEFS AND ASSUMPTIONS

In the Greco-Roman and Western world, the thriving Greek interest in the philosophical foundations of knowledge, ethics, esthetics (the true, the good, and the beautiful), and including with Aristotle and his successors an attempt to understand "nature" and to understand and reform politics, was continued in Imperial Rome until Christianity became an officially established religion. Then, for over a thousand years in Europe, faith and belief became monopolistic and mandatory. Such "heresies" as appeared were in any event mainly concerned with strictly theological matters. The Church became authoritarian and hierarchical in organization, and countenanced (and blessed) authoritarian hierarchies represented by feudalism and the establishment of monarchical and increasingly absolutist national states.

Although historians of medieval Europe would dispute the common view of an atrophy of secular thought and practical innovations, a common view leading to what Robert Nisbet has called "The Myth of the Renaissance,"[2] Nisbet appears to find few medieval precursors of what he calls the "intellectuals" who, from the 15th century, challenged both religious dogma and the foundations for quasi-secular authority. And certainly the Protestant Reformation began to offer a variety of competing religious communities and an increasingly uneasy relationship between church and state. Both wealth and power were at stake in the contests between organized religion and the increasingly secular state, but religion had generally become less powerful both through competition in doctrine within Christianity and through increasing secularization in the form of active questioning or even hostility and in the form of what we might call "disengagement" through preference for the more practical concerns of economics and politics. Even where Protestant churches became "established churches," as did the Lutherans in some pre-unification German states and in Scandinavia, and the Church of England (which did not renounce Catholic doctrine so much as the authority of the pope and the Catholic hierarchy), religious toleration gradually became the policy in Protestant countries and in most Catholic countries. Within the last century, overt profession of unbelief has also become less scandalous in popular sentiment and official policy. One would be tempted to say that religion is no longer a cause for war, were it not for the endless hostilities in North Ireland and the religious overtones of Israeli−Arab conflict. Of course these conflicts also involve economic and political issues, as did the so-called religious wars of Europe.

Even Calvinistic Protestantism, with its "worldly asceticism," which Max Weber credited with major influence in the development of commercial and industrial capitalism, was subject to secularization.[3] "By imparting an ethos of planning and self-control to all economic activities, Puritan teaching encouraged worldly success, which in turn undermined the ascetic way of life."[4]

Over 500 years ago, Copernicus had conclusively challenged the Earth-centered model of the universe, but that intellectual challenge to religiously sanctioned wisdom created no great stir until reiterated by Galileo a century later, when he was subject to suppression by the still-powerful Church.

Making Earth a mere unit of the solar system (and that system a tiny portion of a universe of untold immensity) was difficult enough to accept. Charles Darwin's theory of biological evolution, which he discourteously extended to man, was clearly contrary to the Bible's particular creation myth.[5] If man had been "little lower than the angels," after Darwin angels were in some considerable doubt and man became instead "little higher than the apes." Science had carried secularization well into sacred territory.

Here I must allow a small excursus or digression on science and religion. As long as religion is concerned with strictly supernatural beliefs, such as reincarnation or the individual immortality of the soul, science constitutes no challenge. There is no arena for conflict. But, most highly articulated religious systems with sacred books and accumulated interpretations, together with persons especially learned in the texts and traditions, will provide interpretations of cosmology and human history. That provides room for conflict with secular science and scholarship. Moreover, if supernatural intervention in human affairs is believed to be current and (subject to superior divine wisdom and will) possibly available on request, there is a clear basis for conflict between such belief in what is properly magic (not religion) and secular science and its rational use in technology.

Although the questioning of strictly religious belief is an almost pretentious extension of the questioning of all conventional wisdom in the search for increased rationalization, since it can at most end in an expression of uncertainty (agnosticism), the substitution of technology for magic is likely to occur. But, as I observed in Chapter 1, there are sufficient gaps between rational control and the quest for certainty of outcome that some forms of magic, whether embedded in established religion or not, seem certain to persist.

Traditional religion has not been totally defeated in any contemporary society, but its scope and unquestioned position have been widely impaired. This has come about through successful attacks on exact historical accuracy of Biblical texts, the increasing difference between the scientific tempera- ment and that of the credulous believer in sacred tradition, and the substitu- tion of pragmatic problem-solving for supernatural intervention in natural processes. Except for part of the clergy, religion became a functionally dif- ferentiated aspect of social life both in terms of societal structure and in terms of personal involvement.

As various forms of rationalization are occurring or assiduously promoted in newly developing countries, secularization may be expected. That expecta- tion arises from the dual circumstance that traditional beliefs and religiously sanctioned practices are certain to provide some barriers and points of con- flict with strictly secular goals and processes, and the high probability that the "rational spirit" will be difficult to contain, limited to narrow and safe un- dertakings. I am sufficiently lacking in detailed scholarly knowledge of the world's religions to be able to specify the existing or probable future points of conflict, and certainly not able to predict the outcomes. That secularization is bound to be completely victorious is logically erroneous and empirically false, for goals, individual and collective, are essential to human existence and social survival; they may be changed but not totally abandoned. To suppose, for example, that the officially atheistic communist regimes are completely secularized is simple nonsense. Apart from the hardy, if often covert, survival of traditional religions, nowhere is orthodoxy so carefully articulated and vigorously imposed. Questioning of course does occur, for rationalism is encouraged and institutionalized in safe areas and is hard to contain, but scriptural purity, as interpreted by ideological experts, is rigor- ously maintained with respect to the official canons of political legitimacy.

THE PROBLEM OF LEGITIMACY

Legitimacy may be defined as the rationale, the belief system, whereby those exercising political power claim the right to rule. That claim may be as crude as "Might Makes Right," but then coercion is the sole basis for securing compliance which means at best reluctant and minimal obedience, under realistic threat of harsh penalties for failure, a substantial administrative cost in maintaining total surveillance, and the omnipresent risk of surreptitious sabotage and terrorism if not overt revolt. Any such *de facto* regime will seek as quickly and cleverly as possible to become *de jure*, not primarily to be "recognized" by other countries but to assure a large measure of internal compliance as owed to a legitimate government. A military or militarily backed occupation by a foreign power will generally attempt some form of indirect rule, "coopting" sympathetic or venal locals with some credibility as leaders, who then set up "puppet" governments that will alleviate somewhat the burdens of rule.

Foreign military occupation with direct, coercive rule represents a limiting case in political systems, for the right claimed is merely the right of conquest, although that can be readily and self-confirmingly extended to the superiority of those in power. Domestic military regimes, which abound in the contemporary world, invariably claim to rule in the national interest, holding themselves aloof from and superior to various ethnic, class, or other divisions.

With the possible, and troubling, exception of foreign military rule, the legitimacy of any moderately enduring political regime rests upon non-rational beliefs. Of Max Weber's three "ideal types" of political legitimacy—the traditional, the charismatic, and the rational-legal—most political regimes throughout human history have been primarily or exclusively traditional.[6] Among these, some variant of the "divine right of kings," continued through hereditary succession, has been most common. Charismatic rule, based upon the perceived exceptional (and possibly super-human) personal qualities of a leader, depends for continuity on a successful "routinization of charisma."[7] Otherwise, there is a "succession crisis," which may be followed by a "reactionary" establishment of approximately the prior traditional order, or a new and thus technically revolutionary basis of legitimate rule. The historically most successful case of routinization of charisma has been the doctrine of apostolic succession in the selection of Roman Catholic popes, the electors in each instance of vacancy presumably being guided by the Holy Spirit to select a pope who already has, or will be accorded, special divine authority as Christ's current chief apostle.

Although charismatic regimes are specifically anti-traditional, they may attempt to assure continuity by quickly institutionalizing "new traditions"—a self-contradictory notion—such as the attempt of Hitler's Nazi regime to lay the foundations for the Thousand Year Reich. Or traditions, real or recast, older than those supporting the regime replaced by charismatic rule, may be rescued from the desuetude into which they had been allowed to lapse, in order to establish links with the heroic past. Thus, Hitler's attempt to refurbish pre-Christian German mythology (upon which Richard Wagner had based many of his operas), folk medicine, and racist notions of German genetic homogeneity and superiority were intended to make him appear more a revivalist than a revolutionary.

Secularization impugns tradition as the source of legitimacy, particularly as traditions often have supernatural overtones to account for their origin and possibly their continuation. It appears that Weber regarded what he called rational-legal regimes as the product of secularization. The qualifier "rational" seems to reflect the formally rational bureaucratic structure of political administration, and could not be faulted on that score. This leaves open, however, the basis of legality. Bureaucracies, as noted in Chapter 7, do not in principle set their own goals or govern their own accountabilities. In bureaucratized political systems, those goals and accountabilities derive from a legal order.

Weber's argument is essentially that legality rests upon legislative ascendancy, which does indeed formally institutionalize impersonality and a "government of laws, not of men."[8] That, as noted in Chapter 1, does not resolve the issue of legitimacy. It simply shifts the basis from one traditional non-rational principle—e.g., monarchy by divine right—to another, presumably more flexible but still non-rational, principle, that of representative government. Bureaucratic administration, being a rationalized tool, is not in fact linked to what we may now more correctly call "legislative legality," or, to introduce the actually appropriate traditionalism into the designation, "legislative and constitutional legality." Bureaucracies serve the party oligarchs of the Soviet Union and the People's Republic of China, the pope and the college of cardinals of the Roman Catholic church, and a host of military regimes, to say nothing of monarchical empires.[9]

It can be admitted that a representative government is a considerably secularized form of political legitimacy, as Reinhard Bendix argues in his *Kings or People.*[10] That is, it puts men—or more properly, the people collectively—in charge of their own political destiny. That is especially true in a British-type political system, with the principle of absolute Parliamentary sovereignty and no formal constitution, less so in the American case with a constitution interpreted as superior to legislative acts and difficult to amend. The British, however, have seen fit to restrain secularization not only by maintaining an expensive and symbolic monarchy—the low countries and Scandinavia have done the same—but also by careful attention to "the constitution," which comprises tradition and legal precedents.

Since Weber's typology of the forms of political legitimacy is widely known and used, I must insist that his quasi-secularized form is misnamed and therefore confusing. The belief in the superior legitimacy of representative democracy is as non-rational as any other claim to legitimacy. It does have a semantically and perhaps functionally better fit with social systems otherwise highly rationalized or on that course. Indirect testimony to that congruence is apparent in the rhetoric, if not the reality, of "people's republics," "people's democracies," or "democratic republics" of spuriously communist states. Further testimony comes from the avowedly temporary character of military regimes (sometimes coyly called "guided democracies") until the society is ready for self-government. Bendix does point out Weber's recognition of the importance, for political effectiveness, of "beliefs in the legitimacy of a system of domination,"[11] but Weber plainly failed to note the non-rational character of those beliefs in his quasi-secularized mode. This failure may well derive from his troublesome and deeply confusing distinction between *Zweck-rationalität* and *Wertrationalität*.

Zweckrationalität we may call "instrumental rationality," which is what we have been discussing in this book. *Wertrationalität*, or "value rationality," apparently means consistency among a number of values, but those values represent goals and beliefs held by individuals (perhaps by all or a majority in a collectivity), but derive from no instrumental calculation. Thus, Weber writes that "Legitimacy may be ascribed to an order by those acting subject to it . . . by virtue of a rational belief in its absolute value, thus lending it the validity of an absolute and final commitment. . . ."[12] The adjective used in the German original was *wertrational*; the sentence makes superior sense by deleting the qualifier "rational."

The partial secularization of political legitimacy has led to a kind of dialectic in both scholarly and popular political philosophy. The one view, which I have been arguing on strictly logical grounds, is that political legitimacy ultimately rests upon non-rational beliefs and values. The other view, represented in some forms of neo-Marxist "revolutionary" movements but also in what may be called "interest group politics," is a purely instrumental view of political process and institutions, leaving open any collective goals or a more or less consensual legal order.

The failure to distinguish clearly between spheres of authority proper to religion (God's realm) and those proper to government (Caesar's realm) was not willful stupidity. Both claim "final" authsority over individual destiny, and no religious theology—even "salvation by faith" or "salvation by the predestined will of God"—abdicates all concerns for mundane human conduct. And as both Schmuel Eisenstadts[13] and Edwards Shils[14] insist, partial secularization of government and the state does not entirely eliminate its "sacred" character. Weber's legal order thus rests on what Robert Bellah calls a "civil religion."[15]

The attempted functional and organizational separation of the sacred and the secular, and the consequent undermining of the traditional foundations of secular authority, lead to some form or degree of "crisis." At least, many highly articulate scholarly observers see some kind or degree of crisis in the highly secularized national states of the modernized world. Eisenstadt traces modern revolutions and contemporary revolutionary ferment to what I might call the ideology of popular sovereignty, and he notes especially that socialism constitutes the "revolutionary symbolism in modern civilization."[16] However, he also notes the "weakening of revolutionary transformation" in what he calls late modern or late industrial societies.[17] In that view he is joined by Bendix, who correctly argues that "society is ripe for revolution in the *early* phase of industrialization and democratization, however protracted that phase may be."[18] It may be added, perhaps not gratuitously, that neither Eisenstadt, who is persistently concerned with protest and conflict, nor Bendix, who has an enduring interest in nation-building,[19] appears to take seriously the gravely erroneous Marxist view of increasing polarization in capitalist societies. They treat that doctrine with the ultimate sign of contempt: silence.

The critical feature of a revolution is a fundamental change in the basis of political legitimacy.[20] Other qualifications are necessary, such as confrontations and violence to distinguish between revolutions and such processes as the centuries-long contest between the British Crown and Parliament for ultimate ascendancy—although that struggle was marked by several periods of genuine revolutionary conflict and restorations before representative government finally won.[21] The special feature of revolutions for the last 250 years has been the "populist" rhetoric of the leaders and presumably commitment by the supporters. In this, Bendix and Eisenstadt, the two chief experts on comparative political dynamics I have been citing in these paragraphs because I generally admire their dispassionate scholarship, clearly agree. But, if they are silent on the Marxist doctrine of increasing polarization, they are also silent on what are conventionally viewed either as "revolutions of the right"—that is, fascist regimes, or as "merely" military "national unity" regimes. This failure, I believe, derives from the lack of a clear and succinct definition of revolution (which has been readily available in my work since 1963,[22] and I had predecessors). However, there are two important points: (1) All revolutions in this century—and by the succinct definition there have been several times as many as the spate of books on revolution would lead the innocent reader to believe—have shared in the populist rhetoric and to some degree in its implementation. (2) All revolutions actually involved charismatic leadership and authoritarian regimes, with or without a facade of a representative parliament. (Japan in this, as in some other respects regarding modernization, may represent a partial exception, but the imposition of parliamentary democracy by the American occupation would make that transformation, not a "revolution from above," as was the Meiji restoration of monarchy, which became a military-industrial oligarchy, but a "revolution from without" or revolution as a cost of conquest.)

Now, where were we? My argument is that the secularization of the divine, super-human, or, at least, traditionally sacrosanct bases of political legitimacy may lead to revolts and "successful" revolutions. Revolutions do change the grounds of legitimacy and do have other far-reaching structural consequences, but in no recent case has a revolution established a successful parliamentary democracy, to say nothing of a "direct democracy." Moreover, Bendix and I agree that the revolutionary potential is highest at early "stages" of modernization, which I now prefer to call secularization as an aspect of rationalization. And Bendix would seem to agree with Eisenstadt that protest, if not revolution, is almost certain to be an accompaniment of political rationalization.[23]

What about highly rationalized societies, which may be rife with protest but by no means ripe for revolution? Here we have widespread disenchantment, terrorism by minute minorities, the "twilight of authority,"[24] the "fall of public man,"[25] and what is commonly called "interest-group politics" which I should characterize as the "instrumental state." Robert Nisbet argues that populism leads to a derogation and distrust of *all* authority, deriving either from expert knowledge or, especially, from wealth, social position, and a tradition of public service.[26] His analysis reminds me at times of the dismay of José Ortega y Gasset, by no means a monarchist, at the consequences of the *Revolt of the Masses*.[27] Richard Sennett, apparently and startlingly innocent of Nisbet's many works, argues that disenchantment with political processes and bureaucratic "big government" in the United States (with side glances at Western Europe) has led to a kind of "personality cult" that centers not on a charismatic leader but on self-exploration—as if, apart from social learning and social participation, there is anything worth finding—and on intimate relations within a narrowly circumscribed band of family and friends, and with no sense of public involvement.[28] Alan Wolfe, writing from an avowedly Marxist perspective, correctly perceives the purely instrumental character of much of political participation in Western countries, naively thinking it an evil of capitalism and arguing for more popular democracy, not less.[29]

Weber's anxiety about the future course of ever-increasing rationalization was of an ever-more-pervasive bureaucratization, with impersonal efficiency destroying tradition and the affective components of community and interpersonal relations.[30] That is by no means a worry without foundation.[31] The social critics to whom we have just been giving our guarded attention, some conservative and some radical, have detected a crisis in legitimacy of the ultimate authority to which public bureaucracies are presumably directly accountable, and private ones indirectly so.[32] William James may not have been the first to seek a "moral equivalent of war"[33] and President Jimmy Carter's futile attempt to get the "energy crisis" popularly accepted on that basis may not be the last, but it remains true that a real and present threat to national independence and cultural integrity does serve to calm petty self-seeking and various strains and conflicts within a national state. (Possibly real, in a far-seeing sense, but certainly remote threats in East Asia or Indo-China presented, on the American evidence, not a unifying force for the citizenry but a basis for increased distrust of those who rule, and even of the political system that presumably legitimates their rule.)

The idea of political modernization or political development has attracted considerable scholarly attention, but often from the normative viewpoint that development consists in movement toward stable parliamentary democracy.[34] That kind of argument by final conclusions, which of course underlies convergence theory in general, has the musty odor of 19th century theories of social evolution, in which progress consisted of becoming "just like us." Post-colonial societies must embark on "nation-building," by no means an easy task since most new nations are multi-ethnic in composition.[35] Of course that is also true of many old and relatively stable parliamentary democracies, which have been able to maintain a national identity while permitting considerable cultural diversity. New nations have the additional problem of attempting rapid rationalization through commercialization and industrialization and the other aspects of rationalization we have been discussing. Although the pace of rationalization was slower in the older affluent societies, they, too, had and continue to have organized protest movements, including violent and sometimes revolutionary ones.[36] Although a mixed economy—a combination of foreign and domestic private enterprise along with intensive governmental initiatives—is the situation in many new nations, officially socialist regimes are not wanting. Indeed, a generalization that has a high predictive probability—that is, there are few exceptions—is that the later a country starts on the path of wide-ranging structural rationalization, the greater the proportional influence of the state in the process.[37]

Thus what Germani calls political mobilization has important instrumental functions in support of developmental goals articulated by political authorities.[38] Some forms of mobilization may be more nearly containment, as the behavioral and cultural disruptions deriving from rapid rationalization and the very instrumentalism intrinsic to rationalization combine to foster political activism. Although Alex Inkeles is correct in his perception of increasing surveillance and control by the state everywhere,[39] in highly rationalized societies this more nearly fulfills Weber's gloomy forebodings concerning the expansion of mechanical (or perhaps better, wooden) standardization of impersonal controls than it represents avid popular political participation. Some national regimes in relatively underdeveloped countries may well envy the apathetic and numbly compliant behavior of citizens in the Western world.

The repeated association between deliberate economic development and extreme nationalism is surely not accidental. Nationalism presents an essentially non-rational unifying force that may ease and justify the hardships of personal change. Neil Smelser writes that only "a very generalized and powerful commitment" is able to pry individuals from deeply rooted traditional modes of integration.[40] In his view "xenophobic national aspirations" and political ideologies such as socialism are the functional equivalents of religious values such as Protestantism. In new nations the forms of nationalism include using the former colonial power as a scapegoat for present dissatisfactions and the attempt to establish an older history and continuity of traditions prior to the interregnum of the colonial period. And, it is especially in former colonies that a prior sense of national, or even cultural, identity scarcely existed. When the transition to independence is also accompanied by extensive efforts at economic rationalization, various intermediate social structures that captured loyalties in the pre-industrial system are undermined. Nationalism—often in the garb of Arab or Indian or African socialism—is offered as a source of identity to substitute for the tribe or village. Lenin or Mao have become patron saints, foreign but presumably now universal in their efficacious magic. When combined with a deliberately cultivated sense of national identity and destiny—and sovereignty is dearly cherished everywhere in the contemporary world—the chosen universal saint becomes nationalized and political legitimacy possibly established. Given the utility of external conflict, border skirmishes and other forms of muscle-flexing are probable.

When protest and revolt arise from "reactionary" religious and ethnic divisions, or from conflicts between representatives of the traditional and of the modern, or from "class" conflicts within the rationalized sector of the economy, military regimes often take power and claim legitimacy on the dual basis of modernization and national unity. The military, it should be noted, is likely to be highly rationalized, not only technologically in the narrow sense but also in administrative organization. In fact, it is much easier to explain the high probability of military regimes in countries attempting rapid rationalization than it is to formulate a plan for their replacement by rationally effective *and legitimate* civilian governments.

THE QUEST FOR MEANING

Secularization may result in questioning the historical authenticity of sacred texts, declaring the mythical origins of hallowed traditions to be mere myths not requiring acceptance, and even doubting the existence and/or efficacy of deities. Yet dismissing beliefs as superstitions does not necessarily remove the perils and uncertainties that beset the human condition or provide *meaningful* answers to human purpose. A naturalistic explanation of human origins through biological evolution does not resolve all mysteries, including questions concerning the meaning of human existence and destiny. As far as we know, only human beings keep asking, Why? A geophysical explanation of earthquakes, volcanic eruptions, tidal waves and other devastating floods, or lightning does not totally resolve doubts: Why here, now, these people?(At law, natural disasters are "Acts of God," which raises interesting questions of how legal theorists perceive the character of God.)

The limits of rationalization are evident not only in the logical sense that reason alone cannot determine ultimate goals and values but also in behavioral manifestations. In late 1978, more than 900 U.S. citizens, followers of a charismatic religious prophet, who had established a sectarian community in tropical Guyana, killed the children and then took their own lives after a U.S. Congressman and a small accompanying party of visitors were murdered by cultists. Oriental gurus and other avowedly mystical and holy men attract both followers and their money in the "secularized" Western world. Bands of revolutionary terrorists, adept at murder and, for a while avoiding capture, remain vague as to the shape of the better system that will emerge after the destruction of capitalism. Sennett argues that personalities—the more charismatic the better—outweigh issues in the electoral campaigns of the presumably stable and highly secularized western democracies.[41] Weber, a sincere German nationalist, worried about the increasing stultification of a bureaucratic state but did not foresee Hitler, whose regime systematically, with advanced technology, conducted the largest mass genocide in human history, while killing or enslaving additional millions of external "enemies of the Reich."

I have already commented on nationalism as a kind of non-rational salvation for new nations without a common traditional culture, but it also serves as a kind of "civil religion" in long-established polities with relatively stable legal orders and devices for tension-management but still replete with conflicts in both interests and beliefs. Sacrifices for the collective good, including the future collective good, have some effective appeal. "Keeping America Great and Beautiful" or "Building the Socialist Fatherland" may be acceptable, but among those most highly secularized the present benefits may loom larger. Belief in a kind of collective salvation (there are strong elements of that of course in traditional Jewish theology) seems motivationally less persuasive than personal immortality. Traditional religions (Judaism, Christianity, Islam, Buddhism) survive not only in highly secularized countries but even in those that are officially (and sometimes repressively) anti-religious. Death in military action may be a "noble sacrifice," but the bereaved will still mourn and may assuage their grief in more traditional religious terms. "Killed by friendly fire," which may occur with some frequency with today's weaponry for remote destruction, is a little harder to justify in religious terms.

Daniel Bell would distinguish secularization in the narrow sense of separation of religious and political concerns, and what, taking a lead from Weber, he would call "disenchantment."[42] I believe that he underestimates the underlying difficulty of separating the polity from reliance on ultimate belief systems, as I have just discussed with respect to nationalism (or patriotism), nor do I see secularization as a consequence of rationalization and disenchantment or "profanation"—the discrediting of sacred beings, texts, and the paraphernalia of worship—as substantively different in origin. Yet I readily agree that neither secularization nor profanation, to continue Bell's distinction, resolves "the core questions that confront all human groups in the consciousness of existence: how one meets death, the meaning of tragedy, the nature of obligation, the character of love."[43] Bell does not expect the disappearance of religion as "the sum total of human ignorance" as 18th century rationalists appeared to believe, nor does Robert Nisbet, who finds "the sacred" at the center of the cultural foundations of any organized society.[44] That thesis is certainly not falsified by contemporary, nominally anti-religious, "Marxist" societies.

If new religious sects and cults proliferate, and nominally this-worldly sacrificial political groups espouse dangerous "causes," older religious traditions also survive, along with more secular but still non-rational identifications and allegiances. I noted in Chapter 4 that we now find in the Western world a rediscovery and refurbishing of nearly-lost ethnic affiliations, as a counterbalance to highly rationalized differentiation. It was there seen that Orlando Patterson views such recrudescence of ethnicity as "reactionary," which is literally true but he intends the label in the full, pejorative sense.[45] I view the reassertion of ethnic identity as another example of the quest for identity that goes beyond technical and highly circumscribed positions and roles, and for "community."[46] That identity-quest is not only current. In the United States, with almost the entire population either immigrants or the descendants of immigrants, ethnic revival has been extended to the search for the past—for "roots." The success in print and on television of Roots by Alex Haley,[47] a descendant of black slaves whose immigration represented forcible uprooting, increased the popularity of genealogical quests by Americans who were not expecting to find an ancestor on the passenger list of the Mayflower or establish eligibility for the Daughters of the American Revolution. Even American Indians (some of whom now prefer to be called Native Americans, whose ancestors can claim priority over the tardy and commonly venal interlopers from Europe) have mounted several active attempts to rediscover some sense of traditional cultural integrity. Some of these attempts at restored community may be faddish, and many may be regarded as pathetic or positively mischievous, but they do provide additional testimony that life in an entirely secularized society would be not only logically fallacious but also experientially insufferable.

134

NOTES

1. Gino Germani, *La Política y La Sociedad en una Epoca de Transición* (Buenos Aires: Editorial Paidos, 1962), pp. 81–83.
2. Robert Nisbet, "The Myth of the Renaissance," in Lewis A. Coser, ed., *The Idea of Social Structure: Papers in Honor of Robert K. Merton* (New York: Harcourt, 1975), pp. 471–496, especially pp. 486–494.
3. Max Weber, *The Protestant Ethic and the Spirit of Capitalism* (London: Allen and Unwin, 1930; reprinted, New York: Scribner's 1958).
4. Reinhard Bendix, *Max Weber: An Intellectual Portrait*, California Paperback edition (Berkeley: University of California Press, 1977), p. 65.
5. Charles Darwin, *On the Origin of Species* (Cambridge: Harvard University Press, 1964); first published in 1859; see also Darwin, *The Descent of Man and Selection in Relation to Sex*, 2nd ed. (New York: Appleton, 1930); first published in 1871.
6. Max Weber, *The Theory of Social and Economic Organization* (New York: Oxford University Press, 1947), pp. 124–132, 324–392.
7. *Ibid.*, pp. 363–386.
8. See Bendix, *Max Weber*, cited in note 4, pp. 419–422.
9. See S. N. Eisenstadt. "Bureaucracy, Bureaucratization, Markets, and Power Structure," in his *Essays on Comparative Institutions* (New York: Wiley, 1965), pp. 177–215.
10. Reinhard Bendix, *Kings or People: Power and the Mandate to Rule* (Berkeley: University of California Press, 1978), pp. 3–12.
11. Bendix, *Max Weber*, cited in note 4, p. 294.
12. Weber, work cited in note 6, p. 130.
13. S. N. Eisenstadt, *Revolution and the Transformation of Societies: A Comparative Study of Civilizations* (New York: Free Press, 1978), pp. 31–39.
14. Edward Shils, *Center and Periphery: Essays in Macrosociology* (Chicago: University of Chicago Press, 1975), pp. 3–61.
15. Robert N. Bellah, *Beyond Belief* (New York: Harper and Row, 1970), pp. 168–193.
16. Eisenstadt, *Revolution . . .*, cited in note 13, pp. 174–175, 179–189. See also Charles Tilly, Louise Tilly, and Richard Tilly, *The Rebellious Century, 1830–1930* (Cambridge: Harvard University Press, 1975); Charles Tilly, *From Mobilization to Revolution* (Reading, MA: Addison-Wesley, 1978).
17. Eisenstadt, *Revolution . . .*, cited in note 13, pp. 322–323.
18. Bendix, *Kings or People*, cited in note 10, p. 12; emphasis in original; see also Wilbert E. Moore, *Social Change* (Englewood Cliffs, NJ: Prentice-Hall, 1974), p. 85.
19. Bendix, *Kings or People*, cited in note 10, pp. 378–581.
20. See Moore, work cited in note 18.
21. See Bendix, *Kings or People*, cited in note 10, pp. 273–320.
22. The first edition of Moore's work cited in note 18 was published in 1963.
23. S. N. Eisenstadt, *Tradition, Change, and Modernity* (New York: Wiley, 1973).
24. See Robert Nisbet, *Twilight of Authority* (New York: Basic Books, 1975).
25. See Richard Sennett, *The Fall of Public Man* (New York: Knopf, 1977).
26. Nisbet, work cited in note 24.
27. José Ortega y Gasset, *The Revolt of the Masses* (London: Allen and Unwin, 1961); first published in Spanish in 1930.
28. Sennett, work cited in note 25.
29. Alan Wolfe, *The Limits of Legitimacy: Political Contradictions of Contemporary Capitalism* (New York: Free Press, 1977).
30. See Bendix, *Max Weber*, cited in note 4, pp. 458–468.

31. See Henry Jacoby, *The Bureaucratization of the World* (Berkeley: University of California Press, 1976).
32. See Jürgen Habermas, *Legitimation Crisis* (Boston: Beacon Press, 1975).
33. William James, "The Moral Equivalent of War" in his *Memories and Studies* (New York: Longmans, 1911), pp. 265–296.
34. See, for example, Gabriel Almond, *Political Development: Essays in Heuristic Theory* (Boston: Little, Brown, 1970); Szymon Chodak, *Societal Development* (New York: Oxford University Press, 1973); Colin Leys, ed., *Politics and Change in Developing Countries* (Cambridge: Cambridge University Press, 1969); Lucian W. Pye, *Aspects of Political Development* (Boston: Little, Brown, 1966).
35. See Bendix, *Kings or People,* cited in note 10.
36. See Eisenstadt, *Revolution . . .,* cited in note 13; Tilly, *From Mobilization to Revolution,* cited in note 16.
37. See Karl de Schweinitz, Jr., *Industrialization and Democracy* (New York: Free Press of Glencoe, 1964).
38. Germani, work cited in note 1.
39. Alex Inkeles, "The Emerging Social Structure of the World," *World Politics* 27:467–495 (July 1975), at p. 494.
40. Neil J. Smelser, "Mechanisms of Change and Adjustment to Change," in Bert F. Hoselitz and Wilbert E. Moore, eds., *Industrialization and Society* (Paris and The Hague: UNESCO and Mouton, 1963), Chapter 2; quotation from pp. 38–39.
41. Sennett, work cited in note 25.
42. Daniel Bell, "The Return of the Sacred: The Argument About the Future of Religion," *American Academy of Arts and Sciences Bulletin* 31(6):29–55 (March 1978).
43. *Ibid.* , p. 33.
44. Robert A. Nisbet, *The Sociological Tradition* (New York: Basic Books, 1966), Chapter 6, "The Sacred," pp. 221–263.
45. Orlando Patterson, *Ethnic Chauvinism: The Reactionary Impulse* (New York: Stein and Day, 1977).
46. Nisbet, *The Sociological Tradition,* cited in note 44, Chapter 3, "Community," pp. 47–106.
47. Alex Haley, *Roots: The Saga of an American Family* (Garden City, NY: Doubleday, 1976).

THE LIMITS OF RATIONALITY

The brave belief in a purely rational society was seriously entertained by the rationalists of the 18th century Enlightenment. As political philosophers, the rationalists were not unaware of differences in economic interests, but they had considerable confidence in the possibility of a consensual set of rules limiting private conflicts and modes of resolving persistent differences by resort to a representative government. That government would also protect and promote the "general welfare," including the military protection of a free society against the enemies of liberty. As I commented in Chapter 1, the "self-evident truths" articulated in the American Declaration of Independence were not at all historically valid generalizations but rather the statement of a revolutionary set of values that would provide the legitimacy for a "free" and self-governing society. Even those values turned out to be far from consensually held when translated into constitutional and legal principles, as many compromises proved necessary. Aside from the colonial loyalists—who were thereby also royalists—many of whom emigrated and others, less fortunate, were forced reluctantly to submit to an "illegitimate" government—the closest approximation to a consensus that underlay the new American state was that of a secularized, representative government. That, too, was a nonrational basis of political legitimacy, yet the long, erratic, but generally favorable struggle for the ascendancy of Parliament in England had accumulated enough traditional background to pass for a self-evident principle that had not been extended to the transplanted Englishmen in the American colonies. Within a few decades the Constitution, as interpreted by the Supreme Court, became essentially the sovereign. The framers of the Constitution had provided legal procedures for its modification, however, thus almost obviating the necessity of the historical remedies of regicide or revolution to challenge political legitimacy. And certainly the procedure of reasonable debate had more congruence with the vision of a rational society than did the resort to violence, although that might have an equal or greater claim to instrumental rationality.

I use the American example, not out of excessive parochialism, but because it was, as Seymour Martin Lipset has devoted a book to substantiating, the "first new nation" of the modern era with its characteristic emphasis on rationalization of such seemingly practical matters as economics and politics.[1] The French Revolution, shortly to follow, owed at least as much to rationalist philosophy in its inception.[2] It quickly became the arena for competing political ideologies in which the losers in debates tended to lose their heads, and was only ended by the charismatic, authoritarian regime of Napoleon.

Marxist political theory represents another form of rationalism, leading in some poorly specified utopian future to the "withering away of the state" in a consensual, classless, and therefore harmonious society. The characterization of the *bourgeois* state as the "executive committee of the ruling class"—the capitalists—and of religion as the opiate of the people appears as the extreme espousal of secularization. In fact, if we take seriously the doctrine of historical materialism, which I have previously characterized as silly since it cannot account for that most crucially distinctive feature of human behavior, symbolic communication through language, rational and beneficial control of the means and instruments of production provides for a rationalized and nonexploitative society. Modern "Marxist" political ideologies and programs for political rule owe much to Lenin and little to the nominal major prophet.[3] The presumably transitional "dictatorship of the proletariat" becomes at most a continuing dictatorship of the party rulers, with a strong propensity to charismatic, personalistic rule and the characteristic tensions of such political regimes when such leaders die or are replaced by a power struggle within the elite.

These failures to achieve a rational society, I argued in Chapter 1, are not simply the result of failures in human perfectability that may yet be progressively alleviated through extensions of rationalized segments of human societies, but rather derive from the (fortunate) ineradicability of human emotion and the incapacity of rational calculation to set ultimate goals, establish values, or provide non-material meaning to human existence. Modernization, I have been documenting, is best understood as a process of structural rationalization, and its full course is not yet run in countless "less developed countries." Highly rationalized societies may have reached, or perhaps exceeded, the limits of the process, as seems to be indicated by the apparently increasing incidence of the "organized emotionalism" of religious cults with supernatural faiths and appeals and of nominally this-worldly, terroristic, often self-sacrificial political cults.

The concluding sections of Chapters 3 through 9 have indicated the limits to the various aspects of rationalization that provide the real meaning to modernization, and I need not recapitulate them here. Rather, by reverting to the general theme that started these proceedings, I am provided with an excuse for attending to some important aspects of resistances and limits given scant attention so far, owing to the central focus on major large-scale processes of structural change.

EXPRESSION AND AFFECTIVITY

Human beings decorate things, and often themselves. They add non-utilitarian decorations and designs to tools and household utensils, to buildings, to boats and any other means of transport, as well as to sacred objects and those thought to have magical powers. What constitutes beauty in nature or in the artifices of human actors is highly variable across societies and cultures, and may also differ within them. Yet no society is without art forms or "music"—perhaps only at the level of "folk art" or popular culture. That, of course, does not mean that everyone everywhere engages in active esthetic expression; some may enjoy (or at least accept) artistic forms passively, or succeed in unpunished indifference, if the art forms have no religious, magical, or group-identification functions.

Where both different styles and different "qualities" of art forms coexist, some correspondence between types of art and the cultural traditions or social standing of distinguishable segments of society is likely to be detectable.[4] But, it does not follow that it is possible, solely from knowledge of the structural features of a society, to predict the precise forms that will be produced by, or interdependent with, those features. Esthetic forms are in fact rather loosely linked to social structures, showing a substantial range of autonomous variability which includes openness to borrowing from outside the system without encountering resistances from the functional interdependence of other structural components.[5] Daniel Bell argues that, under capitalism, the social structure is ruled by rationality but the "culture"—his discussion centers on art—is discretionary and anti-intellectual. This disjunction, in his view, represents a contradiction or even, somewhat portentously, a "crisis."[6] From a sociological analyst who is generally both insightful and incisive, that is a remarkably untenable argument. The esthetic content of art is intrinsically "anti-intellectual," although that does become most apparent where structural rationalization of more mundane concerns is highly developed.

Authoritarian regimes, whether ideologically socialist, fascist, or merely nationalistic military dictatorships, may—and commonly do—attempt to impose limits or actually impose standards on artistic expression. The Soviet Union attempts to demand "socialist realism" in fiction, poetry, and drama—which mix art with some intellectual content—and also in the visual arts. (Classical ballet, however, is cultivated; *Swan Lake* displays little socialist realism.) The insistence that art be consistent with ideology (or perhaps simply with the rather uncultivated esthetic tastes of the arbiters) does link art to the social structure by explicit enforcement, and may even be said to rationalize art by making it an instrument (of dubious efficacy) in accomplishing social goals. It has the same degraded relation to esthetic expression as the extensive "art work" performed in the commercial advertising business.

All forms of esthetic expression, along with athletic participation and viewing, outdoor recreation, indoor games, recreational reading, travel—in short, the whole array of ingenious ways we find of not being useful—are subject to rationalization of procedures. The instruments and materials of the painter, sculptor, musician, or mere avocational handicraft artisan are subject to technification, as are sporting goods and playing surfaces, transportation and communication. And, commercialization is rampant in all of art and recreation in highly rationalized societies, with considerable impact on economically less developed countries that may find sale not only for arts and crafts that may have or have had important symbolic significance in the traditional fabric of life but also for contemporary copies that become trade goods to accommodate the collecting propensities of travellers or simply of the patrons of importers in the gift shops of a cosmopolitan world.

The artists and other producers of *objets d'art* for sale, the "professional" musicians, entertainers, and athletes are engaging in expressive activities, but not purely for their own sake. The mere fact that they may enjoy their work does not automatically distinguish them, at the motivational level, from those whose labor has more "practical" results. Even for the patrons, esthetic or recreational motives may be contaminated by status symbolism, or simply evidence of membership in a social group.[7] Actual participation or performance may still be partially responsive to group pressure, although that presumably is attenuated or non-existent if the activity is truly discretionary with the individual. The limiting case is presumably the artist or performer who not only has no colleagues in the activity, but no witnesses or audience. That behavior is sufficiently rare as to be regarded as socially odd.

The question, however, is not whether expressive behavior takes place in a social setting (it usually does) or even whether it is subject to rationalization (it may well be). The critical question is why it should occur at all, and that logically requires us to recognize that it must be regarded, at least by patrons and by unpaid performers, as having intrinsic value. This is to say that the performance or the product constitute final goals and not simply instrumental ones: *ars pro gratia artis*.

I have been attending to expressive activity (including viewing, listening, and witnessing as a sort of "passive activity") and to what would generally be called recreation. These appear to be social and cultural universals, although the forms and the extent of rationalization of procedures are highly variable. Universal also are ceremonies, public rituals, and holidays—both sacred and profane. Without necessarily accepting all of Claude Lévy-Strauss's "structuralism"[8] with respect to myth and (non-utilitarian) cultural symbolism as constituting the "deep structure" that is more fundamental to social cohesion than are common "cognitive" goals and values, it does appear that non-rational beliefs and conventional manifestations of symbolic collectivity constitute counter-balances to strictly utilitarian explanations and activities. That they persist despite some inroads of rationalization, including secularization as the most fundamental or radical challenge, may be interpreted as testimony to the importance of expressive propensities; regulated emotionalism, the symbolism of collectivity, and even explanations of life's deeper problems of meaning. (Cheek and Burch define, and explain, myths as a kind of back-up belief system that accounts for incongruities between the normal or expected and the occurrence of the unexpected.[9])

Cultural variability, I have noted, abounds in that rather extensive class of behaviors that I have been calling "expressive" activities. Wide differences exist in what constitutes beauty; what activities are fun or creative or adventurous; the rules that effectively define games and contests; the procedures, attire, and symbolic objects that conventionally characterize rituals and ceremonies. Yet, if Cheek and Burch are correct, at least part of this range has remarkably common *social structural* characteristics.[10] That part these authors call "leisure" and I should prefer to call "recreation."[11] Such activities, with high probability, turn out to be organized around bounded social groups, and that remains true within large social aggregates such as tens of thousands of spectators at sports events. Those groups, moreover, are typically "primary" in the sociological sense, that is, they are multi-bonded rather than functionally specific to the occasion, and are characterized by affective (often kin-based) relationships among the members.

Emotion—which for some reason is usually called affectivity in sociological and psychological discourse—is intrinsic to human nature, and in terms of biological evolution may be very much older than consciousness and calculation.[12] As I said in Chapter 1, rationalism, as a political and social philosophy, treated emotion, human "passions," as essentially shameful or pathological. Yet, both the containment and the positive direction of emotional propensities is a universal component of the socialization of infants. That socialization, in turn, is always ideally and usually in fact a duty of family and kinship organizations. Here positive affection is displayed and expected in return, though often not unmixed with fear, including that most damaging fear, the threatened withdrawal of affection as a punishment for misbehavior. Anger and hate probably need not be learned, but the proper occasions and objects require guidance.

The impact of industrialization and other forms of rationalization on family organization and kinship systems has been succinctly summarized by William Goode:

> Wherever the economic system expands through industrialization, family patterns change. Extended kinship ties weaken, lineage patterns dissolve, and a trend toward some form of the conjugal system generally begins to appear—that is, the nuclear family becomes a more independent kinship unit. [13]

Goode, however, is careful to document the diversity of pre-industrial kinship systems and the uneven forms and rates of change in various aspects of those systems. He emphasizes that some change has been exaggerated: the extended kinship system with a multi-generational household unit and comprising several nuclear families at the second generation, presumably characteristic of rural populations in the pre-industrial West, was rare or totally fictitious—a product of distorted nostalgic reconstruction. The conjugal family system actually antedated extensive urbanization and industrialization. [14] Similarly, the destruction of extended kinship is more properly viewed as an impairment, with a shift from mandatory to discretionary obligations beyond the immediate (nuclear) family, but still surviving. Goode, in this connection, properly notes that the nuclear family, defined as comprising only parents and their immature children, has never been either the ideal or the statistical mode; rather the conjugal family that retains some ties between adult generations and among adult siblings is the one that "fits" the modern industrial system. [15] In the predominant Western kinship system, an extended kin network in terms of actual behavior has been able to survive the social differentiation, and probable social inequality, of its constituent nuclear units.

Differentiation and mobility, in fact, are the processes that most critically undermine extended kinship as a single corporate and economic unit, and it is not surprising that the hereditary rich and the hereditary poor may display the most intensive kinship networks.

It is the conventional wisdom of standard textbooks in sociology that industrialization and increasing structural differentiation generally have led to a steady loss of family functions. Although moving most economic production out of the household, providing formal education of the young in schools, confining religion to churches, and seeking entertainment in external associations combine to reduce the (easily idealized and exaggerated) functions of the family as a kind of microcosm of society, the conventional wisdom commonly fails to note some other considerations. The "loss of economic functions" is by no means total. Sociologists, following the lead of economists, have attended to production (and physical production at that) and not to consumption. The family is the basic unit of consumption, and market principles of distribution end at the household door. The family as a household unit is also a leading producer of services consumed by the producing unit (and usually left out of account in national income accounts).

The other important consideration is that with the increasing rationalization and emotional sterilization of virtually every public aspect of social behavior (art, recreation, and religion being partial exceptions), the importance of the family as a prime setting for emotional relationships and expression is likely to increase. There members are treated as individuals, whole and unique. The intensity of interaction, and the concomitant emotional strains, are much more important sources of marital instability or generational conflict than is the supposed loss of family functions.

The shift from marriage by arrangement to marriage at the choice of the partners, based upon affection, is in effect a *reduction* in the rationalization of family organization, and that reduction extends to diminished emphasis on preservation and extension of family property through successive generations. The increased, if reluctant, public acceptance in the Western world of alternative life-styles, such as "counsensual unions" without formal marriage, and reduced emphasis on virginity, chastity, and sexual exclusiveness in marriage, does indicate an increased diversity of familial and quasi-familial patterns. They scarcely represent a lessened demand for emotional linkages and sexual gratification. Whether they are regarded as pathological will depend on how the value balance between convention and tolerance is weighted. They do reflect, perhaps, a pathological emotional starvation in the pragmatic, demystified encounters in highly rationalized public organizations. Daniel Bell's identification of discretionary life-styles as a kind of resistance to rationalization is certainly correct, and may represent more of a crisis than does the relative insulation of artistic culture from the main stream of utilitarian concerns.[16]

The same quest for individual identity and for affective social relationships was discussed in Chapter 7 with respect to the invariable appearance of informal organizations in the cracks and around the edges of bureaucratic work organizations. This may be only a token bridging between Freud's "love and work" as central to personality organization, and which Neil Smelser has noted as seriously disjoined in contemporary rationalized society.[17] Other manifestations are to be found in the persistent quest for "community" in fractionated and residentially mobile populations[18] and the widespread recrudescence of ethnicity, on which, in Chapter 9, I took a rather more benign view than does Orlando Patterson in his worries about ethnic chauvinism.[19] I also suggested there that religious secularization in any sense beyond the (nominal) structural separation of church and state, is severely limited, a view brilliantly elaborated by Daniel Bell in a very recent essay.[20]

Of course, given the extensity of institutionalized rationality, there is always the potentiality for the manipulation of the irrationalities and non-rationalities of others, such as feigned affection in order to acquire the wealth of a prospective marital partner, coopting informal organization in order to increase morale and productivity, or the use of community and ethnic identity to maintain unfair discriminatory practices against *other* minorities. But hardy persistence and novel manifestations of expression and affectivity, and, indeed, of religiosity, testify to the limits of rationality as the sole basis of human goal-seeking or the sole basis for social organization.

TRADITION AND MODERNITY

Reinhard Bendix, although he earlier—along with many others—warned against too sharp and total a contrast between tradition and modernity,[21] recently concludes:

> It is easiest to define modernization as a breakdown of the ideal-typical traditional order: Authority loses sanctity, monarchy declines, hierarchical social order is disrupted. Secular authority, rule in the name of the people, and an equalitarian ethos are typical attributes of modern society.[22]

It is precisely concerning the ideal-typical traditional order that Bendix and others have expressed appropriate doubts, owing to the great diversity of societies and cultures that may have little in common, at the detailed level of structure and belief, except that they are not highly rationalized. Similarly, the commonalities that Bendix attributes to modern societies are sufficiently abstract to conceal a plethora of actual and significant differences.

Among the numerous fallacies in the conventional polarity between tradition and modernity outlined by Joseph Gusfield are the following: traditional societies are and have been static; their value and normative systems are internally consistent; their social structures are homogeneous; modernity presents a confrontation, owing to which the traditional belief or practice is doomed to defeat.[23] To this we must add the false presumption that traditional societies represent a homogeneous category of social systems.

In view of the actual diversity of practices to be found in "traditional" societies, and our repeated observation that some form and degree of rationalization exists in all societies, it is not surprising that some premodern practices need little change in the course of economic rationalization. Bert Hoselitz, like Gusfield drawing his examples from India, finds numerous examples of both continuation and of adaptive blending.[24] Melville Herskovits similarly notes examples of mutual adaptation between the economic initiatives of Western "evangelists" for economic development and the traditional organization of native cultures in sub-Saharan Africa.[25]

The commitment to economic rationalization has now become a cultural and ideological universal, obviously diffused and imitated from the historic success of that dynamic process in the West. It is also now evident that technology and forms of economic organization may move across cultural boundaries, without adopting Western political structures or the less pragmatically oriented aspects of philosophy and ideology. Yet in this international setting the discussion of tradition and modernity commonly takes the form of identifying traditional impediments to rationalization. Thus, constraints and resistances become the "bad old ways," the enemy.

However, let us turn the situation around. Suppose that the effective governing authorities, although committed to economic rationalization, are also committed to preserving traditional practices and beliefs, including the legitimacy of their own "mandate to rule." This is the actual situation in Saudi Arabia, which, almost uniquely among "less developed countries," has a surplus of capital and a shortage of labor. Foreseeing the eventual exhaustion of petroleum, from which the current wealth mainly derives, the government plans two new industrial cities to be located in coastal areas now nearly uninhabited. The plans call for a virtual "turn-key" construction of the capital-intensive industries (initially petro-chemicals to use that now-abundant resource), houses, streets, water and sewer systems, and other public utilities. Before actually going ahead the authorities have paused to ask how destructive to a truly conservative Islamic social structure such a massive physical and economic transformation may be.

We have now learned not to answer "totally"—quickly and glibly, arguing from the predestined configuration of the model modernized society. Extended kinship and tribalism will be eroded, and the household unit will be the nuclear family, which will be no novelty and perhaps not a major change in proportions. Marriage by contract among the male elders is likely to diminish, total sexual segregation and female seclusion will provoke incidents and controversies that traditionalists will lose, and women will increase their educational qualifications and labor force participation. New forms of political participation, including labor unionization, will appear, either clandestinely or rebelliously if not condoned by a partially secularized legal system. The fundamentally religious basis, not only of the demands for formal observances such as the five-times daily prayers but also of the legitimacy of the polity, will be subject to doubt and debate. The official urgency behind economic rationalization has ensured some secularization and dissidence by sending very substantial numbers of young men (and a very few young women) for advanced education in the United States or Western Europe. The number studying abroad in late 1978 was approximately 10,000, and the flow continues, with a virtually total repatriation of those completing their degrees.

Some of these predictions derive from the experience of other nearby Moslem countries, such as Syria and Lebanon, Iraq and Iran, Egypt, Tunisia, and Morocco.[26] Some flow from historical and comparative precedents, and some from theoretical consideration of structural interdependencies.

Caution is proper, however. The Moslem countries taken as precedents have had more intensive experience with Westernization, over a longer time, and under overt or indirect colonial dependency. The Ottoman hegemony over Saudi Arabia was thin, incomplete, and at least nominally Islamic. Because Islam, in its full extent and purity, represents a total culture and not merely a theology and set of sacred myths, any change of daily behaviors and forms of social organization is likely to be viewed as dangerous secularization.[27] Some "interpretations" of doctrine and accommodation in practice are clearly possible, because they are occurring, but this may prove to be a kind of unintentional experiment in segmental rationalization and its containment far short of the experiential and theoretical limits of that process that has hitherto been contagious.

The Saudi Arabian experience may turn out to be segmental in a sense now common in newly developing countries: the impetus to modernization coming from a small, urban, Western-trained elite that attempts to foster, and indeed impose, at least economic change and political mobilization in a predominantly rural, village-based social system. Such has been the situation in Burma, as analyzed by Manning Nash.[28] Here, in a Buddhist culture, where also religion is a pervasive influence and not provocative of rationalism or instrumental change, rationalization may be slow, somewhat superficial, and lead to a substantial disjunction between a frustrated modernizing elite and a traditional peasantry defensively protecting a traditional style of life. As in Saudi Arabia, rural poverty is not severe and the demand for change does not originate with the peasants or get echoed by them.

We are left, then, in a rather unsatisfactory state of uncertainty, which is the common condition of developing areas of science and scholarly inquiry. Rationalization is such a pervasive and generally inclusive force in the contemporary world that we are on surer ground in determining its limits and excesses than we are in determining its viable minima, the preservation of an integrated "traditional" structure at an acceptable and increasing level of material comfort without either internal or external contamination of the rest of a society's important concerns. Social systems are demonstrably looser than our conventional interdependence models would lead us, naively, to expect, but they retain genuinely systemic properties. They are never eclectic aggregations, fortuitously selected or stumbled upon without regard to pattern or integration. Always there are inconsistencies, conflicts, tension points and areas. Enduring systems owe their success less to integration than to developing tension-management mechanisms. Those who endeavor to establish novel combinations can be certain that the "fit" will be imperfect, and that at least one further step toward rationalization is appropriate: the deliberate adaptation or outright invention of ways to contain tensions without intolerable disruptions.

COLLECTIVE GOALS AND VALUES

One gloomy vision of the future is that of the standardized, routinized, depersonalized, bureaucratic administration of everything. Max Weber expressed such worries[29] and, a few years ago, Richard Goodwin interpreted the spread of bureaucracy as a kind of inevitable force, trapping executives and administrators as surely as the victimized client who has no effective right of appeal or other recourse for redress of grievances.[30] The idea of a technocracy, managed by technicians with primary regard for rational efficiency, is much admired by some engineers and managerial specialists, for that would put them in charge.

There is a fatal defect in that reasoning, as I indicated in the preceding chapter. Public administrative agencies generally do not have their own sources of funds, and are politically accountable to legislatures and governing officials, whose legitimacy in determining policy and allocating resources does not rest on rational grounds. Some governmental agencies may enjoy a considerable and durable autonomy, not as a matter of right but as a consequence of slovenly surveillance and enforcement of accountability on the part of political authorities. That relative autonomy is not as great as that enjoyed by some private business corporations, which do have a source of funds as long as customers buy their goods and services, and may be run with a high and sensitive regard for the organization's own interests—that is, primarily for the benefit of the employees of all levels and types.

It is the function of political authorities to articulate collective goals and mobilize the resources for their attainment. Those goals will include, at minimum, such strictly political concerns as national defense, internal order, and the maintenance of the legal or other foundations for legitimacy of the regime. Additional goals that are likely to be considered public responsibilities are sometimes called by economists "social overhead capital" or "infrastructure." They are more instrumental in character: monetary and banking systems, taxation and other revenue systems, transportation and communication, water and sewage systems, fire protection. Education may be regarded as a kind of capital investment or as a distributive benefit, along with information services, welfare systems, and support for various special interests that have sufficient political influence to lay claim on the public purse. Many of these activities of governments may be cast in the language of rational calculation, of cost—benefit analyses of alternative courses of action.

And some policies are sufficiently instrumental to other goals to be judged by rational criteria.

Yet it is a "mere prejudice," that is, a non-rational value judgment, to hold that a national state should survive as a sovereign entity, that a central government should not be overthrown with consequent anarchy, and especially that farm prices need public support in fairness to food producers or that those unable to support themselves economically should not simply be permitted to starve. Are law-makers and law-enforcers also bound by law? Do citizens have rights against the state? Is "justice" a universal right or a privilege based upon financial ability to pay? Again, those questions will be answered by affirmation of values, though occasionally a semblance of rational judgment may be made by demonstrating or at least persuasively arguing that the consequences of a "wrong" answer would be to destroy or damage another, even more crucial, value.

The predominance of "interest group" politics in contemporary Western parliamentary democracies, the loss of confidence in the honesty and orientation toward public interest of public officials, and abrasive contentions over the equity of distribution of income and other social rewards may indeed constitute a crisis of legitimacy. And it is arguable that these perceived problems in the body politic may derive in large measure from rationalization, from the instrumental view of government rather than a view of the state as a good in itself.

Patriotism has accumulated a good deal of tarnish in the older democracies, and perhaps especially in the United States. Sacrificial efforts to resist a "real and present danger" to national independence would probably still be the predominant reaction, although already in World War II craven capitulation and collaboration with an enemy manifestly superior in power occurred with a frequency dismaying to patriots. National sovereignty may be the last bastion of defense against political secularization, with one of its potential consequences, international war—the ultimate testimony to human irrationality. The technification of the instruments of war and the rationalization of military organizations make warfare a dangerous and even disastrous symbol of nationalism, a damaged mechanism for display of pomp and circumstance (the symbolic trappings of power), a passion play dramatizing good and evil which ends with no heroes for lack of survivors. Soccer matches and chess contests do not command the awe accorded marching troops and military weaponry of technical sophistication beyond most citizens' comprehension; they are safer ways to represent and symbolize identity and participation.

There are of course safe and significant ways to represent collective identity at some current sacrifice. Actions to preserve natural areas, monuments of the past, and investments for the long-term future represent a belief in collective survival beyond the lifetime of anyone now alive. Were we to take seriously Thomas Jefferson's aphorism, "The earth belongs to the living," there would be no excuse for restraint on plundering all natural resources, destroying monuments as costly testimony to irrational sentimentality, putting all space to its current economically optimum use, and polluting air and water to a point just short of impairing the longevity of the living. That some modest restraints are imposed on such eminently rational behavior does bespeak a kind of belief in a worldly "collective immortality." The restraint reflects an act of faith, not of reason, and faith is sometimes hard to find these days.

NOTES

1. Seymour Martin Lipset, *The First New Nation: The United States in Historical and Comparative Perspective* (New York: Basic Books, 1963).
2. See Charles Tilly, *From Mobilization to Revolution* (Reading, MA: Addison-Wesley, 1978).
3. Vladimir I. Lenin, *The State and Revolution: The Marxist Theory of the State and the Tasks of the Proletariat in the Revolution,* in his *Collected Works,* 4th ed. (Moscow: Progress, 1964), Vol. 25, pp. 381–492; first published in Russian in 1917.
4. See Neil H. Cheek, Jr., and William R. Burch, Jr., *The Social Organization of Leisure in Human Society* (New York: Harper and Row, 1976), pp. 142–147.
5. See Wilbert E. Moore, *Social Change,* 2nd ed. (Englewood Cliffs, NJ: Prentice-Hall, 1974), pp. 77–80.
6. Daniel Bell, "The Cultural Contradictions of Capitalism," in Daniel Bell and Irving Kristol, eds., *Capitalism Today* (New York: Basic Books, 1971).
7. See Cheek and Burch, work cited in note 4.
8. See, for example, Claude Lévy-Strauss, *The Raw and the Cooked* (New York: Harper and Row, 1969).
9. Cheek and Burch, work cited in note 4, pp. 180–194.
10. *Ibid.,* especially pp. 94–121.
11. For a brief discussion of these concepts, see my "Foreword" to *ibid.,* pp. xiii–xv.
12. For a brief exposition, see Loren Eiseley, "The Cosmic Orphan," *Saturday Review/World* pp. 16–19 (February 23, 1974); also Eiseley, *The Immense Journey* (New York: Vintage Books, 1973).
13. William J. Goode, *World Revolution and Family Patterns* (New York: Free Press of Glencoe, 1963), p. 6.
14. *Ibid.,* pp. 6–26.
15. *Ibid.,* pp. 10–26, 70–81.
16. Bell, essay cited in note 6.
17. Neil J. Smelser's unpublished paper is summarized in "Love and Work in Adulthood," *American Academy of Arts and Sciences Bulletin* 31(3):4–21, on pp. 18–19.
18. See Robert A. Nisbet, *The Sociological Tradition* (New York: Basic Books, 1966), Chapter 3, "Community," pp. 47–106.
19. Orlando Patterson, *Ethnic Chauvinism: The Reactionary Impulse* (New York: Stein and Day, 1977).
20. Daniel Bell, "The Realm of the Sacred: The Argument About the Future of Religion," *American Academy of Arts and Sciences Bulletin* 31(6):29–55 (March 1978).
21. Reinhard Bendix, "Tradition and Modernity Reconsidered," in his *Embattled Reason* (New York: Oxford University Press, 1970), pp. 250–314.

22. Reinhard Bendix, *Kings or People: Power and the Mandate to Rule* (Berkeley: University of California Press, 1978), pp. 10–11.

23. Joseph R. Gusfield, "Tradition and Modernity: Misplaced Polarities in the Study of Social Change," *American Journal of Sociology* 72:351–362 (January 1967).

24. Bert F. Hoselitz, "Tradition and Economic Growth," in Ralph Braibanti and Joseph J. Spengler, eds., *Tradition Values, and Socioeconomic Development* (Durham, NC: Duke University Press, 1961), pp. 83–113.

25. Melville J. Herskovits, "Economic Change and Cultural Dynamics," in *ibid.*, pp. 114–138.

26. See Reinhard Bendix, *Kings or People,* cited in note 21, subsection "Arab Nationalism and Socialism," pp. 558–594; S. N. Eisenstadt, *Revolution and the Transformation of Societies* (New York: Free Press, 1978), subsection "The Islamic Civilization," pp. 134–139; William J. Goode, work cited in note 13, Chapter III, "Changing Family Patterns in Arabic Islam," pp. 87–163.

27. See Ishtiaq Husain Qureshi, "Islamic Elements in the Political Thought of Pakistan," in Braibanti and Spengler, eds., work cited in note 24, pp. 212–242.

28. Manning Nash, *The Golden Road to Modernity: Village Life in Contemporary Burma* (New York: Wiley, 1965; Phoenix Edition, Chicago: University of Chicago Press, 1973).

29. See Reinhard Bendix, *Max Weber: An Intellectual Portrait,* new ed. (Berkeley: University of California Press, 1977), pp. 464–466.

30. Richard N. Goodwin, *The American Condition* (Garden City, NY: Doubleday, 1974).

11 PERSISTENT PLURALISM

Are industrial societies becoming alike? That question must have a rather unsatisfactory answer, unfortunately common in social analysis: Well, yes and no. That, of course, is no help in understanding or prediction, unless it is possible to specify the respects in which either an affirmative answer or a negative answer is warranted, and why. That has been my mission in this essay on modernization as a process of structural rationalization, with the logical and empirical limits to that process. Even if there were no differences in social goals, beliefs, and values, and no trace of emotion and expression in the human psyche, carrying out the rationalization process in numerous distinct quasi-autonomous social units (nominally sovereign national states) would still be very unlikely to produce uniform results. Any difference in relative conditions, such as size, resources, population distribution, or access to markets would alter the appropriate mechanisms for achieving the common goal. The "state" of the social structure at any point arbitrarily chosen as the beginning of modernization would at the least affect both the order and the tempo of subsequent changes. (Starting points are arbitrary, since no society, historical or contemporary, has been totally lacking in rationalization, at least with respect to food production, environmental coping, care of the young, and measures for protection from "natural" and human threats.)

In support of increasing commonalities in the world's societies, one can go through a kind of check-list of major "institutions" or functionally differentiated aspects of social systems, such as economic structures, urbanization, the bureaucratic state, education, the family and kinship. This is the approach I have used in some previous writing,[1] adding to these structural features such normative principles as achievement orientations, affective neutrality, "universalistic" standards of placement, and "functionally specific" role assignments and relationships. Although I had earlier surveyed the research materials on labor recruitment and motivation,[2] the character structure of "individual modernity" has been developed by Alex Inkeles and David Horton Smith in an impressive six-country comparative study, confirming their guiding hypothesis that factory work itself works as a socializing agency in inducing attitudes appropriate to the "modern man."[3]

And, in a world with increasing trade with all but the most remote or willfully self-contained areas (e.g., Burma, mainland China prior to another "opening" in 1978, and Soviet-bloc countries in varying degrees), consumer goods, and services such as fast-food chains and hotels, become somewhat internationalized. What we might call the Hilton-and-Coca-Cola syndrome makes it possible for the tourist to travel extensively and never leave home, with only a slight care in selecting an itinerary. This kind of cultural diffusion is of course discretionary—not determined by transformation of the central structural features of society.

The approach I have adopted in this book, although managing to attend to most of these growing commonalities among industrialized societies, views them as uniformly the consequence of structural rationalization. That approach has the dual advantage of permitting an examination of the processes of modernization and not simply the results (characterized in Chapter 1 as the "model modernized society"), and of specifying how and explaining why the question that began this chapter also has a negative answer.

There is another view of increasing commonality in the course of large-scale structural change: what Szymon Chodak calls "increasing systemness," marked by growing differentiation and interdependence, but also by conflict.[4] Curiously, Chodak does not see the limits to commonality imposed by differing goals and values,[5] although he perceives the exaggeration in the "rational man" model of human behavior: "Sane systems which encompass human beings have to be systems of irrational beings pretending that they are rational."[6]

The structural uniformities that have seemed to support "convergence theory" represent, at best, contingent predictions: they are the common consequences *if* modernization "succeeds." Yet that success is by no means assured for the less-developed countries, and in any event need not—nay, certainly will not—follow the historic course to modernity. As noted succinctly by the historian William McNeill, in the specific context of the effects of modernization on human migration:

> There exists no single, standard pattern of modernization to which all peoples must conform, and this despite a habit of mind that remains widespread in English-speaking lands and that expects all peoples to follow along a path already trodden by Britain and the United States.[7]

The pluralism of this chapter's title refers not to the situation in those fortunate societies that have achieved a measure of tolerance for internal differences but to the (not wholly fortunate) avoidance of a look-alike world.

FAILED INITIATIVES

In the history of Western Europe the process of economic rationalization
evolved very differently over the course of several centuries after 1400 A.D.
The Italian city states, particularly Venice, had a lively Mediterranean trade
and had developed banking for pooling investments and clearing accounts.
By 1500, Spain and Portugal had begun to establish and exploit their overseas
empires, including the African slave trade, commercial ventures in the
Orient, and raw materials (especially precious metals) from the Americas.

These initiatives atrophied for a variety of reasons, difficult to weigh in
their several influences. Italy was a linguistic and geographical unity but not a
political one until after 1861. The perennially impoverished southern part
provided cheap labor but not an affluent internal market, and the late venture into colonialism in the eastern Mediterranean and northeast Africa
probably represented a net drain on the national economy. Spain and Portugal's American empires yielded diminishing revenues after the most readily
available precious metals were shipped to the home countries but not "wisely"
invested in domestic enterprises. The establishment in the New World of an
essentially feudal social order was more suitable for authoritarian rule than for
encouraging diversified economic enterprise, and the political climate on the
Iberian peninsula did not favor capitalist enterprise. The African colonies,
after the end of the slave trade, probably were as poor a bargain as the Italian
empire. It is necessary to add, with the same proviso concerning uncertain
weight, that the Catholic Church was a powerful *secular* force in all three
countries as well as a theological influence that did not encourage popular
political participation or economic activism as a form of "mastery" of the
world. Political instability and, in some instances such as Argentina, repeated "false starts" toward sustained economic growth have continued to
plague Latin America.

British and Dutch, and later French and German, colonialism did establish
trading relationships between the colonies and the metropole, although over
the years the net economic balance may not have run very heavily in favor of
the colonial power. Since the cost of protecting overseas shipping, colonial
peace-keeping, and governmental administration tended to be mainly supported out of the metropole's public treasury (aided in some measure by
taxation in the colonies) and the benefits in trade went to private investors,
colonialism probably resulted in a form of indirect income redistribution.
Whether the net balance of costs and benefits in the colonies, now mainly

formally independent, has been seriously negative is debatable, and probably differs among highly diverse situations. American colonialism probably ran a fairly strong negative balance for the national economy (though, again, with some indirect public subsidy for private enterprise), possibly about even for the Philippines, favorable to the now "Freely Associated State" (Estado Libre Asociado, rendered into English as Commonwealth) of Puerto Rico, strongly favorable for the Canal Zone.

Greece, Yugoslavia, and much of Eastern Europe have suffered over several centuries from political instability, colonialism, and (relatively innocent) involvement in "great power" contests. Only under recent Marxist regimes (except in Greece) has economic rationalization been a matter of public policy, without spectacular success.

Whether all of these cases, briefly mentioned, represent truly "failed" initiatives, certainly none has achieved a high degree of economic rationalization as measured by standard economic indicators. They qualify as more highly rationalized by various "social" indicators. All, of course, are highly bureaucratized; the European countries and former American colonies have major commitments to public education; and the relatively poor countries of Europe mainly have completed the transition to rationalized mortality and fertility control.

Asia (other than Japan), Africa, and the islands of the Pacific (excluding Australia and New Zealand) share in varying degrees a number of deficiencies: many have multi-ethnic or multi-communal populations, with few mechanisms for accommodation or self-government after independence from colonial administration; declining death rates with little erosion of high birth rates, leading (especially in Asia) to increasingly dense agricultural populations and "over-urbanization"; initial poverty and low-technology production; thin mineral and energy resources, and minimal capital accumulation or mechanisms for mobilizing what savings exist. The combination of several of these deficiencies—the simplest case being poverty and rapid population growth—leads to simple or complex "vicious circles," making general improvement of economic well-being slow or virtually non-existent.

Simon Kuznets has recently summarized the "state of the art" (both theory and empirical evidence) with regard to the prospects for the less-developed countries, and his conclusions are temperate but not optimistic.[8] Wassily Leontieff, using available trend data and computer simulation for various assumptions regarding international trade and capital transfers, works out "scenarios" for the economic future of developing countries.[9] None is very hopeful for his "Class II" developing countries—those that are poor with few natural resources. Only with a change in the price of raw materials relative to manufactured goods—such as the OPEC countries have achieved—and with massive capital transfers could these countries avoid an increasing gap by the end of this century between their gross domestic product per capita and that of the "developed" countries. Even under the most optimistic assumptions regarding growth in per capita income, and assuming very modest economic growth in the developed countries, Levy has pointed out that it would take a very long time for poor countries to "catch up" with those that had a long head-start or even with those that have grown rapidly under favorable circumstances of space and other resources (for example, the Soviet Union), and/or strong and centralized governmental mobilization (both Japan and the Soviet Union).[10]

DEPENDENCY THEORY

Previously, I characterized the avoidance of a look-alike world as "not wholly fortunate," precisely because of the poor prospects for many poor countries. Inevitably, some neo-Marxist scholars have formulated a "conspiracy" or "scandal" theory to account for this indubitable inequity. It goes by the polite name of "dependency theory." As formulated by André Gunder Frank[11] or Immanuel Wallerstein,[12] and succinctly summarized by Orlando Patterson who seems thoughtlessly to accept the theory, "the major reason for continued backwardness in the developing world . . . is the exploitative nature of the past and present relationships between poor and rich countries."[13] Daniel Chirot, elaborating on Wallerstein's conceptualization, divides the world into the core countries (rich and exploitative), a semi-periphery comprising countries partially free of domination by the core and valiantly trying to achieve economic development, and the true periphery (a kind of international proletariat). Chirot, it should be noted, does not follow the standard Marxist eschatology by forecasting a world proletarian revolution.[14]

The mechanisms of exploitation alleged are colonialism (on which I have previously commented that the record is mixed) and some sort of "purchasers' cartel" that holds down the prices of raw materials, combined with a "producers' cartel" that fixes the prices of manufactured foods, a dual conspiracy for which there is no evidence at all.[15]

Dependency theorists seem to take little or no account of some significant variables and historic facts: (1) Countries in their present boundaries, as often fixed by arbitrary and forcible decisions and compromises, are very unevenly endowed with resources. Some of those boundaries are a consequence of colonialism, but there is no evidence that the boundaries represented a calculated policy of "divide and exploit." (2) Nationalism, particularly in new nations, has been difficult to attain and so uneasily maintained that sensible regional free trade and combined enterprises are almost untried.

(3) National sovereignty is given at least formal deference in international affairs, so that even small countries can, if they will, determine the conditions for foreign investment and even set the price of exports. To say that these rules are violated by bribery of officials, often undoubtedly true, is also to say that the local officials are corrupt. To say that such governmental interference with free trade is contrary to classical economic theory is to be flagrantly irrelevant. (4) Acceptance of the supposition that a socialist world community would somehow do away with both inequity and iniquity would require persuasive arguments outlining paths and mechanisms, not so far advanced. The protagonists of such a program should somehow explain, and try to discount, the internal colonialism of the Soviet Union and its imperialism in Eastern Europe. Virtually no contemporary Marxist "scholar" seems to attend to that not insignificant, contemporary situation.

In short, there is no doubt that there is a grossly inequitable inequality in the distribution of income in the world, according to any of the standards of equity professed in the Western world. It would be a great help to clarity of thought, to honesty of scholarship, and perhaps to consideration of creative solutions—not to mention reduction of the noise level in the proliferation of pretentious publications—if glibly doctrinaire simplifications of complex situations could be treated with scant notice.

The growing interdependence of the world is not to be confused with dependency theory. The United States, for example, is a major exporter of "primary" products: grain, tobacco, and other agricultural products, lumber, and coal. On the whole, highly rationalized economies become more intensive trading partners than any does with a "dependent" raw materials producer.[16] This interdependence has produced no integration in the political sense (though some regional integration, such as that in Western Europe, moves along at a very slow pace), and certainly no convergence in the structural or cultural sense that is explicit in "convergence theory."[17]

What we face, rather, is a fractious and disorderly world political situation. Conventional divisions, such as the ideological confrontation between "East" and "West" (including competition for clients or dependents in the "Third World") or what we may call the equity confrontation between rich and poor countries, sometimes characterized as "North" versus "South," implies far greater homogeneity and common purpose *within* the contending categories than reality supports. Incidentally, with respect to the division between rich and poor countries, Kenneth Boulding has correctly noted that the proper geographical distinction is that between the temperate zone(s) and the tropical belt.[18] Boulding foresees increasing homogeneity among the affluent societies, "in spite of their diverse political philosophies," with the tropical belt falling further and further behind and facing the possibility of collapsing into "famine, internal war, and massive disorganization."[19]

INCREASING CONVERGENCE AND ACCENTUATED DIVERSITY

I have been discussing the wide divergence in the economic performance of the countries of the world, and the small likelihood that they will disappear in any foreseeable future. I did note that some other forms of rationalization, such as bureaucratization, education, and at least partial rationalization of mortality and fertility controls, probably show less disparity among countries and a narrowing gap rather than a constant or increasing one, but those developments too may well become further failed initiatives for lack of economic growth. This discussion was therefore not precisely responsive to our initial question—"Are industrial societies becoming alike?"—but rather to its extension, by way of what has passed for modernization theory, to the global query: "Are all societies becoming alike?" To that question we may safely answer, "more than they used to be," but as a trend toward a common destination, "No."

Not all of the continuing diversity of the less-developed countries is owing to failure to "complete" the various rationalization processes, whatever that could mean in view of the differences in goals, values, and principles of legitimacy (I take those differences much more seriously than Boulding apparently does) and in view of the "human nature" constraints on purely rational behavior. Some of the limits may be deliberate. Japan, for example, from the time of the Meiji Restoration (1868) until World War II set about a centralized and carefully calculated plan of economic modernization under strictly domestic control, while equally carefully modifying but conserving traditional familism and refurbishing "nature-worshiping" Shintoism and the cult of emperor worship as befitting a divine being.[20] Saudi Arabia, as I mentioned in Chapter 10, although heavily dependent on foreign workers and foreign markets, seeks not only an autonomously controlled and rapid economic rationalization but also, similar to the earlier Japanese effort, the preservation of the conservative Islamic way of life, which allows for little, if any, secularization, and of the religiously authenticated royal rule.

These are only extreme examples of a common desire to preserve cultural traditions, particularly those that are distinctive and symbolic of identification with a meaningful collectivity. That desire is seriously disputed only by "total" radicals, who would destroy all in order to create their own shiny new utopia. Nationalism, as was earlier observed, has become the "secular religion" of new nations, while old nations continue to cherish it. "We are thus provided with a further reason not to expect political homogeneity or convergence, and that reason is simply that national leaders *will* that it not be so."[21]

I return, then, to the initial question, limited to industrial (highly rationalized) societies. Of course, the common processes of rationalization, and their interplay, will yield somewhat common, or at least comparable, results. But the pseudo-Marxist eschatology of a single, Communist, stateless world society is certainly not according to the canonical scriptures of the major prophet, for Marx was rather insistently a historical relativist. No society or culture completely escapes its own history. This is equally true of post-revolutionary regimes, for revolutions do not change "everything," and the revolution itself has an enduring historical effect. And the continuing changes that may take place, deliberately or in a quasi-evolutionary fashion, are strongly constrained by the circumstances of time and place. In fairness it must be added that the homogeneous world society without exploitative sin is little, if any, more utopian than the "model modernized society" that has implicitly informed convergence theory, and its logical derivative— modernization theory.

Because of the strong and abrasive ideological differences between the Soviet Union and the United States (or the "West" in general), and because of highly hazardous political tensions between them in an age technologically equipped to produce massive slaughter and destruction, there has been con-siderable interest in the structural convergence—rather than a collision— between them. There is, of course, the standard check list of similarities: commercialization (with significant differences), technification, bureaucrati-zation, partially secularized education (no state eschews the opportunity of teaching its own ideology and sacred myths in its schools), demographic rationalization, secularization. Yet as Alex Inkeles has concluded, "The evi-dent durability of the Soviet system after more than fifty years has surely confounded the prediction of those who . . . asserted that the Soviet and American sytems were going to converge on some common position."[23]

That convergence will not occur, and the danger endures. Israeli statesman Abba Eban once commented when he was serving as Israeli ambassador to the United Nations, that, "National states may sometimes be persuaded to act rationally after they have exhausted all other alternatives." If the alternatives include trying a nuclear holocaust, the wisely cynical comment is not com-forting. Even rational action is not to be totally trusted, for rational calcula-tion is always subject to the possibility of ignorance and error, and impeccably rational conduct may be devoted to the most nefarious goals. The best hope of compromising, if not resolving, the "East—West" confrontation and a host of others rampant in the contemporary world is that of rationality with a significant admixture of humane passion. Auguste Comte, who coined the term "sociology" in mid-19th century, sought to establish a "religion of humanity." It was an unrealistic idea, but the motives were honorable and the recognition of the importance of values commendably perceptive. Op-timists will profess some slight movement toward universal respect for human life and human dignity, and pessimists will correctly note that we fortunate survivors are living in the bloodiest century, by far, in human history. The wit who asked, "Is there intelligent life on Earth?" might be given a partially favorable answer, but intelligence, I have been arguing, is inadequate or downright dangerous if not contained by compassion.

At the risk of ending this discourse on a less exalted note, it may be comforting to know that an economy may be rationalized without Coca-Cola or MacDonald's hamburgers, and that American tourists can still travel—if they get a few miles away from international airports and the centers of cosmopolitan cities—without the awful feeling that they never left home.

NOTES

1. Wilbert E. Moore, *The Impact of Industry*, (Englewood Cliffs, NJ: Prentice-Hall, 1965); Moore, "The Singular and the Plural: The Social Significance of Industrialism Reconsidered," in Nancy Hammond, ed., *Social Science and the New Societies* (East Lansing: Social Science Research Bureau, Michigan State University, 1973), pp. 117–130.

2. Wilbert E. Moore, *Industrialization and Labor: Social Aspects of Economic Development* (Ithaca, NY: Cornell University Press, 1951; reprinted, New York: Russell and Russell, 1965).

3. Alex Inkeles and David Horton Smith, *Becoming Modern* (Cambridge: Harvard University Press, 1974).

4. Szymon Chodak, *Societal Development* (New York: Oxford University Press, 1973).

5. *Ibid.*, especially pp. 307–308.

6. *Ibid.*, p. 145.

7. William H. McNeill, "Human Migration," *American Academy of Arts and Sciences Bulletin* 31(8):8–7 (May 1978); quotation from p. 15.

8. Simon Kuznets, "Notes on the Study of the Economic Growth of Nations," in Manning Nash, ed., *Essays on Economic Development and Cultural Change in Honor of Bert F. Hoselitz*, Supplement to Vol. 25 of *Economic Development and Cultural Change* (Chicago: University of Chicago Press, 1977), pp. 300–313.

9. Wassily Leontieff, "Natural Resources, Environmental Disruption, and Growth Prospects of the Developed and Less Developed Countries," *American Academy of Arts and Sciences Bulletin* 30(8):20–30 (May 1977).

10. Marion J. Levy, Jr., *Modernization: Latecomers and Survivors* (New York: Basic Books, 1972), pp. 11–21.

11. André Gunder Frank, "The Development of Underdevelopment," in R. I. Rhodes, ed., *Imperialism and Underdevelopment* (New York: Monthly Review Press, 1970), pp. 4–16; also Frank, *On Capitalist Underdevelopment* (New York: Oxford University Press, 1975).

12. Immanuel Wallerstein, *The Modern World-System: Capitalist Agriculture and the Origins of the European World System in the Sixteenth Century* (New York: Academic Press, 1974).

13. Orlando Patterson, from a summary of an unpublished conference paper, in "The Transformation of the Idea of Progress," *American Academy of Arts and Sciences Bulletin* 31(1):10–29 (October 1977); quotation from pp. 21–22.

14. Daniel Chirot, *Social Change in the Twentieth Century* (New York: Harcourt Brace Jovanovich, 1977).

15. See Gustav F. Papanek, "Economic Development Theory: The Earnest Search for a Mirage," in Nash, ed., work cited in note 8, pp. 270–287, especially p. 275.

16. See Alex Inkeles, "The Emerging Social Structure of the World," *World Politics* 27:467–495 (July 1975).

17. In addition to *ibid.*, see Chodak, work cited in note 4, especially pp. 252–315; Karl Deutsch, "Social and Political Convergence in Industrializing Countries—Some Concepts and the Evidence," in Hammond, ed., work cited in note 1, pp. 95–115.

18. Kenneth E. Boulding, "The Gaps Between Developed and Developing Nations," in C. S. Wallia, ed., *Toward Century 21: Technology, Society, and Human Values* (New York: Basic Books, 1970).

19. *Ibid.*, p. 129.

20. See Reinhard Bendix, *Kings or People: Power and the Mandate to Rule* (Berkeley: University of California Press, 1978), pp. 431–490.

21. Moore, "The Singular and the Plural . . .," cited in note 1, p. 129; emphasis added.

22. Inkeles, "The Emerging Social Structure . . .," cited in note 16, p. 493. See also, Inkeles, *Social Change in Soviet Russia* (Cambridge: Harvard University Press, 1968), especially Chap. 20, "Russia and the United States: A Problem in Comparative Sociology"; Paul Hollander, *Soviet and American Society: A Comparison* (New York: Oxford University Press, 1973).

METHODOLOGICAL NOTE

It will not have escaped the notice of the attentive, and perhaps even the casual, reader of this book that I have not displayed any statistical tables or other signs of measurement of modernization. My excuse for this conduct, unfashionable in any of the several social science disciplines, is that this has been intended as a theoretical and conceptual argument, not a research report as such is now conventionally understood. It is not difficult to reconfirm the systemic character of country units by finding moderately high correlations among such indicators of development as gross domestic product per capita, proportions of the adult population that are literate, mortality and fertility rates, kilowatt hours of electricity or telephones per capita. Rank-order correlations among a number of countries on these or other convenient measures will also reconfirm that some countries are substantially better off in these indicators of modernization than are others. Yet, increasing the number of measures is likely to reduce the predictive power of the combined (or any) measure for the whole set, precisely because in situations of rapid structural change, not everything changes at the same time or at the same rate (and, I have been arguing, some perhaps scarcely at all).

Aside from a cultivated caution in the use of numbers of dubious accuracy, the cross-sectional calculations in conventional use are of minimal relevance for measuring dynamic processes. The relationships that need to be tested are not primarily those of interdependence (which is not demonstrated but must be hazardously inferred from a high correlation coefficient) but rather those of causal relations in a temporal and sequential order.* These would include time-lagged correlations and other time-series analyses, as well as analyses of stochastic processes (sequences of probability distributions), including Markov chains. Some leads may also be found in cybernetics models, the economists' approach to "linear programming," and from "general systems analysis."

In addition, I have not offered suggestions for measures or indicators of the various types of rationalization discussed. Simple ones readily come to mind: changing proportions of the total output of goods and services subject to monetary exchange, with attention to the changing composition of the commercialized transactions; measures of investments in identifiable technologies, by type; changing proportions of the total economically active population that are wage and salary earners as an indicator of bureaucratization, possibly supplemented by distributions by size of various distinct governmental or industrial and business organizations; changes in fertility and mortality rates, morbidity rates, and indicators of efficiency of health-service delivery systems; literacy measures, years of school completed, numbers and distribution by type of specialization of "high-level manpower." Measures of secularization will require considerable ingenuity and experimentation if they are to go beyond membership and participation in religious organizations.

I have not at any point argued against systemic linkages, but only that they must be demonstrated and not assumed from an untenable integration model, and that processes mean sequential linkages and not merely point-of-time correlations. A proper set of measures of modernization, the appropriate technology, will certainly include the interplay among processes of change and the effects of that interplay in dampening or accelerating trends, the latter known as synergistic effects.

The point of developing measures appropriate to the theoretical conception of modernization that I have elaborated in this book is both theoretical and practical. I have argued that the theory of modernization now commonly used is deeply flawed by its derivation from convergence theory. Attempts should now be made to give an empirical grounding to the processes of rationalization and their limits, which will unfortunately not lead to greater simplification of theory—merely to greater validity. From a practical viewpoint, consideration of the actual current state of any country seeking increased rationalization, and estimation *under those circumstances* of the consequences of alternative courses of action are bound to result in more responsible, if less pleasant, advice than our current alternatives of "do everything" or "do anything." The first alternative will generally prove impossible and in any event wasteful and probably needlessly disruptive, and the second misleading and probably fruitless.

*See Wilbert E. Moore, "Toward a System of Sequences," in John C. McKinney and Edward A. Tiryakian, eds., *Theoretical Sociology* (New York: Appleton-Century-Crofts, 1970), Chapter 6, pp. 155–166.

INDEX

A

Accounting
  as aspect of commercialization, 41–43
  in allocating production costs, 66
Achievement orientations, 150
Adams, John, 9
Affective neutrality, 150–151
Affectivity, *see* Emotion
Africa, 37, 49, 115, 116, 143, 152
Age of Reason, 8
Alienation, 12, 50, 58–60
Almond, Gabriel, 135
Anderson, C. Arnold, 89
Argentina, 152
Aristotle, 7–8
Art, *see* Expressive activity
Ashley, W. J., 18
Asia, 153
Attitudes, toward modernization, 24, 26,
  49–50, 60, 84–85, 151
Australia, 21, 153
Authority, 4–5, 14, 91–98, 104, 124–131,
  146–148

B

Bacon, Francis, 8
Beliefs, 2–7, 10–11, 14, 132–133, 150
Bell, Daniel, 64, 76, 132–133, 135, 138,
  142, 148

Bellah, Robert N., 15, 134
Belshaw, Cyril S., 34, 36–37, 45
Bendix, Reinhard, ix, 126–129, 134–135,
  143, 148–149, 159
Bentham, Jeremy, 9, 18
Berelson, Bernard, 115–116, 119–120
Berliner, Joseph S., 45
Blau, Peter M., 52, 61, 89
Blauner, Robert, 60, 62
Boas, George, 18
Bogue, Donald, 114, 120
Bottomore, Tom, 61
Boulding, Kenneth, 155–156, 159
Bowman, Mary Jean, 89
Braibanti, Ralph, 17, 149
Bronfenbrenner, Urie, 89
Broom, Leonard, 61
Buddhism, 145
Buhler, Roald, 18
Burch, William R., Jr., 140, 148
Bureaucracy, 13, 51, 58–59, 90–104, 126,
  129, 146, 150, 153, 156, 161
Burma, 21, 145, 151

C

Cannan, Edward, 61
Caribbean, 115
Carney, Martin, 80, 89
Carter, Jimmy, 129
Change, sources of, 3–7

Charisma, 4–5, 14, 17, 125
Cheek, Neil H., Jr., xi, 140, 148
China, 5, 17, 21, 53, 58, 80, 86, 108, 113, 115, 126, 151
Chirot, 154, 158
Chodak, Szymon, 135, 151, 158–159
Clark, Colin, 50, 61
Class, 53–56
Coke, Edward, 10, 18
Coleman, James, 89
Colonialism, 20–22, 37, 74, 79, 152–153
Columbus, Christopher, 20
Commercialization, 33–45, 53
  of expressive activity, 139
Complexity, of organizations, 91–92
Comte, Auguste, 157
Conflict, see Protest; Revolution
Conformity, 4
Constas, Helen, 105
Convergence theory, 26–29, 47, 150–158
Copernicus, Nicholas, 8, 123
Coser, Lewis A., 134
Cushing, Robert G., 61
Cutler, S. J., 61
Cutright, Phillips, 32
Cybernetics, 161

D

Darwin, Charles, 46, 123, 134
Davis, Kingsley, 52, 61, 110, 119–120
Demographic transition, 113–116
Dependency, 74, 154–155
Descartes, René, 8
Deutsch, Karl, 25, 31, 159
Development, economic, 23–27, 30
Deviance, 4
Dickson, William J., 61
Differentiation, 19–20, 25, 46–60, 87, 90–91, 94–95, 141, 151
  of products, 67–69
Diffusion, 29–30, 151, 158, see also Westernization
Distribution, of goods and services, 70–71
Diversification, of labor, 50, 52, 95
Division of labor, 12, 34, 47–52, 95, see also Differentiation
Dorn, Harold F., 119
Duncan, Otis Dudley, 89, 119
Durkheim, Émile, ix, 44–45, 47, 60, 84, 89

E

Eban, Abba, 157
Economics, classical, 9–14, 155
Education, 30, 51

as aspect of modernization, 77–88, 144, 146, 150, 153, 156
Egypt, 5, 78, 145
Eiseley, Loren, 15, 18, 148
Eisenstadt, S.N., 127–129, 134–135, 149
Emotion, 1, 8, 13, 39, 44, 72, 118–119, 129, 137, 140–142, 150
Engels, Friedrich, 59–60, 62
England, see Great Britain
Enlightenment, the, 8, 80, 87, 136
Ethnicity, 53, 55, 57–58, 133
Europe, medieval, 5, 52–53
  modern, 111–112, 116, 129, 144, 153, 155
Evolution, social, 3, 14, 19, 46–47, 71
Exchange, non-monetary, 34–35
Exploitation, 12
Expressive activity, 138–140

F

Factory system, 64–66
Family, 33–34, 56–57, 141–142, 144, 150, 156
Feldman, Arnold, x, 22–23, 31–32, 61
Fertility
  control, 110–113
  differentials, 111–112, 153, 156
Ford, Clellan S., 119
Foster, Philip J., 82, 86, 89
France, 20, 152
Frank, André Gunder, 154, 158
Franklin, Benjamin, 9, 87
Freud, Sigmund, 142
Friedrich, Carl J., 104
Functional specificity, 151

G

Galileo, Galilei, 8, 123
Germani, Gino, 121, 130, 134–135
Germany, 17, 55, 67, 125
Gerth, H. H., 104
Glazer, Nathan, 62
Goals, see Values
Goode, William J., 141, 148–149
Goodwin, Richard, 146, 149
Goslin, David A., 89
Gouldner, Alvin W., 104
Great Britain, 20, 67, 88, 126, 128, 136, 151–152
Greece, 153
  ancient, 78
Greeley, Andrew, 62
Gusfield, Joseph R., 143, 149
Guyana, 132

H

Hobermas, Jürgen, 135
Haley, Alex, 133, 135
Hammond, Nancy, 158–159
Harris, Marvin, 6, 18
Hartmann, Heinz, 5, 18
Harwitz, Mitchell, 31, 45
Hauser, Philip M., 119
Health, as universal value, 30, 106–110
Heilman, Samuel C., 119
Henderson, A.M., ix, 17
Hernández, José, 115, 120
Herskovits, Melville J., 31, 45, 143, 149
Higgins, Benjamin, 25, 29, 31–32
Hitler, Adolf, 125, 132
Hobbes, Thomas, 3, 9, 13–14, 17–18,
    44–45
Hollander, Paul, 159
Homans, George C., 35, 45
Hoselitz, Bert F., xi, 17, 24–25, 31, 89, 135,
    143, 149, 158
Human nature, 1, 8–9, 13, 15–16, 140–141
Hunter, Guy, 25, 31

I

India, 5, 20–21, 49, 52, 80, 85, 115, 143
Indo-China, 21, 129
Indonesia, 21
Industrialization, 23, 53, 111, 141, 144
Inequality, 25–26, 52–56
    international, 150–158
Ingelfinger, Franz J., 119
Inkeles, Alex, 26, 32, 84, 89, 130, 135, 151,
    157–159
Institutionalization, of rationality, 64
Iran, 145
Iraq, 145
Ireland, 123
Islam, 144–145, 156
Israel, 58, 123
Italy, 152

J

Jacoby, Henry, 135
James, William, 129, 135
Japan, 21, 44, 53, 58, 67, 78–80, 115, 128,
    154, 156
Jefferson, Thomas, 9, 75, 87, 148

K

Kahan, Arcadius, 89
Kerr, Clark, 28, 32

Kinship, 57–58, 141–142, 150, see also
    Family
Kleinman, Arthur, 109, 116, 119–120
Knowledge, see Technology
Kristol, Irving, 148
Kunstadter, Peter, 18
Kuznets, Simon, x, 23, 31, 153, 158

L

Labor markets, 37
Latin America, 152
Law, as rational creation, 10–11
Lebanon, 145
Legitimacy, 1–2, 4–5, 10–11, 14, 104,
    124–131, 136–137, 146–148
Lenin, Vladimir I., 131, 137, 148
Leontieff, Wassily, 153, 158
Levy, Marion J., Jr., 28, 32, 72, 76, 81, 83,
    89, 154, 158
Lévy-Strauss, Claude, 140, 148
Leys, Colin, 135
Likert, Rensis, 49, 61
Linear programming, 161
Lipset, Seymour Martin, 31, 61, 137, 148
Locke, John, 9, 11, 18
Longevity, as universal value, 106–110
Lowe, Adolf, x

M

Machlup, Fritz, 64, 76
Madison, James, 9
Magic, 4, 16, 123–124
Malaya, 21
Malinowski, Bronislaw, 4, 17, 18
Malthus, Thomas, 11, 18
Mao, Tse-tung, 131
Markets, 38–39, see also Labor markets
Marx, Karl, 9, 11–13, 18, 48, 53–54,
    59–62, 65, 157
Marxism, doctrine and theory, 11–13, 20,
    22, 39, 50, 53–56, 59–60, 88, 113,
    127–128, 137, 154–155, 157
Marxist regimes, 3, 40, 53, 124, 126, 133, 155
Matsas, Judah, 114, 116–117, 120
Mayo, Elton, 49, 61
McClelland, David, 26, 32
McKinney, John C., 119, 161
McNeill, William, 151, 158
Mechanization, 63, 65–66, see also
    Technification; Technology
Merton, Robert K., 104–105, 134
Military regimes, 125, 131
Mill, John Stuart, 9, 18
Mills, C. Wright, 104

Mobility, 26, 51–52, 84–85, 141
Model modernized society, 26–29, 151, 157
Modernization
   as economic development, 23–25, 28–29
   as rationalization, 1, 29–31
Monetization, of exchange, 34–41
Money, 35–37
Moore, Wilbert E., x, xi, 17–18, 24, 31–32,
      45, 60–62, 75–76, 89, 105,
      119–120, 134–135, 148, 158–161
Morbidity control, 107–108
Moriyama, Iwao, 107, 119
Morocco, 145
Mortality control, 108–110, 153, 156
Moynihan, Daniel P., 62
Mumford, Lewis, 63, 75
Myths, 2–3, 121–122, 125, 131, 140, 156

N

Napoleon, 137
Nash, Manning, xi, 25, 31, 89, 145, 149,
      158
Nationalism, 30, 59, 130–133, 155–156
Netherlands, 152
Newton, Isaac, 8
New Zealand, 21, 153
Nisbet, Robert A., 60–61, 122, 129,
      133–135, 148
Norms, 4, 7, 9, 44, 47, 91–97, 103
Notestein, Frank W., 113, 120

O

Oakeshott, Michael, 17, 45
Occupation, see Division of Labor
Organization, informal, 65, 103
Organization of Petroleum Exporting
      Countries (OPEC), 74, 153
Ortega y Gasset, José, 129, 134
Orwell, George, 75

P

Papanek, Gustav, F., 158
Parsons, Talcott, ix, 11, 13, 17–18, 45, 60
Particularism, 102
Passin, Herbert, 89
Pathologies, of bureaucracies, 102–103
Patterson, Orlando, 58, 62, 133, 135, 142,
      148, 154, 158
Philippines, 153
Philosophy, Greek, 7–8, 12
Planning, 43, 99–101
Plato, 7–8
Polarization, 53, 128

Political regimes, and modernization, 24–26,
      30, 59
Population growth, 47, 108, 112–116
Portugal, 152
Prestige, occupational, see Inequality
Protest, 128–130, 144, 151, see also
      Revolution
Puerto Rico, 153
Purpose, see Values
Pye, Lucian W., 135

Q

Qureshi, Ishtiaq Husain, 149

R

Rationalism, 2, 7–17, 136–137, 140
Rationalization
   defined, 1
   limits, 1–2, 136–148, 150–158
   as modernization, 17, 29–31, 144,
      150–151
   over-rationalization, 137
Rational-legal type of authority, 5, 125–127
Recreation, 140
Religion, 3, 121–127, 132–133, 137,
      144–145, 156, see also Values
Revolution, 11–12, 53, 125–129, 137, 157
Ricardo, David, 10, 11, 18, 48–49, 61
Rituals, 140
Roethlisberger, F. J., 61
Rosenblum, Gerald W., 61, 89
Rossi, Alice, 118–120
Roth, Guenther, ix
Rousseau, Jean-Jacques, 9, 13, 18
Russia, 21, 79, see also Soviet Union
Ryder, Norman B., 112, 116, 119–120

S

Saudi Arabia, 144–145, 156
Schweinitz, Karl de, 135
Science, 123, see also Technology
Secularization, 3, 121–133, 144, 156
Sennett, Richard, 129, 132, 134–135
Sexuality
   and recreation, 118–119
   and reproduction, 110–111, 118
Sheldon, Eleanor Bernert, 119
Shils, Edward, 127, 134
Sigerist, Henry E., 89
Simon, Julian, 115, 116, 120
Slavery, 152
Smelser, Neil J., 31, 61, 130–131, 135, 142,
      148

Smith, Adam, 10, 48–50, 52, 58, 60–62
Smith, David Horton, 26, 32, 84, 89, 151, 158
Social Science Research Council, x, 23
Socialist regimes, 39–40, 42–43, 53, 59–60, 130, *see also* Marxist regimes
Socialization, 151
Sociobiology, 77
South America, 115–116
Sovereignty, *see* Nationalism
Soviet Union, 21, 40, 44, 53, 86, 126, 138–139, 154–155, 157
Spain, 152
Specialization, *see* Differentiation; Division of Labor
Spengler, Joseph J., 17–18, 31, 149
Stephan, Frederick F., 18
Strafa, Piero, 61
Stratification, *see* Inequality
Symbols, 15
Syria, 145

T

Taeuber, Irene B., 119
Target workers, 37, 49
Taxes, 33–34, 37
Taylor, Frederick Winslow, 48–50, 61
Technification, 63–75, *see also* Technology
Technocracy, 146
Technology, 3–7, 11–12, 30, 47, 63–75, 83, 123–124, 144
  technological alternatives, 71–73
Teleology, 101
Teleonomy, 101
Tension-management, 10–11, 145–146
Thompson, Warren, 113, 120
Tilly, Charles, 134–135, 148
Tilly, Edward, 134
Tilly, Louise, 134
Tiryakian, Edward, 17–18, 119, 161
Traditionalism, 4–6, 125–126, 143–146
Treiman, Donald J., 61, 89
Tucker, Robert C., 18, 62
Tumin, Melvin M., 61
Tunisia, 145

U

Udy, Stanley H., Jr., 34, 45, 104–105
Unemployment, as consequence of mechanization, 67
UNESCO, 24
United States, 67, 85, 111, 116–117, 129, 144, 147, 151, 155, 157
  Bureau of the Census, 115, 120
  Department of Labor, 61
  Public Health Service, 107
Universalism, ethical, 151
Urbanization, 50–51, 53, 111, 141, 150
Utilitarianism, 9, 12

V

Values, 7, 13–14, 16–17, 30, 33, 75, 77, 106–110, 117–118, 124–133, 137, 140, 146–148, 150–151, 155
Veblen, Thorstein, 102

W

Wagner, Richard, 125
Wallerstein, Immanuel, 154, 158
Wallia, C. S., 159
Washburn, S. L., 88
Weber, Max, ix, 4–5, 17–18, 36, 42, 45, 94, 104, 105, 123, 125–127, 129–130, 132, 134, 146
Westernization, 20–22, 53, 79, 113, 143, 145, 151
Westoff, Charles F., 18
Whitehead, T. N., 61
Whyte, Lynn, Jr., 7
Wilde, Oscar, 37
Wilensky, Harold L., 55, 61
Wilson, E. O., 88
Winter, D. G., 32
Wittich, Claus, ix
Wolfe, Alan, 129, 134

Y

Yinger, J. Milton, 61
Yugoslavia, 153